LOU WHITTAKER

Memoirs of a Mountain Guide

Lou Whittaker
with
Andrea Gabbard

THE
MOUNTAINEERS

Published by
The Mountaineers
1011 SW Klickitat Way
Seattle, Washington 98134

8 7 6 5 4
5 4 3 2 1

Published simultaneously in Canada by Douglas & McIntyre, Ltd.,
1615 Venables Street, Vancouver, B.C. V5L 2H1

Published simultaneously in Great Britain by Cordee,
3a DeMontfort Street,
Leicester, England LE1 7HD

Manufactured in the United States of America

Edited by Linda Gunnarson and Kris Fulsaas
Drawings and maps by Dee Molenaar
Cover design by Betty Watson
Book design, typesetting and layout by The Mountaineers Books

Cover photo by Bob and Ira Spring; inset photo by Preston Spencer

Library of Congress Cataloging in Publication Data
Whittaker, Lou.
    Whittaker : memoirs of a mountain guide / Lou Whittaker with Andrea Gabbard.
        p.   cm.
    Includes bibliographical references and index.
    ISBN 0-89886-396-1
    1. Whittaker, Lou. 2. Mountaineering guides (Persons)--United States--Biography. I. Gabbard, Andrea. II. Title.
GV199.92.W47A3   1994
796.5'22'092--dc20
[B]   94-10546
                                                   CIP

To Mom and Ingrid

Security is mostly a superstition. It does not exist in Nature, nor do the children of men as a whole experience it. Avoiding danger is no safer in the long run than outright exposure. Life is either a daring adventure, or nothing.

—Helen Keller

CONTENTS

FOREWORD

For more than forty years, Lou Whittaker has been regarded as an outstanding mountaineer and something of a philosopher, too.

Lou started his climbing at a very young age—as a Boy Scout when he was twelve years old. He had climbed all the major peaks of Washington State by the time he was eighteen and began guiding climbs on 14,410-foot Mount Rainier at age nineteen. Today, on Mount Rainier, his name is a legend and he has conducted thousands of people to the summit of that great mountain in every variety of weather and snow conditions.

Lou may be less well known worldwide than his twin brother, Jim, who was the first American to reach the summit of Mount Everest. Yet to climbing initiates, Lou has a resounding reputation in his own right. He has been involved in formidable ascents in Alaska, the Himalaya, and the Karakoram. He led the first American ascent of the North Col of Mount Everest in 1984, and today, at age sixty-five, he's in the midst of planning yet another expedition, this time to an unclimbed peak in the Himalaya.

Lou has a strong personality, yet appears rather humble with a warm sense of humor and a remarkable flair for building up the confidence of his inexperienced climbers. He knows that fear can often be a stimulating factor. It can enable you to extend yourself far beyond what you thought possible. In any case, fear is all part of the motivation. If you don't feel afraid now and then, why go to all the discomfort and effort involved in getting up a high mountain? Better to stay down sunbathing at the beach.

Lou sums up his philosophy very effectively when he says, "There's a certain amount of risk involved in life. When it comes down to dying, I want to know what it is like to have really lived."

I also like his approach when he says, "Invariably, a novice climber will say to me, 'I'm afraid of heights.' I always reply, 'I am, too. That's why I'm still around.' " With that sort of approach, Lou and his climbers should be around for a very long time yet.

Sir Edmund Hillary
Auckland, New Zealand
October 1993

Co-author's Preface

It was a late afternoon in early June 1992. I was huddled with a group of twenty climbers inside the small wooden bunkhouse at Camp Muir, the encampment at 10,000 feet on Mount Rainier that serves as a base of operations for Lou Whittaker's guide service, Rainier Mountaineering, Inc. We'd been confined to the bunkhouse since the night before, when our summit attempt had been foiled by a blizzard with winds gusting between fifty and sixty miles per hour. The blizzard had continued to buffet the walls of the bunkhouse all day and made the 100-foot crawl to the privy on the hill outside a major effort.

Suddenly, the bunkhouse's heavy door burst open and a tall figure, swathed in spindrift and backlit in snowy glare, stepped inside. "It doesn't get much better than this!" thundered Lou Whittaker. "The mountain is really showing off!"

He spent the next several hours regaling the group with "war stories," alternately terrifying and entertaining us with his mountaineering exploits. Then, he tucked us in for the night with a profound statement about how the summit may be the goal, but the journey is the adventure. "You may not have made the summit this time, but the mountain will be here for you another day." And, with that promise, he opened the door and disappeared into the blowing storm, to sleep alone in his tent on the mountain.

A fellow climber turned to me and said, "Somebody should write a book about this guy."

Six months later, Lou and I sat before a tape recorder. "Let's start with your childhood," I said. He laughed, and the fun began.

Over the next several months, Lou and I met regularly, on Mount Rainier and at his home in Ashford, Washington. I recorded Lou's stories as well as recollections from family, friends, and associates who know him best. When asked to describe Lou, most people smiled and commented about his sense of humor. Several mentioned his compassion. And others talked about his natural sense of leadership.

One friend said that there was a part of Lou that is only known through silence, through time spent alone with him. There's a sense of greatness about Lou, the friend added, that Lou has nothing to do with, other than just being who he is.

My impression of Lou is that he became his own best friend, took the road less traveled, and found his inner guide long before it became fashionable to do so. Lou's internal compass is set on a positive bearing, and he does not veer from that course. His passion for life is infectious. The more you know the real Lou Whittaker, the more you are confronted with the challenge, "Are you doing what you love?"

In writing the story of Lou's life, in Lou's words and the words of those close to him, I found that I could answer that question with a resounding "Yes!"

Andrea Gabbard

PREFACE

I figured out early on that I'd probably check out by age fifty, living the life of a mountaineer. But here I am, more than a decade beyond that, still hanging around. There's an old mountaineering saying that rings true for me: "There are old climbers and bold climbers. There are no old, bold climbers." I've learned a lot about survival from a life in the mountains.

It's said that challenge is the mainspring of all human endeavor. If there's a wrong, we right it. If there's an illness, we cure it. If there's a mountain, we climb it. It is our nature to want to do these things.

After all these years, I can truthfully say that the thrill of challenge is as strong now as it was when I was just getting started in the mountains. It's not necessarily the exhilaration that comes at the moment of reaching the summit that keeps me coming back for more. For me and the other mountaineers I know, I think climbing helps define who we are. Maybe it's something as simple as that a mountain represents such a concrete goal that you can work toward. And most other goals we seek in life are not as easy to define.

There's a certain amount of risk involved in mountaineering, as there is in life in general. The philosophy I've developed over the years is that life is a gift. It's a gift that will be taken back at some time by the Giver. People who aren't living their lives fully don't like the idea of that gift being taken back. If your life is taken back without having earned some happiness from that gift, why, it's your own fault. But if, as an old philosopher once said, you "warm both hands before the fire of life," you'll know what it means to have lived when it comes your time to check out.

Everything I know, everything I believe in, I've learned in the mountains. The mountains have given me my health, my confidence, and my triumphs. They have also given me the opportunity to help other people overcome both real and self-imposed obstacles. To me, there is no greater satisfaction than seeing the joy on a person's face upon reaching the summit of Mount Rainier, a journey that seemed impossible to that person at the start. In writing this book, I hope to share my journeys and the lessons learned from them.

There's a passage from former Supreme Court Justice William O. Douglas's book *Of Men and Mountains* that further defines my motive for recording my life experiences: "If man could only get to know the mountains better, and let them become a part of him, he would lose much of his aggression. The struggle of man against man produces jealousy, deceit, frustration, bitterness, hate. The struggle of man against the mountains is different. Man then bows before something that is bigger than he. When he does that, he finds serenity and humility, and dignity, too."

Lou Whittaker

Acknowledgments

The authors wish to thank friends and family members who contributed their time, recollections, love, and support toward the completion of this book.

We are especially grateful to Lou's mother, Hortense Whittaker, for her memories and photos of Lou's childhood; to Ingrid Widmann, for her strength, humor and assistance; to Matie Daiber, for her years of devotion and meticulous record-keeping; to Sir Edmund Hillary, for his generous response; to Jim Wickwire, for his personal recollections, professional opinions and photographs, dates, and other pertinent information; to Mary Lou Wickwire, for her generous insights; to Peter and Win Whittaker, for their honesty, insight, and support; to Jerry Lynch, for his contributions and encouragement; to Dr. Otto Trott, for his entertaining and informative recollections; to Nawang Gombu, for his faithful support and encouragement; to George Dunn, Dave Mahre, John Roskelley, Pete Schoening, and Eric Simonson, for their courage, generosity, and honesty; to Laslo and Susan Pal, for background information; to Barney Whittaker, for his insights; to Dee Molenaar, for excellent maps and sketches; to Keith Gunnar and Ira Spring, for outstanding photographs; to Ted Kennedy, for his support; to the Russian climber Ed Myslovsky, for his support; to Paul DeLorey, for his persistence and generosity; to Preston Spencer, for his support; to Linda Gunnarson and Kris Fulsaas, for their editing expertise; to Margaret Foster, for her patient guidance; to Jerrold Parry, for the pleasure of his company; to Frank Paul, for his illuminating insights; and a special nod to Jim Whittaker and Kim Whittaker, with love and understanding.

Thanks also to Sally Jeans, for timely, invaluable tape transcriptions; to Pam Montgomery, for "being there" throughout the project; to Sharon Leicham, for her encouragement, especially at the beginning; to Lacey Gabbard, for her uplifting verses when things got hectic; and to Francey Blaugrund, for her love, friendship, and steadfast belief in our ability to complete the project on time.

Lou offers particular thanks and undying love to the memories of all the friends who warmed their hands before the fire of life, but checked out early. And to all the guides, cabin persons, and staff of RMI, sincere gratitude for their faithful support and boundless energy.

Last but not least, we owe a debt of gratitude to Skip Yowell, who planted the seed and helped it grow.

Lou Whittaker

Scouts Jim and Lou, age sixteen (Photo courtesy Whittaker family)

◆ 1 ◆

Beginnings

My brother Jim and I were wombmates. Jim was born first, by ten minutes. I came next and I've hated waiting in lines ever since.

Most people could never tell us apart, although I'm right-handed and Jim is left-handed. When I was in grade school, we were playing hide-and-seek and I ran into a guy and broke my nose. It was the first time that Jim and I looked a little different, because I had a bump on my nose. It didn't get fixed until I was in the military and had a bout of tonsillitis. The doctor said that I wasn't breathing through one nostril, so, while he had me under for a tonsillectomy, he also performed a rhinoplasty.

Mom rarely dressed us alike, and in school we were put in different classes. They said it was to encourage us to develop our own personalities, but I think it was mostly done so that teachers would be able to distinguish Lou from Jim. You'd think the years would have changed us some, but here we are now in our sixties, and people still get us confused. We've been saying "Hi" to both names for most of our lives. It's just easier that way and less embarrassing for the person caught in the mix-up.

I often get the credit for having been the first American to reach the summit of Mount Everest. Jim and I have been on four major Himalayan expeditions each, and I did lead a successful climb of Everest in 1984. But it was my twin, Jim, who was the first American to summit the world's highest mountain, with Sherpa Nawang Gombu, in 1963.

Sometimes, the confusion over our identity has proved to be convenient. There were a few times when Jim would tire of the parades and personal appearances that followed his Everest success, and he'd ask me to fill in for him. Only our families and closest friends ever knew the difference.

Jim and I were born to Charles Bernard and Hortense Elizabeth Whittaker eight months before the Great Depression, on February 10, 1929. The family lived in the small community of Green Lake, outside Seattle, until I was about three years old, when Mom and Dad bought a tiny house on a large lot in West Seattle for $380. Mom, who is in her nineties, still lives there, surrounded by what has become a rhododendron forest. Dad died in May 1982, when I was on my first Everest expedition.

Hortense Whittaker (Photo courtesy Whittaker family)

*Charles B. Whittaker
(Photo courtesy Whittaker
family)*

Jim and I share a brother, Barney, who is three years older. We three were close and rarely argued or fought. Jim and I were exceptional in that we were, and are, the only twins in our family. Neither our father or mother had any history of twins in their families, and there haven't been any twins born among the grandkids.

Mom always has said that I was the more enthusiastic and outspoken of the two of us, and a lot of people say that this is still true today. Jim tends to be a little more reserved. But when we were kids, Mom says it was more like having one person around.

This is probably because identical twins share more than just a physical resemblance. Being a twin is a unique experience. You know you're two separate individuals, but you often feel like one. Jim and I would think and speak alike, and even finish each other's sentences. We'd just have to look at each other to know what the other was thinking. When one of us accomplished something, the other felt like he had done it, too.

Jim and I were competitive from the beginning and remain so to this day. Part of this comes from being twins, but I think part of it is also natural inclination and is what has motivated us to achieve more, to go beyond what we thought were our capabilities.

Our parents encouraged all three of us to be active and adventurous. They would caution us to be careful, but they never stopped us from trying something, whether that meant climbing a tree, walking a picket fence, or scrambling up a cliff. Mom and Dad both loved the outdoors, especially the ocean. On vacations, we'd go to the Oregon coast. Jim, Barney, and I would climb the cliffs above the water and we'd get scared, but we'd push each other onward. Even at age six or eight, I liked getting up high and feeling danger—and surviving it. It gave me a sense of accomplishment and helped build my confidence and courage.

I fancied myself as "The Scarlet Avenger." I wore a cape—an old towel tied around my neck—and climbed and swung from a rope in the old tree in the backyard. I rescued many an imagined victim. Mom likes to tell the story of when I was eight or nine and "rescued" her:

"I accidentally cut off the tip of my finger with a sickle, while I was working out in the yard. The boys were horrified at all the blood. I wrapped a pillow slip around the finger and asked, 'Will one of you boys go with me to the doctor?' Lou stepped right up. 'I'll go,' he said, in his best Scarlet Avenger voice, and you could see the look of relief on Jim's and Barney's faces."

Of course, to rescue your own mother is the paramount act of heroism for a boy. There wasn't anything any of us boys wouldn't have done for Mom. She was, and still is, warm, loving, and very understanding of her boys and their escapades.

Dad was happy and outgoing, and on the road a good deal of the time, selling and installing burglar alarms. This left Mom with the challenge of raising three active boys. She loved to walk, and we lived in a hilly area above Puget Sound. Mom walked us all over those hills.

Our favorite trek was to the beach. We'd start out downhill, full of energy that we'd expend playing and swimming at the beach. We'd go in the freezing water of Puget Sound as early as April. On the way home, we kids struggled to match the uphill pace set by

Mom. Keeping up with her caused us to develop a bounce in our step. We rode streetcars to school, but we still had to walk downhill to catch them and uphill about seven steep blocks to get back home. Sometimes we'd come home for lunch and walk back again. Being tall and gangly, even in elementary school, Jim and I were teased a lot about our bouncy walk.

As an installer of bank burglar alarms, Dad was well employed during those Depression years. We were considered a middle-class family. Even so, our home was small and fairly humble. The best part was the clear view from the front room of Puget Sound and the Olympic Mountains. After Jim and I started climbing in our teens, we'd sit in the front room and identify the peaks we'd climbed. We'd go from left to right, from Ellinor to Washington to The Brothers, working our way along the mountain silhouette. After we ticked off one peak, we'd sit and plan our next ascent.

Mom cooked on a wood stove. My two brothers and I shared a room that we still call "the bunk room." Barney slept in the twin bed in one corner and Jim and I had the bunks. The bunks were built into a nook in the wall. I slept in the bottom bunk, Jim up top. By junior high school, we suddenly started growing taller, and we became embarrassed by our height. If we didn't get a seat on the school bus, we'd have to stand with our knees bent to keep our heads from hitting the top of the bus. We got into the habit of standing and walking with a slump.

Jim, Lou, and Barney at the beach, 1931 (Photo courtesy Whittaker family)

In high school, our heads began hitting the wall in the nook where the bunks were, and we started getting really despondent. We thought that if we pushed against the walls with our feet and heads, that would keep us from getting taller. Eventually, our parents noticed our discomfort and Dad knocked out the wall to lengthen the bunks. Jim and I stopped growing at six-foot-five. Barney stopped an inch shorter. One day, a stranger came up to me and Jim and said, "Don't be embarrassed to be tall. Stand up straight and be proud of your height. You have no reason to be embarrassed." The advice stuck and we straightened out.

In 1943, when Jim and I turned fourteen, we got jobs at Mr. Ruddy's neighborhood grocery store. We enjoyed working there. We could earn enough to pay for our recreation and we had fun with the customers. A shopper would see me stocking shelves in one aisle, then she'd get around a couple more aisles and run into Jim stocking shelves. She'd ask, "How'd you get over here so quickly?"

It's a strange feeling to walk into Mom's house today and see it as it was when I was a boy. There are pictures of grandkids and great-grandkids on the walls, alongside pictures of me and my brothers at different stages in our lives. It's strange, but somehow reassuring, to be able to see your beginnings as tangible things.

Going back home makes me think of all the love our parents gave us and how lucky I was to have grown up in such a loving family, in a simple, wonderful time. The doors to our home were never locked and I'm not sure that there even was a key. In those days, adventure was a natural high. To explore a tide pool or sit around a campfire in the evening after a long day's hike was enough. We didn't need drugs or alcohol to feel at peace with ourselves.

I can't remember Mom and Dad ever telling us boys not to use alcohol or to smoke. It was just something that, as kids, we did not do. Barney was in the military during World War II, while Jim and I were in high school and working at Mr. Ruddy's. When Barney returned from duty and was smoking, I asked him to please purchase his cigarettes elsewhere. I've been anti-smoking ever since.

Dad introduced us to reading, particularly poetry, at an early age. This was the pre-television era, so evenings were spent reading. We each had our favorite reading spot in the living room. We subscribed to the *Saturday Evening Post,* and would read it from cover to cover. When Dad was home, he'd read us poetry.

Dad would sometimes compose his own poetry. Being on the road, he really got into those old Burma Shave signs. He composed several verses himself, and sent them to Burma Shave. They used a couple of them, such as, "Why does Hitler/rant and rave?/The poor galoot/needs Burma Shave." And "A peach looks good/with lots of fuzz./But a man's no peach/and never wuzz./Burma Shave."

On climbing expeditions, you often get stuck in your tent during days on end of bad weather. To fight the boredom, you tend to read anything you can get your hands on, from books to soup can labels. I read poetry. Unlike most novels, you can read poetry over and over again. I've memorized many a verse. I especially enjoy William Shakespeare, Robert Service, Rudyard Kipling, and the romantic poets—Shelley, Charles Lamb. As a boy, two of my favorite verses were "The Cremation of Sam McGee" and "The Spell of the Yukon," by Robert Service. I also liked Jack London's books and often visualized myself in the remote wilderness areas that he described.

Our religious training was somewhat casual. We attended the neighborhood Congregational Church. The minister was a woman. A rare occurrence, but she could spout fire and brimstone as well as any man. She always wore a big black robe. The image of her up there in the pulpit has never left me. To me, she was scary and such a contrast to my mother, who tends to be easygoing and pleasant. Mom is self-assured and expresses her point of view, but not with the vehemence of a preacher.

Mom suffered from hay fever and we boys had it, too. Luckily, Dad was free of it. Jim and I also developed asthma. The doctors said it was brought on by the hay fever, which was brought on by dust, pollens, and grasses. Jim and I would nearly always get asthma attacks at the same time—and not because we were twins. The attacks would most often come at night, after we'd been playing outside all day on the lawn, in dirt and grass. We'd sit up in our bunks for hours, wheezing and gasping for breath. At times it felt like you weren't going to get enough air to stay alive. It was a horrible, suffocating feeling.

To our eternal relief, we discovered the Boy Scouts. Scouting not only got us out and away from pollutants, it also helped strengthen our vital capacity, a priceless commodity for a climber. And it introduced us to the mountains. A lot of old-time climbers got going through scouting.

Barney, being the oldest, joined the Boy Scouts first. In 1939, when we were ten years old, Jim and I got to go on a weekend trip with Barney's troop, up into the mountains. Jim and I discovered that we could breathe really well up there. The next weekend, we went again and found that we could breathe clearly for a few days after we got back, before the asthma hit again. So we joined the Boy Scouts. Our doctor encouraged us, and told us to go up into the mountains as often as we could. By the time we turned eighteen, Jim and I had climbed most of the major peaks in Washington State and our asthma had disappeared.

We were members of Troop 272, led by Scoutmasters Ray Myers and Ed Ebert. They took us on hikes throughout the Olympics and Cascades. Years later, I sent them postcards from Mount Everest that said, "Look what you got us into."

By age twelve, Jim and I were taking seven-day hikes with the scouts. Because the mountains are so close to Seattle, outings were convenient. On one trip, we nearly ran out of food and only had oatmeal to eat for a couple of days. On another, our lean-to caught fire—we thought maybe one of the guys was smoking, but we never proved it—and all our gear was burned up. We had to hike out in stocking feet. After I told my dad about it, he wrote a humorous poem, in the style of Robert Service's "The Cremation of Sam McGee."

During junior high school, Jim and I also discovered basketball. Mom had gotten a job as a camp counselor at a Presbyterian church camp on Horsehead Bay in Puget Sound during part of the summer, and signed up me and my brothers for a stay. One of the other counselors also coached basketball at the YMCA in town and invited us to play while at camp. We were crummy shots, but we were tall. After camp, the counselor asked us to join the YMCA team. We never had time to go out for basketball at school, because we worked afternoons at Mr. Ruddy's store. But the YMCA schedule fit ours, and allowed us to play.

We could handle the ball, and eventually improved our shooting, thanks to our coach's patient teaching. Our team started going to meets around the city, and eventually we beat our own high school team.

Our adventures on the basketball court and in scouting proved to be great learning experiences. Basketball was a great outlet for my natural competitiveness. It also taught me the value of teamwork in achieving a goal. I learned to value winning, but to value even more the sense of having done my best. In scouts, I'd come home from an outing and realize that life is pretty simple in the city. You have food, shelter, water that comes out of a tap. The more time I spent in the outdoors, the more my confidence broadened. I learned to believe that there isn't a problem that can't be solved if you put your best effort into it. When you become confident in yourself and confident in nature, you carry that back with you, to the city and your everyday life.

We scouts would always gather at Ray's home for meetings and to dream up trips. It was only fitting, then, that all the surviving members of Troop 272 met at Ray's home on Vashon Island one day in the summer of 1992 to reminisce and say goodbye to him. He'd had a stroke and died shortly after our get-together.

Ray and Ed introduced us to several men who became our mentors—men such as Ome Daiber, Max Eckenburg, Sam Eskanazi, Wolf Bauer, Dr. Otto Trott, and Dee Molenaar. Some of these guys had learned to climb in their European homelands, and became a source of inspiration and technique for us.

Ome Daiber was a carpenter, scoutmaster, and climber, as well as an inveterate punster. "Snow some more, I don't get the drift," or "My name's Cliff, drop over some time" were part of Ome's standard repetoire.

Ome got his name in high school, when he was an Eagle Scout. One day, he asked a friend, "Would you owe me a quarter?" The friend said, "I don't *owe* you a quarter." Ome said, "I know, but if you will, I'll pay you back tomorrow." Ome had a habit of mixing up his words and this time one of his mix-ups stuck. His friend loaned him the quarter but also pinned him with the nickname

Ome. Ome later had it legally changed because that's what everybody called him. I never did know his real first name.

Ome taught us how to handle ourselves in the mountains. He used to take out our scout troop. We were green as hell, but in good shape, so we could keep up with him. We just didn't know how to do anything. Ome would point out the route and say, "Go that way." He'd remind us, "Look back to memorize your route. That's how it will look on your return." We'd say, "Okay," and head off, not knowing that it was a test and immediately forgetting to memorize our route. We'd climb to the top of a mountain and Ome would ask, "Okay, who wants to lead us out?"

I volunteered once and promptly went the wrong way. Ome didn't say anything. We were tired and hungry and had been wandering around on this mountain all day. Around five in the afternoon, Ome stopped us and asked, "Okay, you guys, how many think that Lou is headed in the right direction?" About half the troop did. Ome informed us that I was lost.

He said, "Who wants to lead now?" And another guy took over. I thought he was going in the wrong direction, but didn't say anything. It was getting late, almost dark. Ome finally stopped us again and said, "Well, you guys, I told your parents you might be a day late. Right now, I don't think we're going to make it back by dark if we keep heading this direction."

We were pissed as hell at Ome, but he was giving us the best lesson we could ever have. If we had remembered to memorize what we had seen on the way up, we'd know the way back down. Now, we were dependent on him. When Ome asked us, "What if something happened to me?' he drove home the lesson. He finally led us down off the mountain in the dark, with flashlights.

At age fourteen, Jim and I were still playing basketball on the YMCA team, but we were losing interest in scouting and wanting to climb more. Ray and Tom decided to form an Explorer troop for kids our age, to offer us more challenge. They taught us some rope work and rock climbing. There is a city park in West Seattle called Camp Long that included a rock "mountain" called Monitor Rock (it's now called Schurman Rock, after Clark Schurman, chief guide on Mount Rainier from 1939 through 1942). I guess you could call it the first artificial climbing wall in this country. We practiced there a lot.

We met Tom Campbell and Lloyd Anderson through scouting. Tom was a member of the Mountain Troops. He had lost his arm in a climb in Europe, but he still climbed, with a prosthetic. He'd unscrew his gloved hand, then screw in a hook and climb with that and his good hand. To us boys, Tom was a swashbuckling hero. Lloyd was one of the founders of Recreational Equipment, Inc., a cooperative retail store based in Seattle that specializes in equipment and clothing for outdoor sports. Jim later worked for REI for twenty-five years, rising to president before he retired and moved on to his own business.

Jim and I did our first real climb in 1943, when we were fourteen, on a scout outing led by Lloyd and Tom. The war was still going on, and gas was being rationed. A few of the guys pooled their rationing tickets and took two cars, with me, Jim, Barney, and a few other scouts, to Snoqualmie Pass in the Cascades.

At Snoqualmie, we climbed The Tooth, a sharp rock fang three miles in from the road. The Tooth sits at 6,000 feet with a 1,000-foot east face and technical route and a medium south face about 300 feet high with a good "fat man's misery" ledge, a spot where the ledge narrows and the wall bulges. The west and north sides are what climbers consider to be good belay routes without protection needed, but good exposure. This means that there are high, challenging cliffs, but with intermittent ledges to stand on. You don't have to use pitons or other hardware to anchor yourself to the rocks as protection against a fall. A rope is sufficient protection.

We did the north ridge first. Nowadays, with rubber lug-sole boots, you'd climb the smooth, slab faces of the large boulders to get to the base of the route. Back then, our heavy leather "Triconinail" boots were no good on flat rock. They had special nails inserted into the soles with brads and screws. They'd screech and spark as they slid around on a friction slab. So to get to the route, we had to avoid the slabs and scramble over the rubble of the rock slide. We did the north route in nails, but the south side required only tennis shoes. Lloyd once did the south side in stocking feet when he forgot his tennies.

We roped up on the top of the rockslide in the shade, but saw the sun on the granite above and climbed to it. Our ropes were 120 feet long, made of five-eighths-inch manila hemp. They had no stretch and deteriorated 40 percent a season, unlike today's nylon kermantle ropes, which drop about 2 percent in strength each season under normal use.

We "leapfrogged" up the route, as we had been taught at Monitor Rock. One climber would tie himself into the rope and lead a section of the route, while the other climber "belayed" by running the rope around his waist, slowly paying it out and controlling the slack. We took turns, leading and belaying, all the way up. It was butterflies and just the right amount of doubt that made us really feel good when we topped it off. Nature showed off with hundreds of rock peaks around us, including the big peaks and glaciers of Rainier, St. Helens, Adams, Glacier Peak, and Baker, all rising over 10,000 feet, with the highest, Mount Rainier, at 14,410. I can still taste the potato salad that Mom had sent with us and feel the warm breeze coming up that 1,000-foot east face.

On top, Tom was still tied in to Jim and me. We watched with real horror and apprehension as Tom deliberately backed up and hung the heels of his nailed boots over the 1,000-foot face. He balanced on his toes like a diver on the edge of a diving board for a back flip. He laughed as Jim and I grabbed for rock handholds to keep from getting pulled off when Tom peeled. I asked Tom how he could be so casual and he said, "You'll be able to do the same thing when you get to be better climbers."

I still get good butterflies my first few days on a wall if I haven't climbed in a few months. I never want to lose those instincts that keep us alive—one instinct being the fear of heights. The climber who has lost that fear is a dead climber. Jim and I learned to become used to a vertical environment. We controlled our self-preservation instincts. For some, fear turns into a phobia, and that's no good. That's as bad as having no fear at all.

Although he was on The Tooth with us, Barney did not follow Jim and me into climbing. As a child, he had been injured jumping off the running board of a car. A driver had offered Barney a ride up the hill to our house. He told Barney to jump on and he'd let him off at the house. Our house wasn't right at the top of the hill, so when the driver didn't slow down there—he wanted to get to the top of the hill before he stopped—Barney jumped off the running board. He had been told never to accept rides from strangers, and he figured this was one ba-a-ad guy. Barney broke his cheekbone and jaw and was in the hospital a few days. I think the experience increased his fear of being injured in a fall.

I learned early on that to be afraid of a cliff is natural. That's what instincts are for, to make us more alert. Barney just didn't enjoy climbing as much as Jim and I did. He didn't like the exposure on The Tooth, and a later climb on Mount Baker was, to Barney, a dreary combination of hours of walking and more hours in a cold sleeping bag at timberline, before the climb even began.

Today, when Barney is asked why his brothers climb and he does not, he says, "Lou and Jim had an advantage. They both had P.B.D.—Permanent Brain Damage. Anyone who would subject himself to such torture most surely has such a condition."

In 1945, at age sixteen, our "P.B.D. condition" propelled Jim and me into our first ascents of Mount Rainier, the highest peak in Washington, and Mount Olympus, the highest peak in the Olympic Range.

Our Rainier climb was with a Seattle-based climbing club called The Mountaineers. There were nearly thirty of us on the climb. We camped out the night before at the base of the mountain, so we could get up early to meet the guy who would be leading our rope. He wanted to go fast, using the Emmons Route, the most popular route on the east side of Rainier. Our group left early in the morning, and ascended from our camp at the White River Campground to our next camp at Steamboat Prow, at 9,500 feet. We set up our tents, lit the stoves, and ate dinner under a million bright stars. I could have sat up all night on the mountain, I was so entranced by its beauty. But bed came early, because we were set to rise at the ungodly hour of one o'clock in the morning to make our summit attempt.

We roused ourselves on time, tossed down some hot drinks, and roped up in the dark. Jim and I followed our eager-beaver rope leader and were up on top four hours later, several hours ahead of the last of the six rope teams. We caught up on sleep on top, waiting for them.

Mom knew we always got hungry and thirsty in the mountains, so she had packed about two pounds of green seedless grapes in our lunches. Sure enough, on the summit rim, we were dying of thirst from our speedy ascent. I was also feeling a little nauseated from the altitude, so I wolfed down a big bunch of the grapes to get the juice out of them. Bad idea. Within minutes, I threw them all up. The story got around later that I ate the ones that came back out whole, but that's not true. I did feel better, though, having emptied my stomach. After that, I learned how to pace myself eating and drinking on a climb.

On the Mount Olympus climb, we were to be dropped off afterwards in downtown Seattle. As we drove into the city, we heard a loud siren and all sorts of commotion. We stopped to ask somebody what was going on. We were told, "The war is over!"

The streets were full of military men and everyday citizens. Everyone was celebrating, kissing, and hugging each other, and here were Jim and I, let out in the middle of it all. We were wearing grubby clothes and carrying our packs. We'd been out in the mountains about a week. We were only sixteen, but we looked big enough and old enough to be in the army. We were suddenly struck with the fear that somebody would think we were draft dodgers who'd been hiding out in the woods. We caught the first streetcar that came along and headed for home. When we got there, the first thing Mom said to us wasn't, "How was the climb?" but, "How'd you get that lipstick all over your face?"

It wasn't long before our climbing adventures led to mountain-rescue work. Our European mentors were very active in rescues, so we naturally followed them. While we were still in high school, Jim and I joined a two-week search for nine people who had bailed out of a military plane on Mount Rainier. The plane had gotten in trouble during a bad storm and all the passengers and copilot decided to bail. As it turned out, the pilot righted the spin and landed at McChord Air Force Base. All but two of the passengers and crew had made it out safely. We went in after the other two and found one alive, hanging from his chute in a tree. The other, the copilot, was finally located after the search had ended. His chute hadn't opened.

The rescue effort was based at a nearby school gymnasium at Fairfax. We were fed great food, like steaks, potatoes … and coffee. Military coffee. This is when I got hooked on the stuff. I also got hooked on real butter, which had been rationed during the war. It was much better than the white Nucoa margarine that we usually ate.

We'd sleep in the school gymnasium and eat these big meals while waiting for our turn to go up on the mountain, where we'd sleep in the snow and try to stay alive in the rain, snow, and cold while searching for these two guys. It was prime discomfort, but it was also high adventure and I, The Scarlet Avenger, thrived on it. At one time, we all got soaked in our sleeping bags. Since it was my turn to tend the bonfire we maintained at our snow camp, I also got the job of drying out our bags while the rescuers went out searching.

I spent all day dragging dead snags from the forest over the snow to the fire. By the end of the day, I had done such a good job of keeping the fire going that, when the others returned, they found me standing in a ten-foot-deep pit. The fire had burned all the way down through the snowpack to the ground. They got a great laugh out of that. Later Max Eckenburg told me, "Next time, find a stump to build the fire on or, if you can, a raft of green logs."

Jim and I received a letter of commendation from the military for our work on that rescue. It was published in our school bulletin and we were heroes for a week or so.

Many of the outings with Otto Trott and the other guys were in pure fun. They once took us on our first ski mountaineering trip, up to Mount Margaret, by Snoqualmie Pass. These guys were experienced in all methods of mountain travel. They used canvas socks over the backs of their skis or seal skins on the bottoms to give them traction going up the mountain. Jim and I bought canvas socks and managed to keep up with them, although we flailed around a lot.

Once we got to the top, the guys took off their skins and said, "See you at the bottom. Have a good ski." They took off down a steep run, skiing gracefully through the trees.

Jim and I looked at each other. We were just getting beyond snowplow turns on open slopes. How the hell were we to get down through these trees? We'd never have disgraced ourselves in front of our mentors by walking down. It was now or never. So we took off in a feeble attempt to follow their route. Down we went, falling, crashing, grabbing branches along the way. Our clothes were torn ragged by the time we made it to the bottom. This was more dangerous than climbing!

We straggled into the parking lot long after the others had arrived. Otto said, "We've been talking. We think we should take you up to Snoqualmie and teach you how to turn so you won't kill yourselves having so much fun." Max Eckenburg spent a weekend with us that winter, doing just that.

Sometimes we'd ride to the mountains with one of our mentors, Sam Eskanazi. He was one of the better skiers of the group and had good judgment in the mountains. He also was a lover of longhair music, and we'd listen to it on the two-hour drive to our destination. Jim and I looked at these Europeans as true aristocrats. They loved good food and good music, they loved the ruggedness of the mountains. To this day, I enjoy classical music—especially Chopin, Rachmaninoff, Beethoven, and Tchaikovsky—and associate it with the mountains.

Other times, we'd ride with the Ochsner brothers, Marty and Louie. They didn't ski, but they loved climbing. The first cars available after World War II came out in 1946. Marty bought a new Ford that year. A real beauty. Our first trip in that car was to a climb on Mount Adams.

What a memorable drive that was. We had to travel over an old gravel road about forty miles from the main road to the base of the mountain. We scraped over a high center and broke the fuel line in Marty's new Ford. When the car died, Marty found the trouble and fixed it with chewing gum and tape from my first-aid kit.

Undaunted, we drove on in and climbed the north side of Mount Adams, 12,300 feet, via the Adams Glacier. We glissaded down a 4,000-foot couloir and were home the same evening.

By the time World War II had ended, Jim and I were sixteen, and we had left the Explorers to become junior members of The Mountaineers climbing club.

The Mountaineers issued a pin for climbing the six highest mountains in Washington, called "The Major Peaks." After you got that, there was a ten-peak pin, for the ten next highest, then a twenty-peak pin, and a thirty-peak pin. It was fun to collect the summits. If you got the six major peaks, you got your name in The Mountaineer membership book printed in capital letters. Then you got an asterisk alongside your name for the next ten peaks and another notation for the next ten and so on. It was a challenge to get those capital letters and all the asterisks.

In 1947, at age eighteen, Jim and I had met that challenge. We also were still playing basketball. At the game where we beat our own high school team, there happened to be a coaching scout from Seattle University. Afterwards, he approached me and Jim and offered us scholarships. By then, I was working nights at the Boeing Company, guiding in the summer, teaching skiing on weekends in the winter, and participating in rescues, and I hadn't really thought about going to college. Jim and I had been used to working since we were eight, when we had our own newspaper routes. Mom and Dad never pushed us to achieve grades. If the scholarship had been based on scholastic achievement, we'd have been out of luck.

I started thinking about college. It's 1947. I'm eighteen and what am I going to do with my life? Seattle U. was a Catholic college, and Jim and I weren't Catholic, but we both decided to accept the scholarships.

We chose pre-med majors and education minors. Pre-med seemed logical, because we had developed an interest in first-aid during our mountain-rescue work. Otto Trott, a doctor and fellow climber, would take Jim and me into the anatomy lab at the University of Washington and have us work on cadavers. He'd say, "Okay, Lou, this is a dislocated shoulder." And he'd dislocate the cadaver's shoulder, then teach me how to reduce the dislocation. He made me practice over and over again on those cadavers. I paid attention and caught on quickly.

Some of our climbing friends didn't take to this phase of training so easily. One day, Otto had a bunch of us in the anatomy lab and, in the middle of a demonstration, one of the guys keeled right over. Otto said, "Let him be, he'll be all right," and finished the demonstration.

Our basketball career at Seattle University was less than illustrious, even though Jim once became high point man. During the first season, the coach informed us that we would have to choose between basketball and skiing. He was afraid that we would hurt ourselves skiing. Because we were getting paid on the scholarship, we reluctantly agreed not to ski.

I say reluctantly because we were back on the slopes within a weekend or two. We figured we'd never get hurt and the coach would therefore never know. Hindsight always reveals the folly of youth.

Jim and I were headed out for a ski weekend, in different cars. There were several cars between us on the mountain road. A freak avalanche rolled down the mountainside and hit one of those cars, knocking it over the cliff. I was in a car behind the scene, and I knew that the avalanche must have gotten someone. But Jim, who had stopped ahead, waved to me that everything was under control.

Jim headed down the hill to the rescue. On the way down, he lost his ski boots in the deep snow, but he was able to dig out two people from the wreck and get them to safety. The avalanche closed the road, so I had to turn around and go home. Jim, whose car was stopped on the other side of the avalanche, got a great weekend of skiing at Stevens Pass, *and* was also awarded a Purple Star from the Ski Patrol for the rescue. By the time he got home, the story was plastered all over the Seattle papers.

Back at school, the coach confronted us: "You've got to make the decision, now. Skiing or basketball."

Jim and I didn't even have to discuss it. We said, "I guess we'll ski."

The coach was surprised at our decision, but we stuck to it. We had more fun skiing, anyway.

We stayed at the university and earned bachelor of science degrees, supporting ourselves and paying our way through school by working summers at Boeing, guiding, and teaching skiing. The mountains have always been my first choice, and they've been good to me ever since.

◆ 2 ◆

LEARNING THE ROPES

In 1948, when we were nineteen and in our second year of college, Jim and I became charter members of the newly founded Mountain Rescue Council. Wolf Bauer, a ceramic engineer who was also an avid climber and active in rescues, formed the council in an effort to organize and standardize mountain-rescue procedure in the Pacific Northwest. Up until then, rescues had been done informally, by a group of fellow climbers. Somebody would hear about an accident and call somebody else. We'd all converge at a pre-arranged site and ride together to the rescue.

Ome Daiber was the second founding member, and was designated head of technical operations. Ome's wife, Matie, created the answering service for rescue operations. Jim and I were still living at home, so to contact either of us, Matie would call Mom. Dr. Otto Trott, who had been a member of Ski Patrol here in the United States since 1939, became the third founding member. Otto brought his medical expertise to the council.

Just as scouting had introduced us to the outdoors and climbing, mountain-rescue work introduced us to advanced climbing technique and first aid. It also reinforced our love for the mountains, especially for Mount Rainier. Just out of high school, Jim and I also found that there were people who would actually pay to be led up the mountain! By 1948, we were guiding during the summers. It not only helped pay our way through college, but

Lou and Jim geared up for a rescue, 1947 (Photo courtesy Whittaker family)

also introduced me to what would become a lifelong vocation.

Guiding kept us close to rescue work. Most of the time, we'd see the same guys on rescues. A lot of regular climbers didn't participate in rescues. And a lot of rescuers only went out when there was a rescue in effect. Jim and I did both because it gave us an opportunity to climb and to learn alpine technique.

Down lower, in the forest, it took more people than technique to do the searching. Often you would find the lost or injured persons after they had stumbled out onto one of the many roads in the forest—unless it was in the middle of Olympic National Park, where there aren't that many roads. But up higher, above the treeline, you had to depend on alpine skills for your safety and success.

Not all the lessons I learned on rescues involved climbing technique. I'll never forget the first time I saw a dead body. It was in the Olympics, on a peak called The Brothers. Dee Molenaar and Otto Trott were cracking jokes and I was just mortified. All I could think was "this poor guy ..." After seeing my first two or three bodies, I'd dream about them, and awaken from nightmares. But after handling a lot of bodies, I came to accept that death is part of nature, part of the process of life. I felt fortunate to have gained at an early age the gut-level realization that I, too, was going to die someday. It was better to have realized my mortality then, rather than having it sneak up on me in my old age. I never wanted to look back and regret not having lived my life fully.

This doesn't mean that I learned to take death or our rescue efforts lightly. I had a hard time with certain things, such as Dee taking photos of the victim's body. I once told him, "If I ever make a mistake out here and you take my picture, I'm going to come back and cut off your nuts." He couldn't believe it. "What's wrong with you?" he said. "I always take pictures for the record." I told him he was sick.

I eventually learned to joke along with the rest of the guys. You try to distance yourself as much as possible from death, and joking is the best way.

On some rescues, the humor didn't have to be manufactured. When I was with Dee and Otto on The Brothers, on my first rescue involving a dead body, I accidentally broke Otto's toe, and ended up having to rescue him.

Dee and Otto had elected me to climb up to the ledge where we had located the victim. I was to lower him down to them with a rope. The young man had been climbing with a friend when he fell and was injured. His climbing partner had left him at the site in a sleeping bag and gone for help. While the friend was gone, the injured climber fell asleep, rolled over, fell another 400 feet, and died. If his partner had anchored him to a rock, it wouldn't have happened.

The combination of my first encounter with a dead body and the realization of how easily this death had occurred made me a little nervous. I tied the body's feet together and prepared to lower it head first, using a hip belay, but I let the rope slide a bit too fast. The head came down and smacked Otto on the foot, breaking his toe. It was a long hike back, and we had to carry the body. Otto limped, moaned, and groaned all the way, while Dee and I needled him.

As we approached the Hamma Hamma Ranger Station on the east side of the Olympics, we encountered two rangers with two horses. They were on their way to meet us. One horse was for the body. Otto commandeered the other one to relieve his aching toe, although all he knew about a horse was that one end bites and the other end kicks. Otto let the reins go, and assumed that the horse would follow the one in front of it.

I don't know how it happened, but suddenly the saddle slipped and slid underneath the horse, with Otto still hanging onto it. The horse spooked and took off, with Otto crying bloody murder. Dee and I were up ahead, so we jumped out in front of the horse, waving our arms. Luckily, it stopped.

Otto later told everyone that Dee and I had saved his life. I was just glad to have been able to neutralize the act of breaking Otto's toe by rescuing him. I believe that was Otto's last horse ride.

Another part of the attraction of rescue work was the fact that we never had a dull moment with these guys. Otto was a wild man in a car, and the worst driver of the bunch. One time, he was driving to a rescue in heavy fog and drove into a barn. He thought he was following a road, but it turned out to be a farmer's driveway and it led right through the open doors of the barn. Otto simply backed up, turned around, and continued on, while the rest of us in the car nearly died of laughter.

Otto would sometimes let someone else drive his car to a rescue while he caught a nap in the back seat. He had taught himself to fall asleep immediately—a good technique for a doctor. He could catnap anywhere and wake up refreshed. Made us all as jealous as hell. On one early morning rescue, he'd been on call all night, so he crawled in the back seat and promptly fell asleep. A few minutes later, he suddenly awakened and mumbled, "Low left tire." We all said, "Whaaat?" He repeated, "Low left tire. Pull over."

I looked out the window and, sure enough, the left rear tire was going down fast. Otto had sensed it in his sleep.

Another time, Otto was driving us to Mount St. Helens to rescue Art Jesset, a preacher's son. We were racing like mad because, last word we had, Jesset was still alive. There was traffic, so Otto tried to pass a car through the left-turn lane, but ended up straddling the center divider. We had a permit from the State Patrol to use portable red flashing lights that you could stick on top of the car roof. So away went Otto, whizzing down the center divider, flashing lights and all.

We heard a strange noise, sort of like a buzz saw, then—*clang, clang, clang*! A red light flashed in the oil gauge on the dash. Otto pulled off the highway and into a service station, to discover that the oil had completely drained from the car. The oil pan was intact, but the cap had been unscrewed by the center divider. Undaunted, Otto bought another cap, filled the car with oil, and off we went again on our mad dash to the rescue.

This madcap mood changed as soon as we reached Mount St. Helens. Then it was all business as we geared up and got organized. Ome agreed to let me and Jim shoot out ahead to see if we could get to Jesset in time to save him. Jim and I were young and hardy and spent most of our spare time climbing, so we'd often volunteer to get out front and go fast to the rescue site.

We decided to climb unroped on the lower glacier through the crevasses below the Lizard Route because it would be faster. (This route is no longer there. In 1980, when St. Helens erupted, that side of the mountain was blown away.) After the rescue, Ome told us that he was pissed at the sloppiness of our climbing technique. He chewed us out good. He had taught us never to travel over a glacier unroped, not for any reason.

Jim and I had been lucky to safely reach the crevasse where Jesset had fallen in. There were foot tracks around a small hole, about two feet in diameter. His climbing buddies hadn't been able to get him out, and had left an ice axe stuck in the snow by the edge of the crevasse before going for help.

We were supposed to yell down the mountain to the others if the guy was still alive. Both lips of the crevasse were overhung and the sides curved in, out of sight, about sixty feet, so we couldn't see anything but blue ice. By then, we were roped together, and we flipped a coin to determine who would go in. Jim won and was over the lip in a minute. I belayed him and he stopped about eighty feet down, out of sight. "I can't see him," he yelled back up. We knew that Jesset had to be there because the party had marked the crevasse with the ice axe.

A few seconds later, Jim yelled, "I found him." He had finally

Mountain Rescue Council members. Left to right: *Wolf Bauer, Max Eckenburg, Otto Trott, and Ome Daiber, circa 1948 (Photo: Bob and Ira Spring)*

noticed some fingers sticking up through the snow. He was standing right on top of Jesset and didn't know it. Apparently, in an attempt to locate him in the crevasse, Jesset's buddies had enlarged the opening and knocked snow down on him. They said he was still alive when they left, but he was dead now. Frozen. When you make an opening up top on a crevasse, you're supposed to pull snow back out instead of knocking it into the crevasse.

Jesset had been dead for three or four hours. He was wedged in almost vertically, so Jim dug down underneath him and looped a rope around his ankles. Jesset was a big guy, but we had planned to pull him out. Jim positioned himself beside the body, stemming with his crampons, one foot on each side of the narrow crevasse. He yelled, "Pull!" and I pulled, then I heard him shout,

"Stop, stop!" His voice sounded odd, so I called, "Are you okay?"

After a couple of seconds, Jim said, "Yeah, I'll be okay." When I had started pulling, Jesset's lungs had collapsed and let out a moan of air. It scared the hell out of Jim, because he had already checked Jesset's vital signs. He checked again. Sure enough, Jesset was still dead.

I couldn't pull him out alone, so Jim climbed back out and we waited for the others. We all brought Jesset down the mountain, and the reporters—who are always the hardest to deal with—were waiting. They wanted to open the body bag and take pictures of Jesset. The father, a minister, was there, waiting. He was in his robes, leaning over his son, crying. The photo was on the cover of a national magazine. It was pretty grim and is the part we have always hated about rescues. The press can be like vultures.

Otto was great fun as well as a serious climber and a physician. Most of my first-aid skills came from Otto. One day, we had a call on a boy from Paraguay who had fallen off a rock while fishing and had been badly injured in a waterfall. We all took off in Otto's car, mountain-rescue style. Jim and I reached the boy first and had him stabilized by the time Otto and the others reached the scene. Otto's nod of approval was worth more than any commendation we could ever have received.

Other Perspectives: Otto Trott

The day we got a call to rescue an injured boy from Paraguay, I drove to the scene as fast as was safely possible. Lou and Jim were part of the rescue team and struck out ahead of the group. By the time the rest of us arrived where the boy had fallen, Lou and Jim already had made a huge fire against a stone wall by the river. Although the boy had a concussion and a severe cut on his head, they knew he was hypothermic, and dealt with that first. They got him out of his wet clothes and got him warm by the fire. Hypothermia is the most dangerous affliction. You take care of that first, then deal with other problems. That's what the Whittakers did. They were only about eighteen years old.

From then on, I knew that these Whittakers had perfect knowledge of what's important in mountain rescue and first aid. They

continually impressed me with the application of their learning. It
was part of their natural leadership ability.

It took me years to learn to distinguish between Lou and Jim.
They were so alike in walking, in speaking, in behavior, in skiing and
climbing. It didn't matter who did something, they always did it the
same way. By and by, I learned to differentiate. First of all, Lou is
much happier. Jim is more serious. Lou is and always has been more
outgoing, more approachable. Jim is more reserved. Now, as they get
older, they look a little different. To me, it wouldn't be possible to
mistake them anymore.

Another thing about the Whittakers that impressed me, and does
to this day, is how they always give thanks to those who taught them
about the mountains. They always have given credit to other people
for what they do so much better than anyone else.

Since we had full certifications for first aid from our mountain-rescue work, Jim and I were able to join the National Ski Patrol at Stevens Pass. We were often put in charge of directing rescues and first-aid efforts on weekends. We'd sometimes get as many as twenty fractures during a weekend, thanks to the good old long thong bindings used at that time. Either the ski broke or the leg, but never the binding. This unfortunate fact gave us the opportunity to really hone our first-aid skills.

Some of our skill was also used off the mountain. Since our major in college was pre-med and the Jesuits knew of our mountain-rescue work, we'd sometimes get involved in a "rescue" on campus. One time, one of the Jesuits came to get me out of class, saying, "Could you come with me? A girl just slipped on the ice and hurt her leg as she was getting out of her car in front of the university. I think it's a sprain, but could you take a look?" Turns out, the leg was broken, a fracture of the tibia and fibula, both bones of the lower leg.

On ski patrol rescues, we'd often send a self-addressed post-card with our diagnosis along with the injured skier, requesting the physician to confirm our diagnosis. For instance, I'd splint a leg and send the guy down to the hospital with a postcard on which I'd write my diagnosis. I'd ask the doctor to please confirm or correct it and send back the card. Most of them would do it, and that feedback really helped me learn the basics of first aid and what is called second aid, which involves reducing dislocations and aligning fractures.

Always being the rescuer and never the "rescue-ee" was beginning to make both me and Jim feel somewhat invulnerable. It took only one incident, in 1949, when we were twenty, to correct that. Jim and I came close to checking out of this life on a peak called Index near Stevens Pass. We had spotted this beautiful rock peak from the highway, driving in for ski weekends. It looked to have a good 1,000-foot face with some great overhangs. The route was on the North Tower of Index, and our fascination with it grew every time we drove to Stevens Pass that winter.

By summer, we had summoned up enough courage to give it a try. We invited three other guys around our same age, whom we had met on other climbs with The Mountaineers. We parked at the trailhead to Lake Serene, which lies near the base of the North Tower. By late afternoon, we had hiked in and set up camp beneath the cliff face. While the others fixed dinner, Jim and I volunteered to climb up a little ways and lay in the route we would use the next day.

We leapfrogged to a point about 400 feet above our camp. There, the climbing became more technical and exposed. I placed our first piton below and left of an overhang, for protection. Above that, the route looked good, but more extreme than we were used to climbing. We would tackle it the following day.

That night, Jim and I had one of our most intimate talks. We knew tomorrow would be dangerous, even life-threatening. I had been on numerous rescues by then and I thought my life philosophy was set. I told Jim that if I bought the farm tomorrow, I would still be happy. It would be worth it, I said, it's such a great peak. Jim agreed.

We both had inherited the "gentleman's code of honor" from Dad. He had told us that a man should never talk or brag about any women he may have made love with. Even as twins, that was one confidence we hadn't yet broached. So, without mentioning names, Jim and I confessed to each other that we were no longer virgins. We could die without regrets.

In the morning, we all agreed that we'd split up into one rope of two and another rope of three. Jim and I would be together and start first. Since I had led the day before, Jim stepped up and grabbed a handhold while I belayed him. The sun was just touching the peaks to the west of us as we leapfrogged again to my last lead near the overhang. My belay position was a one-foot-wide ledge for my feet and a "hip hole," a depression in the rock face where I could lean in with my hip for more support. Once I leaned in, though, I couldn't see Jim.

The rope had stopped moving, so I leaned out to check on Jim's progress. He was about sixty feet above me and had worked quite a ways to the right and bypassed my piton. He was on an over-hang, which was pushing him out. Gravity was doing its best to pluck him loose. One of his legs was starting to jump, or "sewing machine," a term we used to describe the way a leg vibrates up and down from strain, like it would on an old treadle-driven sewing machine.

Positioned as he was, he had to move up or fall. "Jim," I yelled, "you're too far right!"

"I know, I have to jump for a hold!"

A great rush of adrenaline and rage hit me and these thoughts raced through my mind during the space of a few seconds: We've screwed up. I'm not anchored. He'll freefall 120 feet and pull me off. We'll maybe hit once on the 400-foot fall. I'm not mad at Jim, I'm mad at *us*. He's my twin. It took both of us to start our leapfrog lead opposite from yesterday, and my leaning in and not watching him, and my assuming that I didn't need to protect my belay… I'm quite sure we won't make it, but that's to be found out—"Go ahead!" I shouted, bracing myself for his fall.

Jim jumped out and up, one hand grabbing and scratching for a handhold on top of the overhang. With both feet dangling free, he pulled himself up and over, and disappeared.

Shaking with anger and relief, I leaned into my hip hole and paid out another ten feet of rope as I felt Jim climb higher. Then he stopped. I heard faint voices float up from the three climbers a couple hundred feet below me, and I realized that they knew nothing of our predicament. As it turned out, we never told them.

Then a weak voice from above said, "On belay, climb." I fol-lowed the route I had laid yesterday, to the left of the overhang. When I reached Jim, he was sitting in a good hip belay and looking pale. We stared at each other a long time before either of us spoke.

"We screwed up good," I said.

Jim nodded. We stood, and with renewed caution, finished the route, summitting the North Tower of Index.

I laugh now to think how arrogant we were to believe that we had done everything in life we wanted to do when we were twenty years old. We had thought we were willing to die for a peak! Through the years, as we polished our climbing technique, the sloppiness of our North Tower climb settled in as one of those life lessons that lurks nearby, ever vigilant, keeping you alert and humble. Nothing reinforces the awareness of your own mortality like a close brush with death.

I also realized that I wanted to live so that I could continue to see a girl I had met that summer. My sense of self-preservation was becoming heightened by a new desire.

I had met Pat at The Sand Pit, the beach where Mom had always taken us as kids to walk. Pat was an attractive eighteen-year-old girl who had just moved with her parents to Burien, Washington, from Venice, California. When I met her, she was visiting her grandmother, who lived near my parents.

I started talking to Pat right away, but it took me a while to work up the courage to ask her on a date. We started going to dances and skiing. She was my first real girlfriend. During high school, Jim and I hadn't dated girls or gone to the prom. In our spare time, we worked and played sports. We didn't drink beer and carouse. This all started to change when we got to college. When I met Pat, I fell in love quickly, and I fell hard.

That's when I started getting really motivated to have a car. Since Jim and I still lived at home, we had been bumming rides to the mountains and riding the bus to the university. Right after I met Pat, I bought an old 1937 Plymouth coupe, so that we could go on real dates.

I was soon working a twelve-hour shift at Boeing during summers to save enough money to buy an engagement ring. Looking back, I think if I hadn't had such a strong sex drive, I wouldn't have married so young. In those days, you didn't make love unless you were married. That's how I was raised, and I wanted to honor my parents' beliefs. Pat and I fudged a little, but we made a commitment to each other and stuck to it. In my mind, marriage was the only way we could legitimately continue to make love.

Pat and I married in Seattle in 1950. I was twenty-one, still in college, and the first of the three brothers to get married. Pat was nineteen. We honeymooned by train to Mount Hood in Oregon, and skied.

I worked at Boeing during the summers of 1947, 1948, and 1949. By the summer of 1950, both Jim and I were guiding on Mount Rainier in the summer and participating in rescues whenever we were called. I also took a part-time job at a sporting goods store in Seattle called Osborn and Ulland. On days off, we skied or climbed. Pat liked to ski and, luckily, she understood my devotion to mountaineering.

She also understood my devotion to my twin brother. After we were married, Pat and I rented a house only a few blocks from my parents' home, and we visited quite often. Everyone liked Pat and the feeling was mutual. Even so, making that jump from the nest, away from Jim and the family, was tough on both me and Jim. Mom told me later that Jim took it pretty hard. He would sit by the fireplace and stare at the fire, and was depressed for quite a long time. The separation was a little easier on me because I had a love interest. Instinctively, I knew that, as twins, it was important for me and Jim to stay as close as possible, but also to lead separate lives. I knew we would always share many of the same interests, but we needed to also develop some other interests on our own.

I took the responsibility of marriage very seriously. In 1951, about a year after my marriage, I was able to buy a house in the Green Lake area of Seattle for $500 down. This meant moving farther away from Jim and the family, but it also meant an investment in the future for me and Pat. Pat and I settled into a very active life-style. We had a great time together, partying and skiing with our friends from college and, of course, with Jim.

During that time, Jim met a girl at the university and fell in love. She was Catholic and he decided to convert to Catholicism before they were married. Jim and I had some great arguments about religion at that time, as you do in college when you're trying to figure out what life's all about. We had been raised Protestant, but here we were, at a Catholic university where there were very few non-Catholics. The atmosphere was ripe. The pressure was on to convert.

Most of our professors were Jesuits, and they were good educators. I avoided the religious ceremonies, or rituals as I called them. At the time, my religious beliefs already had begun to take root in the natural world. In my mind, the laws of nature applied to human life as much as they did to the rest of the universe. Religious dogma didn't interest me, except for the sake of argument.

Jim invited the whole family to the ceremony for his conversion. The Jesuits had provided a limousine for Jim to ride in to the church. Barney drove the car behind with me, Pat, and a despondent Mom and Dad. Barney decided that things were getting way too serious, so he turned on the headlights, as though we were in a funeral procession. Mom was crying in the back, Barney was laughing up front. We saw Jim turn around in the limo and gesture at us, as if saying "Turn off the damn lights!" Jim later broke off his engagement, but he remained Catholic.

My concern about Jim's conversion was that he and I would never go climbing or skiing together again, because on Sundays he'd have to be in church instead. As is turned out, Jim would get up at five in the morning and go to early mass, then we'd meet and head for the mountains.

We even started taking one of the Jesuits skiing. Father Snarenger ended up going quite often and would sometimes hold mass at the ski area. He actually was a good skier. I'd argue with him, too, about epistemology, about the ten proofs of the existence of God and things like that. Jim would get mad when I argued with the Jesuits. I saw it as good fun.

The separation from Jim and marriage to Pat helped mature my outlook on life. I had always taken my commitments seriously, but with a sort of boyish intensity. Now I saw myself as a husband and a provider, and I paid even closer attention to my own safety.

I still sought the adrenaline rush of high risk and adventure, but learned to temper it with judgment. That judgment mostly came from rescue work. Rescues invariably brought up the questions "How did this guy die?" and "How can I prevent this from happening to me?" I learned many lessons on rescues that I later passed on to my climbing students and other guides who came to work for me.

One of the lessons I learned from rescues is the value of sharing each other's strength. You get a little tired, a little blue, and the other guys lift you up. It helps control egos, too, when you learn to help each other, rather than just concentrating on your own needs.

Some of the lessons I learned were very practical ones, such as the proper use of equipment. When I was twenty-three, I participated in the rescue of a man who had been killed when he and his climbing partner had used an upholsterer's cotton cord, about the size of a clothesline rope, as an anchor rope around a rock. They had made four turns with the rope around the rock, but only used a single knot to tie it off. Their rappel rope was okay, but the cotton anchor rope frayed on the rock and broke, and the man was killed in the fall.

On another rescue, I learned not to wear a poncho or loose clothing on the high mountain, so that you could always see your feet and where you were placing them. A climber had been on a ledge in pouring rain. He took a high step to another ledge and stepped on his own poncho, tried to straighten up, couldn't, fell off the ledge, and killed himself.

Incidents like these taught me that most deaths in the mountains occur as the result of simple mistakes or errors in judgment—made by novice as well as accomplished climbers.

As much as I've learned about the dangers of lightning, I'm still a little jumpy in lightning storms. I've had St. Elmo's fire come off my metal skis and ice axe, and it makes me spookier than hell. I've spent the night in a cave on a mountain during a storm, knowing that lightning could come in and scour out the walls, but figuring it was safer in there than being exposed on the mountainside.

Lightning was the cause of the death of the first friend I ever lost in mountaineering. In 1952, a college buddy, Paul Brikoff, was struck and killed by lightning. Paul had been climbing with another friend, Bob Grant. A lightning storm had moved in on the peak they were climbing, and both men were struck. Bob managed to roll down the slope a ways, away from the strike zone. Paul was not so lucky. Bob later told us that Paul had been struck at least five times. The lightning melted the metal of Paul's pack.

This was my first introduction to grief. It reinforced the realization that I could just as easily have been the person who had been killed. The person who dies climbing never thinks that it's going to be him or her and doesn't suffer the loss that the friends and relatives do. The dead are free of worry and grief. The survivors have to deal with patching the hole in their lives caused by the unexpected death of a loved one.

As a rescuer, once you've located the victim, the easiest part of your job is over. The toughest part lies ahead, telling the families and friends of their loss. It's a job I've always dreaded, but I've never shied away from it. Still, I can't help thinking, "What if it had been me? What kind of grief would I be causing my family and friends?"

I think I've saved about half the people I've gone after. That makes you feel good. You get rewarded now and then by realizing that if you hadn't been there, that person wouldn't have made it. That's a good feeling. It cancels out some of the negative ones.

Some of the rescues Jim and I were involved in received a lot of publicity and some were kept quiet. The quiet ones usually involved military aircraft. We were security-cleared to be flown in to different military crash sites in the Cascades and Olympics. A foot was about the biggest piece of anything we'd ever find. More often, we'd find a guy's wallet, a finger ring, or something like that. We'd bring out anything that might help verify the identity of the victim.

There are planes—private, commercial, and military—stacked all over the mountains of the Northwest. Some of the military craft were still armed when we went in. There would be rockets lying all over the place. On one rescue, out of four men in two airplanes, two had bailed out safely, but they weren't sure about the other two. In the wreckage, I found a piece of skull, so we knew that one of the guys didn't make it. While we were at the site, I got a radio call telling us that the other guy had just been found out on a road. In five days, he had walked out fifty miles and flagged down a car. Amazing guy.

I talked to him later and discovered that he was from Florida and was afraid of bears. He told me that he had sat up all night, holding a club. I told him, "You don't need to be afraid of any bears out here." He was sure they were going to kill him before he made it to safety.

On that rescue, I had been lifted out by helicopter. I was in wilderness, and twenty minutes later, I was having breakfast. Helicopters are good on rescues, although they tend to crash, too.

We didn't always find the people we set out to rescue. Many are still out there, on Mount Rainier and Mount St. Helens. In 1952, when Jim and I were about to graduate from college, we were facing a comprehensive, four-year exam that you had to pass to graduate. Two days before the exam, we were on a ski ascent with some friends on Mount St. Helens when one of our party, Willy Rosenstein, took a fall near a rock outcropping called Dog's Head and suffered a spiral fracture of his tibia and fibula, thanks again to those long thong bindings.

We put a splint on Willy's leg and used his skis as a sled to slowly take him down the hill. We spread out, single file, and, as usual, assigned a rear guard—a person responsible for making sure that no one skied away from the rest of the party. We got down to our cars with no mishaps, only to discover that one of our party, Joe Carter, was missing.

We didn't find out until later that Joe was diabetic. We went back all the following week to search for him, on the mountain and in the woods. We slept in the woods on bark laid on the snow, but we never found him. Somehow, he had skied off to one side and the rear guard hadn't seen him. He might have gone into a diabetic coma and suffered hypothermia. We'll never know. It was heartbreaking.

During the rescue, Jim and I missed the comprehensive exam, but the university decided to grant us an extension and let us take the test. Jim and I were put in two separate rooms with the exam. I was about two-thirds of the way done when one of the Jesuits walked in and said, "Okay, Lou, you passed the test last week. If you don't feel like finishing the test, don't."

"What? I can finish it."

"I'm telling you, you don't have to," said the Jesuit. "As far as we're concerned, you've earned your diploma." He was referring to our rescue work. "You've done a great job."

Jim was waiting outside the room, grinning. We were honored at graduation. They said something about how even though we didn't conform to the discipline of basketball, we were among the top athletes at the university.

It had taken Jim and me five years to graduate from college, because we'd taken a couple quarters off to ski in Sun Valley, Idaho. After we graduated, we were faced with the Korean War. Everyone we knew was getting drafted. I didn't want to kill anyone and I knew that I sure as hell didn't want to get shot at. I really wanted to stay out of the war. At one point, Jim and I thought that we might get a deferment if we went for a master's degree. We found out that, except for science, our grades hadn't been good enough to enter the master's program. Our counselor said that we could get in on the G.I. Bill when, and *if*, we returned from the war.

We received our draft notices in the spring of 1952. Our first concern was that we would lose the summer guiding season on Mount Rainier. We had spent the past two years getting established on the mountain. We even had outfitted ourselves with gear from an airdrop that the army had made on the summit of Rainier during a military rescue. We had to return the radios and drugs from the first-aid kits, but had been able to keep the army-issue packs, tents, sleeping bags, and stoves. Now it looked like we'd be using army gear for the real thing.

Jim, Hortense Whittaker, and Lou at college graduation, 1952
(Photo: C. B. Whittaker)

We asked Al Rose, the superintendent of Mount Rainier National Park, for assistance. He wrote a letter to the Department of Defense, stating something like, "These boys are essential to the operation of Mount Rainier National Park and shouldn't be drafted until fall."

It worked. We graduated that spring, and were deferred through the summer. We guided right up until we got our draft notices in the fall. Before we were inducted into the army, Jim married Blanche, a girl he had met at Mount Rainier. We were sent to Camp Roberts in San Luis Obispo, California, for basic training with the infantry, and were able to take our wives with us.

It was soon discovered that Jim and I were competent typists, so we were almost immediately assigned to the Signal Corps. The deal was, if we typed for a half day, three days a week, we could have weekends off. Since our wives lived off base, we were able to spend more time with them. Jim and I were immensely gratified to discover that our wives liked each other. We were able to do things together once again, even if most of it was army business.

During basic training, I wrote letters to a couple of friends who were teaching mountain troops stateside—in particular, Bob Craig and Colonel Ed Link. Jim and I were looking to get assigned stateside, rather than get shipped out to Korea. We sweated it right up to two days before our ship was to leave for Korea. Our commanding officer called us into his office and said that our orders had been cut for Camp Hale, Colorado, to teach skiing and survival skills in winter and rock climbing in the summer. We couldn't believe our good fortune! Pat and Blanche were able to go with us, and the four of us spent most weekends together.

For nearly two years, Jim and I taught skiing and climbing in the mountains of Colorado, which helped us polish our own skills. Whenever we were out on snow, we had to wear camouflage whites. Our skis were wood, painted white, and we used bamboo poles. The soldiers we trained in winter survival and mountaineering were all in top physical shape. They were members of the Tenth Special Forces, career soldiers groomed to go behind enemy lines. Many of them spoke several foreign languages.

These Special Forces guys had a lot of special talents. One of them demonstrated his proclivity toward lock-picking one day when I lost the key to my footlocker. I had bought a heavy-duty, supposedly foolproof, lock after several thefts had occurred in the barracks. The soldier volunteered to open it for me. He used a straightened paper clip and snapped open that lock in about three seconds! I didn't ask him where he'd received that training.

After teaching skiing and winter survival at Camp Hale, we went to Fort Carson in Colorado Springs to teach rock climbing during the summer months. We were starting to get good enough ourselves to think about bigger mountains. Then, in 1953, the news came that a New Zealander named Edmund Hillary had become the first man to summit Mount Everest, the world's highest mountain. We were crushed. That goal had been brewing in the backs of our minds. But in 1953, at the age of twenty-four, we were still too young and inexperienced for an assault of that proportion.

At the same time that Hillary's Everest expedition was being cooked up, an American team was planning the first American expedition to K2, the second-highest mountain in the world. We either knew, or had heard of, several of the climbers on that expedition, including Bob Craig, Dee Molenaar, Pete Schoening, Art Gilkey, and Bob Bates. The climb was to be led by Dr. Charles Houston, an eminent Himalayan climber. Jim and I were considered for the climb, but the army denied us permission.

Art Gilkey died in an avalanche on that climb. Forty years later, in 1993, his corpse emerged from the glacier about a mile from base camp. It was still wearing the red Eddie Bauer down parka that had been standard issue for the expedition members. Gilkey's remains were evacuated from the mountain and returned to his family.

Jim and I were fated to wait until several years after our discharge from the army to get our first taste of expedition-style climbing. In the meantime, after we had served in the army for twenty-one months, the new superintendent at Mount Rainier National Park, Preston Macy, wrote another letter to the Department of Defense, saying that the mountain desperately needed guides. Jim and I were honorably discharged early in order to return to guide on Mount Rainier. Our stint in the army turned out to be mercifully short.

◆ 3 ◆

A GUIDE'S LIFE

After our return from the army in 1954, Jim and I settled into married life and started looking toward the future. We resumed guiding on Mount Rainier during that summer and going on rescues throughout the Cascades and Olympics. We also got "regular" jobs, in sporting goods. Jim went to work for Lloyd Anderson's REI, and I went back to Osborn and Ulland, to manage a new branch store in Bellevue.

Pat and I sold our house in Green Lake and moved to Lake Sammamish, to put me closer to the store. Jim and Blanche had first moved to Mercer Island after the army but, within a short time, they uprooted and moved almost next door to me and Pat at Lake Sammamish. There was only one house between us, and it was owned by the Jesuits of Seattle University. They used it as a retreat.

Jim and I felt that our close living arrangement might be tough on Blanche and Pat. We didn't want to assume that the four of us would be doing everything together, even though we all got along so well. So Jim and I agreed to make a conscious effort to develop different interests off the mountain. Despite our good intentions, Jim and I ended up spending less time on the mountain together and more time together with our wives. Blanche and Pat had be-

Opposite: *Lou belaying a climber on the Ingraham Glacier (Photo: Bob and Ira Spring)*

come friends, and that drew us even closer together. By the mid-fifties, Jim was devoting most of his time to REI, and rarely guided with me.

He still went on rescues, though, and it was during our first summer home from the army that we were called in on one of the hairiest rescues we'd ever attempted on Mount Rainier, involving a plane crash.

We learned that a scientific party had been camped on the summit, doing a study of volcanoes. One of the group had died of pulmonary edema. A pilot had tried to fly in to assess the rescue, but had crashed. When we arrived at the park ranger headquarters at Rainier, we were told that the scientific party had been led down the mountain by another rescue team, but the pilot and passenger might still be alive.

There were a couple of rangers and three or four other rescuers already at the Camp Muir hut, at 10,000 feet. At Paradise, at the base of the mountain, where Jim and I converged with eight other rescue people, it was raining. We left Paradise and climbed like hell, to get out of the weather and to Camp Muir as soon as possible. All but me, Jim, and one other rescuer turned back on the climb to Camp Muir.

The rain turned to snow as we climbed higher and froze the elbow and knee joints on our clothes. We felt like we were wearing armor by the time we got to the hut at Muir.

There, we greeted Dick McGowan, who had the guide concession on Rainier at the time. Jim and I had been guiding independently that summer, but we liked McGowan. He was a good climber, with good judgment. We told him that we'd be ready to head on up to the summit as soon as we changed into dry cold-weather gear.

"Who else is going?" we asked the group in the hut. Nobody volunteered, not even the guy who had just climbed to Muir with us. By then, it was snowing and blowing outside the hut and nobody wanted to risk it. Except McGowan. He roped up between me and Jim.

We had a radio, so we could keep in touch with the park ranger at Paradise. We climbed to around 14,000 feet before we put in our first call. Because of the high wind, I had to yell into the radio:

"Where do you think the plane crashed?"

The ranger replied, "Around 14,200, just off the summit."

I had been on compass and altimeter, in an effort to keep our bearings straight. We were getting knocked around a lot, but we kept going up. I made another call, to ask the status at Camp Muir. We wanted to know that there would be backup for us when we got back down to 10,000 feet. "Backup" on a rescue means that there are people waiting at designated stations to care for both survivors and rescuers, with first-aid, dry clothing, food, and drink as needed. The ranger said, "Sorry, Lou, they've all left for Paradise."

"Geez, no backup at all?"

"Nope. They've all gone back down to Paradise, but Dave Mahre is trying to get up to Muir."

The rangers and mountain-rescue team at Camp Muir had bailed out, but there was one man who was making his way to Muir in the storm, determined to give us some backup. We had never met Dave Mahre, but we'd heard of him. He was from the Yakima area, and had a reputation as an excellent climber, mountain rescuer, and skier.

In the meantime, McGowan, Jim, and I decided to climb a little higher, to a point just off the rim of the summit. The wind was fierce; we couldn't see anything. Finally I said to the others, "Let's stop trying to show each other up and get out of here. I think we're really sticking our necks out." I figured if anyone had survived the crash, they would only have lived a few minutes out there, unless they were dressed for a 30-below storm, as we were. We all agreed that it looked hopeless, so I radioed down to the ranger that we were calling off the search. "We don't think those guys could be alive," I said.

"Okay, Lou," the ranger replied. "Remember, the parents are here."

It wasn't until about ten years later that we developed a radio code for rescues where we'd call a dead or presumed-dead person a "Breitenbach," after Jake Breitenbach, who became my replacement on the 1963 Mount Everest team, and who died on the second day of the climb. After that, on rescues we'd say, "We've got a Breitenbach here," in case family members were listening in.

When McGowan, Jim, and I got back to Muir, it was colder than hell. Dave Mahre had just arrived and started brewing hot drinks.

The four of us spent the night there, waiting for the storm to let up enough for us to descend. We didn't find our crash victims that night. Instead, I found a lifelong friend in Dave. He later guided with me on Rainier and became a member of both of my Everest expeditions.

It wasn't until the sixth day after the crash that the weather finally cleared enough for a helicopter to take us up top to survey the wreckage. We spotted a wing sticking out of the snow near the summit. We jumped out of the 'copter, dug down to the cockpit, and found two men, squashed against the instrument panel, obviously killed on impact. The rescue was over.

It was not unusual for most of the rescuers to have abandoned the rescue effort when the weather got bad. This has happened quite often over the years, and we sometimes end up having to rescue some of the rescuers. Unfortunately, there are a lot of guys who like wearing the Mountain Rescue Council patch who aren't fit enough to participate in a rescue on the upper mountain. There are lots of jobs on the lower mountain for which they would be better suited. If I'm leading a rescue party, I'll tell them, "If anyone can't keep up with me, you're going to get cut. I'm not slowing down." Because lives are at stake, I want only top people with me.

I thrived on my work in the mountains. Guiding was always my first love and I didn't want to give it up. But at best, it was a good summer job. It just wasn't lucrative enough to be the sole source of support for my family.

In the fifties, we charged $28 for a two-day guided climb to the summit. Today, that same climb costs a little more than $300. In 1950, we also charged $5 per person to go to the ice caves. It was our most popular trip. The ice caves were a series of tunnels on the lower mountain, formed at the outlets of a few streams that emerged from the end of the Paradise–Stevens Glacier. Back then, we'd climb to the summit maybe twelve to fifteen times during the summer, but we'd go to the ice caves twice a day, once in the morning and once in the afternoon. We'd take anywhere from three to forty people each time. It was a three-hour round trip, and our biggest

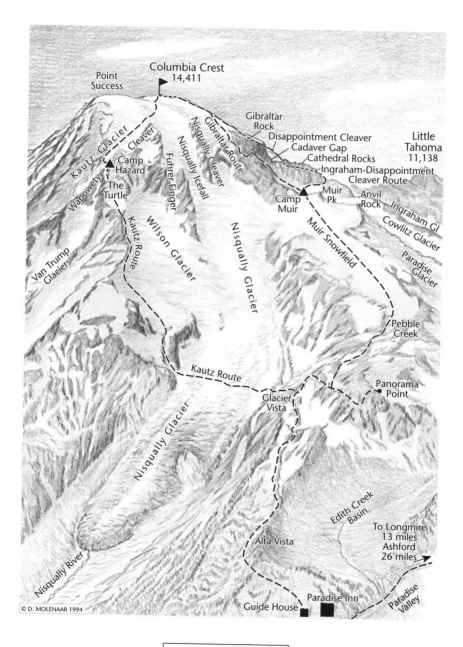

Columbia Crest
14,411
Point
Success
Gibraltar
Rock
Disappointment Cleaver
Cadaver Gap
Cathedral Rocks
Ingraham-Disappointment
Cleaver Route
Little
Tahoma
11,138
Kautz Glacier
Cleaver
Nisqually Route
Gibraltar Route
Nisqually Cleaver
Camp
Hazard
Fuhrer Finger
Nisqually Icefall
Wapowety
The
Turtle
Camp
Muir
Muir
Pk
Anvil
Rock
Ingraham Gl
Kautz Route
Wilson Glacier
Nisqually Glacier
Muir Snowfield
Cowlitz Glacier
Paradise
Glacier
Van Trump
Glaciers
Pebble
Creek
Kautz Route
Panorama
Point
Glacier
Vista
Nisqually Glacier
Edith Creek
Basin
Alta Vista
To Longmire
13 miles
Ashford
26 miles
Nisqually River
Paradise Inn
Paradise
Valley
© D. MOLENAAR 1994
Guide House

MOUNT RAINIER

source of income. The ice caves were closed around 1970, because they had melted back and grown smaller.

In 1950, nearly 200 people attempted to climb to the summit of Mount Rainier with me or Jim as their guide. In 1992, my guide service, Rainier Mountaineering, Inc., or RMI, guided more than 2,500 people. About the same number of independent climbers also attempted the summit. Five or six thousand people climbing for the summit each summer is about average nowadays. The Park Service regulates the number of climbers on the mountain, and we gladly comply, to help preserve the resource.

My love for Mount Rainier has not diminished over the years. It's beauty is stunning, to climbers and non-climbers alike. The glaciated summit rises to 14,410 feet, dwarfing every peak around it. Paradise—the site of the Visitor Center at Mount Rainier National Park, the Paradise Inn, and the Guide House—sits at 5,500 feet. It's the end of the road and the beginning of the climb up the mountain. Timberline is at 6,000 feet, leaving climbers more than 8,400 vertical feet of challenging alpine conditions on which to test their skills. The glaciers, crevasses, icefalls, and steep rocky ridges make it a difficult, and therefore rewarding, mountain to climb.

Mount Rainier creates its own climate. Sometimes when you fly into Seattle, you'll see the peak sticking up above the clouds. It will be raining in Seattle and sunny on the summit of the mountain. We often lead climbing parties up out of the rain or snow at the Guide House at Paradise and into sunny conditions at Camp Muir. At other times, the weather on the upper mountain will be as severe as on any high mountain in the world. That's what makes Rainier such an excellent training ground for high-altitude expeditions.

As a dormant volcano, Mount Rainier occasionally huffs and puffs steam and smoke from its crater. In the summit crater, which is full of snow and encrusted with ice, there are fumaroles, or steam vents, that have been formed in the ice by the pressure of the escaping steam of the volcano. Jim and I didn't lead parties through the network of caves and passageways in the crater because it was considered dangerous, but we were curious about them for years. In 1954, we went into one of the caves a little ways, but turned back when we smelled sulphur fumes. We rolled a rock into another cave and heard a splash. "By God, there's a lake down there," said

Jim. "Yeah," I said, in my youthful exuberance, "and maybe blind mermaids, too!" It wasn't until 1970 that I got the chance to fully explore the steam vents on the summit.

During our early years of guiding on Rainier, clients bunked with me and Jim either in the 12-by-20-foot rock cook shack that had been built in 1929, or in tents at Camp Muir, our "base camp" at 10,000 feet on the south-facing side of the mountain. We'd set up tents on the ridge. The tents were okay for a few weeks, then in the first storm they'd get ripped off the damn mountain and we'd have to retrieve or replace them. We followed this routine until 1970, when the Park Service finally let us build a bunkhouse at Camp Muir.

As guides, Jim and I did everything, from cooking the meals to training the clients. Later on, when RMI became the established guiding concession, I hired "cabin girls" to do the cooking.

When Jim and I were guiding, we rarely climbed together, because we alternated climbs. I brought a party to Camp Muir the first day, cooked dinner, and got them bedded down early. We got up about midnight, ate breakfast, and started up the mountain to the summit. We came back down that afternoon and took a rest break at Camp Muir, then I locked up the cook shack and took the party back to Paradise. A day or two later, Jim arrived with the next party, and did the same routine.

Jim and I did climb together at the end of the season, during what we called the "employee climb." We offered our summit climb at half price to employees of Paradise Inn. Their bosses wouldn't let them climb during the season because they came back too tired to work. So we waited until they got laid off at the end of the season. Our season ended earlier then, on Labor Day weekend. (Today we run to the first week in October.) We'd have seventeen or eighteen people in the cook shack—mostly people we both knew from working at Rainier all summer—and it usually turned into a great party.

During this time, I met Jerry Lynch, who worked for Rainier National Park Company, a concessionaire that supplied different services, including horseback rides and climbing gear. Jerry and I saw each other at Paradise and went to some of the same parties. In those days, the park was sort of a closed operation. You couldn't get in or out of the park after ten at night. You had to make your own social life, which we often did. Jerry and I became friends and, later, business partners.

Jerry eventually became manager of the Paradise Inn. Part of his job was to help promote the horse guides that operated on the mountain. They aren't there any more, but at one time, you could ride to the Skyline Trail, at 6,800 feet, as well as to some of the nearby lakes.

In the fifties, the road to Paradise came up the head of the valley. The buses had to round a corner right below the Paradise Inn. As they slowed down, Jerry jumped aboard, dressed like a cowboy. A horse person he was not. With his horn-rimmed glasses, he looked more like Buddy Holly in cowboy garb. But he gave the tourists a spiel about what there was to do at Mount Rainier National Park: horse trips, ice caves, guided hiking and summit trips.

As if that weren't enough haranguing of the tourists, during meal times at the inn one of us—usually Jerry, and sometimes me or Jim—made another brief presentation. Jim and I did an exhibition "climb" of one of the large timber posts in the high lobby of the Paradise Inn. Those were the days when people stayed at Paradise longer than a day. They came in on buses on Cook's Tours and stayed for three or four days, which was plenty of time to get them enthused about a summit climb. Nowadays, people who come to climb usually have it planned beforehand. You rarely see someone just drop in the Guide House and decide to go on a summit climb.

The routine we followed then on guided climbs hasn't changed that much over the years. There have been changes and advances in gear, clothing, and boots, but the basic techniques and routine remain about the same. Camp Muir has always been our main base camp. This is where we bring the climbing parties on the first day, whether they are on a two-day or a longer summit climb. We get some beautiful views from this spot. You can see Mount St. Helens, Mount Adams, Mount Hood, and Mount Jefferson, the latter two of which are in Oregon.

The weather varies from incredible sun to incredible storm. Sometimes we make it to the summit and sometimes we have to turn back for one reason or another: high avalanche danger, high

Evening climbing demonstration in Paradise Inn lobby with Lou on top, early 1950s (Photo: Bob and Ira Spring)

winds, an approaching storm, or a client who is unable to continue. In college I minored in education, so when I started guiding regularly, I felt that I already had the basis for teaching mountaineering as a professional educator. From the beginning, I tried to set up my guide service as a climbing school, with a formalized teaching program and a structured course, rather than just telling a client, "Follow me and wait till I tell you what to do next."

As my guide service became more structured and grew in size, I was able to pass along my techniques to the guides I hired. Phil Ershler, who joined my guide service in 1970, has said, "Lou didn't teach me that much about mountaineering, but he taught me everything I know about guiding." Guiding is a lot different than mountaineering. You're responsible for a whole group, not just yourself, and you have to constantly think about everything that can go wrong, then try to prevent it.

During the "school" part of a five-day summit climb, we teach self-arrest, which involves learning to stop yourself in a fall by using an ice axe. We have the clients fall down a slope backwards, forwards, and sideways. In each position, they practice stabbing their ice axes into the snow or ice, achieving a pivot point with the axe, swinging their legs around so they're downslope, digging in with their feet, anchoring the ice axe, and holding on. Using this technique, they're less likely to get pulled off the mountain if one of the climbers they're roped to takes a fall or plunges into a crevasse.

There's usually at least one death a summer from an independent, or non-guided, rope team being pulled off the mountain. If you learn how to stop correctly, you not only save yourself but your rope team as well. In the early days, we didn't always teach self-arrest because we actually thought the less the client knows the better. We felt it was too much for them to think about. Concentrating on walking up the mountain was taxing enough. Now, before you can climb Mount Rainier with my guide service, you have to be able to self-arrest.

Once you fall, you want to stop as soon as possible, before you accelerate. Falling for ten feet, you weigh twice as much as you do when you first fall. At twenty feet down the slope, you can weigh the equivalent of 1,000 pounds. So we try to teach a fairly immediate self-arrest.

We also teach how to handle a rope and how to belay another climber to protect them if they fall. To teach rappeling, we fix a doubled rope at the top of a cliff using different types of anchors. For a hasty rappel, we use a friction wrap, where the rope runs around your hip or back, and you monitor the speed with your hands. You can come down a lot faster that way, without the rope running through a belay device such as a carabiner or figure eight. You tend to get more butterflies walking off the edge of a cliff with a friction wrap than you do using a belay device.

For ice-climbing instruction, we go out on one of the glaciers, usually the Cowlitz, to a serac and show the clients how to use crampons. We show them how to front-point using just the two front points of each crampon, and how to ascend using an ice axe and ice hammer, moving just one foot or one hand at a time. We teach two-point suspension using three tools—two crampons and an ice axe. If it's real steep, we use both an ice axe and an ice hammer and both cramponed feet. This is called three-point suspension, just as in rock climbing.

Three-point suspension involves first moving the ice axe, then the foot, then the ice hammer, then the other foot. Moving one appendage at a time gives you more security on an ice wall. Not two at once, or you reduce your points of suspension. This technique really came into play on our Kangchenjunga expedition in 1989, when we encountered a steep, 3,000-foot ice face beginning at 21,000 feet. Six of my RMI guides summitted, after front-pointing on that ice wall for several hours at a time.

When you're climbing ice, you want to climb on the shady side. Ice screws are metal and it's really a scary feeling to look down and see them all melting out, except for the one you just put in.

We also teach clients how to jump a crevasse. We're talking a small crack, of course, not a yawning gap in the glacier. Just a little "rip." We set up a belay from behind, so that if you fall you'll be held by the rope. We always remind clients to build up a little slack in the rope before they jump, so they can reach the other side. We've learned to never assume that a client knows even the most obvious bit of technique.

And we tell clients that if they do fall in, sometimes they can walk around down there in the crevasse. It's like being in a different world. Quiet, cold, surrounded by hard blue glacial ice. It's okay when someone falls in while on a rope, because we're always looking for hero pictures. You always want to bring back some good hero pictures from a climb.

Suspension traverses are the most fun. We string a rope across a crevasse and anchor it on the top of each side. Then we rig up a pulley to which you clip in your harness. You walk off the edge of the crevasse and just slide across to the other side.

We make a point of instructing clients on how to set up a system for a rappel or a traverse, or for a crevasse rescue. They may need to perform a rescue on their own some day, when they're out on a glaciated mountain on an unguided climb. Many times, we don't have to simulate a rescue because a client will accidentally "discover" a crevasse while we're climbing.

We've always risen around midnight or one in the morning on the day of the summit attempt, because it's a long day. You walk for a total of about twelve hours, in rope teams of four to six people. At our first rest stop, at 11,000 feet, we're usually greeted by a beautiful sunrise. Every hour or so, we take about a ten- or fifteen-minute rest break. No longer than that, so you don't lose your body heat. You stop, immediately put on a parka, eat and drink, do maintenance checks on your carabiners, harness, rope, and crampons, look each other over, check knots. Then take off the parka, stuff it in your pack, and off we go again, to the summit.

From the beginning, I thought guiding was the greatest job in the world. So what if it didn't pay that much? I was getting paid to do something I loved, and what could be better than that? I can't say that I wasn't motivated by the dollar, because I definitely was. I didn't want the life of a "climbing bum," who scrapes together barely enough money to exist between climbs. I wanted to support my family. I just didn't want to get stuck in some mundane occupation that had nothing to do with my passion.

◆ 4 ◆

SETTING RECORDS WITH JOHN DAY

By the late fifties, my life had become pretty serious. Pat had given birth to our daughter, Kimberly, in 1957 and our son, Peter, in 1958. I had a wife, two kids, and some freelance guiding that was barely bringing in enough to cover expenses. I still had my job at Osborn and Ulland. In addition to working the sales floor, I also had started working as a sales representative for a few lines in their wholesale division, which put me on the road part of the time. It was starting to look like my passion for climbing was going to be part of my past life.

Then one day a robust fellow wearing a cowboy hat, who looked to be in his early fifties, entered the store looking for me. "I've just been to see your brother, up the street a ways," he said. Jim was working at REI in Seattle at the time. "I'm looking for a guide. I'm interested in making a record on some mountains around here and I hear you and your brother are the fastest in the West."

"What did my brother say?"

"He said he was too busy."

"Well, I'm busy, too, so I guess I wouldn't be interested."

"Well, I'll pay all our expenses and your time."

"I guess I'd be interested."

This was my introduction to John S. Day, millionaire rancher, Boone and Crockett hunter, and all-around outdoorsman from Medford, Oregon. Having watched many of his successful friends and business associates get arthritis and ulcers and die of heart attacks, John had recently divested himself of several of his business interests and had set out to enjoy life in a healthier manner. His home was full of big-game trophies, complete with an engraved plate under each stuffed prize with John's name on it and the date of the kill. Mountain climbing had become his second passion. Now he was standing there in front of me, with one of those offers I'd have been a fool to refuse.

"Whose car are we using?" I asked.

"You want me to rent a car, too?"

"I have a station wagon that will hold all our gear. I can drive you around."

John agreed and informed me that he preferred to stay in hotels. This was starting to sound pretty good to me. I was used to sleeping on the ground the night before a climb. Here was a guy who was willing to pay my way around and let me climb all the peaks that I'd been too busy to climb.

Over the next seven days, we did St. Helens, Adams, and Rainier. Each time we finished a climb, John crawled into the back seat of the car to sleep while I drove us to the next destination. I started getting punchy from lack of sleep. Just before we climbed Mount Baker, I phoned Jim and said, "I need some help. This guy is wearing me out." I warned Jim beforehand, "You'd better be ready, this guy's an incredible athlete." But Jim and I were about half John's age and competitive enough that we managed to keep up the pace and help John set his records.

John generated a lot of controversy with his determination to set records in climbing. At that time, there were some stuffy attitudes about what people should and shouldn't do in climbing. Back then, one of those attitudes was that you shouldn't race up mountains. That wasn't the appropriate thing to do. But some of us felt that it was more fun to do things that were interesting, stimulating, and reasonably safe. Otherwise, you just sort of sterilize your life, and there's no fun in that.

The first time I climbed Rainier with John, I got lost in a snowstorm and headed down the wrong side from the summit. It took me a couple of hours to get my bearings and head back up to the top. Luckily, we were in a cloud, so John didn't realize that we were lost. It wasn't until we had walked all the way back to the top that I noticed that John was starting to drag a little. I told him, "Thanks for being in such good shape, John." A guy who's not in shape and gets lost, everybody knows he's lost. But the guy who is in shape and gets lost can cover ground fast enough to get back before dark, so nobody ever knows he's lost.

Because of the storm, we were on Rainier two days and didn't set a record, but we got back down the mountain in decent time. We had to go like mad. On one part of the descent, John was roped in front of me. It was snowing and we were coming down the Ingraham Glacier, a route that hadn't been climbed that year because it was too broken up to climb on. And there we were, in a storm that's blowing like hell. I was off route again, on the wrong side of Gibraltar Rock, on the headwall of the Ingraham, where it was steep and loaded with crevasses. I could just barely see John at the head of the rope, slowing down before a crevasse—I could see the dark line of the crevasse stretching out on either side of him.

I shouted, "John, what's wrong?"

He said, "The bridge is really thin."

"Christ, I've got you, you're tied to me, go ahead and jump it."

"It's too wide to jump."

"Then use the bridge."

"It looks really thin."

"That's okay, I've got you. Jump!" I was getting impatient because the storm was getting worse and we had to get off this thing. I kept yelling at him to go on across until he finally decided to use the snow bridge. I watched as he tiptoed across, arms stuck straight out from his sides, trying to walk as lightly as possible. He made it.

I came up behind him and got a much better look at the crevasse. The snow bridge stretched about twenty feet across the crevasse, and it was about three inches thick at its thickest part. I told John, "I'm not crossing that," all the while thinking, "Jeez, I've got to watch what I tell this guy to do."

We walked along either side of the crevasse, flipping the rope that stretched between us to keep it from dragging in the snow, until I found a better place to cross. John asked me, "Why didn't you want to cross where I did?" I told him that would be the last place I'd ever cross.

He got a good laugh out of that. I said, jokingly, that I was afraid

Lou and John Day on Mount Rainier, late 1950s (Photo courtesy Whittaker family)

he'd do anything I told him to do. He said, seriously, "You're right. I would."

"John, I should have come down and looked at it first and you should have argued a little more before trying it. Next time, argue more." The crevasse was about 200 feet deep. John had no ascenders, so if he had dropped in, I'd have had to pull him out, which would have taken about a half hour.

Nothing stopped John. After that experience, he was determined to make a better record on Rainier. He knew that one of the park rangers had climbed the mountain in eleven and a half hours, after having had an argument with his wife. We knew we could beat that. I called in Jim to help again. He couldn't resist, with John paying all expenses and our time.

We carried John's gear, so he wouldn't have to carry a pack and could therefore go fast. We made it to Rainier's summit and back in seven and a half hours. John was about fifty-one at the time. Jim and I were twenty-nine. Later, one of my senior guides, Craig Van Hoy, did it in five hours and twenty minutes.

After the Rainier climb, John said, "How about Mount Robson? It's only been climbed four times. Would you guys lead me on that one?" We agreed, because we hadn't been up Robson yet. Robson is in the Canadian Rockies and we attempted it in the summer of 1959, but missed the summit by a couple of rope lengths. An avalanching cornice turned us back.

After Robson, Day said, "How about McKinley?" We hadn't yet been up McKinley, so we agreed to take John. This would be only the twelfth time McKinley had been climbed.

We planned the climb for the following May, in 1960. To go fast and get a good climb, we decided to do it alpine style, making a quick ascent without acclimatizing at support camps at different altitudes. We invited Pete Schoening, who was then in his early thirties, to be the fourth man on the climb. Pete had a great reputation as a strong climber.

In fact, I had named my son Peter after Pete Schoening. Pete had been on the 1953 attempt on K2 and had made one of the most heroic belays in history. He was at 24,500 feet belaying and lowering Art Gilkey, who had been disabled by thrombophlebitis and was unable to walk. He was wrapped in a tent and in a sleeping bag, and while Pete belayed from above, the others tried to pendulum him across an ice slope. One man slipped and his rope entangled ropes of five others, including Dee Molenaar and a few others we knew, all top climbers, who would have died in that fall, but Pete held them all on his anchor rope. They didn't make the summit, and Dee says their principal achievement was getting back down the mountain. Pete was one of the strongest members of that attempt, so we picked him for McKinley. We figured he could help us set a record with John Day.

John bought all of us Eddie Bauer down outfits. Eddie Bauer used to make some great mountain equipment. In fact, they made suits for the Everest climb in 1963. Now they make what we call "urban" mountaineering clothing.

All sorts of things went wrong on the McKinley climb.

We established our base camp at 10,000 feet. On the second day, we reached 14,000 feet and set up our second camp. Our third camp was established on the third day, at 16,200 feet. We carried eighty-five-pound packs to that point, and left most of our gear there. On the fourth day, we stood on the summit. The record for the summit at that time was three weeks. We did it in four days and we did it too fast. We didn't acclimatize. We had flown out of the airport at sea level in Seattle and four days later we were standing at 20,320 feet.

I have pictures of my twin, Pete, and John on the summit that I don't remember taking. I also have a photo of the four of us that was taken by another party of four led by Paul Crews that summitted at the same time.

I do remember that on the way down from the summit, at the top of Denali Pass at 18,000 feet, we decided that it might be safer if we all tied in together. We tied both our ropes together, making one long rope of four guys. It wasn't clear to any of us how the fall occurred, but speculation was that someone took a spill and accumulated enough speed to pull off our whole rope team.

We fell about 500 feet down a wind-scooped wall with a succession of small, steep ice cliffs. We'd slide off one, bounce 8 or 10 feet, fall onto the next one, bounce another 8 or 10 feet. I recall thinking that I wouldn't get pounded as badly if I curled up. I knew that the wall leveled out at the bottom, after about a 500-foot drop. I figured we'd settle on the plateau that stretches to the next wall, a 3,000-foot drop above Peters Glacier.

Sure enough, we finally slowed to a stop at the bottom of the wall. I stood up and said, "Well, at least we're a little closer to camp." The comic relief was lost on the rest of the group. John groaned, "My legs don't feel so good." I actually had the optimism to try to get John to stand up so that we could keep on walking.

"John, can you put some weight on your legs to see how they feel?"

I got him vertical but he was unable to stand. That's when I discovered that we really had a problem. Both of John's ankles were fractured and dislocated. He told us that when he had started falling, he'd jammed his crampons into the hard ice in an effort to stop the fall. Each of us weighed more than 200 pounds. With our big packs, that had made for too much weight for John to hold.

Jim seemed a little shaken, but otherwise wasn't hurt. I had a sore shoulder that I think was dislocated and then reset during the fall. But Pete, we noticed, was semiconscious. One eye was closed from a blow to the side of his head.

I asked, "Pete, what do you think, you all right?"

"Yeah, I'm okay," he drawled, slowly pushing himself into a sitting position.

Now I knew we had a big problem. We were at 17,300 feet at ten-thirty at night. We were climbing in twilight because it never gets completely dark that far north in May. Luckily, it was a fairly calm night, but the temperature was 35 below zero. We'd been climbing for fourteen hours straight, no sleep. We were going to have to leave John there and get back to our tent for food and rest before we could begin a rescue effort.

Pete wasn't very active, so Jim and I prepared a place to leave John for the night. We dug a coffin hole in the snow, big enough to accommodate John in two sleeping bags. Jim and I had learned during our mountain-rescue days to always carry sleeping bags on any climb as a backup in case of a screw-up. We had managed to save a few lives that way. In this case, it was going to help John a great deal because we didn't have the strength to drag him down that night to our third camp. We could have stayed with him, but our best alternative was to get John into two sleeping bags and come back for him in the morning. John agreed. We had to take care of Pete as well, get him down to our tent, which was at 16,200 feet on the West Buttress.

Jim and I aligned and immobilized John's dislocated ankles. When an injury like that occurs, there is an initial, natural anesthesia that seems to occur with shock. That's when you want to do the realignment. Alignment also restores circulation, which is important in helping to keep warm and ward off frostbite. We gave John some pain pills and reassured him that we'd be back in the morning.

Jim was acting a little punchy and unstable by the time we got roped up and ready to descend with Pete. I rigged the rope so that Jim and Pete were in front of me, with me tied in the middle so that I could belay both of them. On the descent, Pete kept asking the same question, over and over again: "What happened?"

"Pete, we had a fall."

And a minute later: "What happened?"

Pete looked strong, walking down the mountain, but he sounded pretty unstable.

We came to a ridge at 16,800 feet, above our third camp at 16,200 on the West Buttress. We were at a place where the ridge becomes extreme and you have to go either to the left or the right. Going to the right led to the 3,000-foot wall above Peters Glacier. The route to the left sloped down a 1,500-foot wall toward our camp. I was about 60 feet behind Jim and Pete. There were no footprints, but my Boy Scout memory training was still intact. I had memorized the slope on the way up. I was quite sure that we were to go to the left of the ridge, and my twin felt the same.

Pete said no, we go to the right.

"No, Pete. I'm sure we go to the left." And as I was standing there, arguing with Pete, I noticed that Jim was untying himself from the rope. He'd had it. He was not going to argue. He was going to the left, back to camp. By himself, if he had to. Pete headed off to the right.

That's when I discovered that blood is thicker than water. I felt an obligation to both of them, but I could only watch one at a time when they started going off in different directions. I untied from the rope and followed my brother.

My plan was to make sure that Jim got back to our tent, then I'd go back and get Pete. We made it to the tent in about an hour. We both were dead tired. Jim crawled in and flopped down on top of his sleeping bag with his boots and crampons still on, and fell right asleep. I decided to just take a little rest there, too, then go get Pete. Anyway, I thought, Pete should show up soon. He'll realize his mistake and turn around.

A half hour later, I jerked awake, realizing with horror that Pete wasn't there. I woke up Jim. "Jim, wake up, Pete isn't here."

Jim mumbled something like "So what." He'd been hit pretty

hard in the fall and was punchy from that and lack of sleep.

I was all fired up. My adrenaline was pumping, from the rage building up inside me. "Damn, from a great climb to broken legs and concussions. We're going to end up with some deaths—what the hell is going wrong?"

I got up, told Jim that I was going to look for Pete, and then started up the damn mountain again. Rage can give you a lot of strength.

I climbed up the same route, yelling for Pete. The wind had picked up and was moaning. I couldn't see or hear Pete anywhere. I climbed all the way back, up above where the ridge split, almost to where we had left John. Then down to the right, the direction Pete had headed, yelling for him all the way. After about twenty minutes, I heard a deep, slow voice: "What do you want?"

I looked down to see Pete, sitting just below the edge of the 3,000-foot cliff above Peters Glacier. He was trapped. He had hiked down the ridge, climbed over the edge and down the face of the cliff, and just sat down on a little rock outcrop with his feet hanging over the edge. The rope was still tied to him and the middle and end knots that Jim and I had been tied in on were also hanging over the edge, swinging in the air.

Pete was sitting there, dusted with snow, looking out over this great expanse of twilighted white. He was conscious, but quite incoherent. Again he asked, "What happened?" I told him that we had fallen and then I noticed that one of his gloves was off and his hand was white. He'd been out more than two hours without a glove, in 35-below weather.

"Pete, can you throw me up some rope? Just coil up a piece and flip it to me?" He tried to coil the rope and then saw that his hand was frozen. He sat there for a few seconds, looking at his white hand. He had trouble using it to coil up the rope, but I didn't want to get any closer to him. I was only about eight feet above him, but it was a real hairy situation. One wrong move and we'd both go off the wall.

"Just throw me a few feet of rope, Pete. You can do it." Finally he coiled enough to flip up behind him. I grabbed it with great relief. "I've got you!"

Thank God, I've got him. Now he'll be okay. That's what I was thinking as I started to pull him up. But Pete got angry and climbed to his feet, saying, "Hey, don't pull me up, give me some slack." He was proud, even though he was semiconscious. To this day, he doesn't remember any of this.

He climbed up the damn wall to show me he could climb it. Then he stopped and asked, "What happened?"

"Pete, we had a fall. We're going back to camp now."

I put him beside me, pointed him in the right direction and he staggered back toward the tent. Stronger than hell, he just didn't know what was happening. As we descended, an old poem by Robert Service, called "Grin," came into my head and reminded me of Pete:

> *If you're feeling pretty groggy,*
> *   and you're licked beyond a doubt—*
> *Grin....*
> *Though your face is battered to a pulp,*
> *   your bloomin' heart is stout;*
> *Just stand upon your pins until*
> *   the bugger knocks you out—*
> *And grin.*
> *This life's a bally battle, and the same advice*
> *   holds true*
> *Of grin.*
> *If you're up against it badly,*
> *   then it's only one on you.*
> *So grin....*

Nobody was going to knock out Pete. He made it to the tent, where I helped him off with his crampons, gaiters, and boots, got him in his sleeping bag, and put a glove on his frozen hand. A close look at the hand told me that he was going to lose a lot of it. We all bedded down for several hours of exhausted sleep.

About ten in the morning, Jim and I woke up, roused Pete, and lit the stove to melt ice and get us all fed and watered. Then we broke camp and started planning the rescue. First move was to climb back up to John, taking all our gear and Pete with us so we could keep our party together.

We found John under a tent. Paul Crews's party apparently had heard or seen the fall and were camped just below where we had come to a halt. During the night, Paul Crews had hiked over and put a tent over John, to give him more protection. By the time we arrived, Crews and his party had continued their descent. One of their party, a woman named Helga Bading, was sick in a camp below and had become part of another rescue effort.

John was really happy to see us. He'd spent a miserable night, throwing up from the effects of shock. He told us that he wondered all night if we'd bother to return for him.

"John," I said, teasingly, "we made a big decision last night and you came out good in it. We figured you're so damn tough that we couldn't just leave you and say that you were lost in a fall. We'd first have to come back up and kill you off—otherwise, you'd crawl down the mountain if you had to, and get us."

We fed and watered John, and set up our tent. John seemed coherent and asked for his radio. Then he announced that he was going to call ex-President Eisenhower. John was rich, he had a lot of connections, and he was going to ask Eisenhower to get us off this mountain. We thought John might be incoherent after all.

"John," I said, "we can haul you off this mountain."

He didn't want it that way. He knew the sooner he got to a hospital, the better. It took him a while, but he got through to Eisenhower and got a military helicopter ordered up out of Chicago. They had never done a lift this high, but it was a big chopper and they were going to give it a try.

The thing flared out trying to get up to us. John heard it all on his radio and his spirits wilted.

"John, we can drag you off this thing." We had Pete's hand dressed and Pete was gaining some strength. The weather was great: clear, winds of maybe twenty miles per hour, temperature 30 below. Typically good for this time of year.

That day, a light plane flew over and dropped a film canister. I retrieved it and found a note inside: "If he's alive, wave. If dead, lay in the snow with arms out like this"—there was a diagram showing arms out at right angles. I waved and the plane flew off. A while later, another light plane flew over and made a drop of military rations. Then Gary King, a friend of ours who owned a sporting goods store in Anchorage, flew up and dropped a big stove with a note on it: "Why don't you guys cook up some dinner while you're waiting?" A rescue effort was being mounted and we had plenty of food, but no plane could land up here.

Jim and I started hauling all the cases of food back to the tent. Each time we brought in a case, Pete would open up a ration, take out the best can of fruit and eat it. I caught him at it.

"Hey, Pete. That food is for all of us. You're eating the best part. Leave some for us."

He said "Okay," and mumbled something about how you don't need a bunch of doctors to get you well.

When I brought back another case, I found that he'd eaten all the fruit out of the case I had just dropped off. The guy's survival instinct was working. Jim and I figured Pete wouldn't be a liability, he'd be an asset in getting John off the mountain. Even today, Pete claims that he never ate all that fruit.

We told John again, "We're going to haul you off."

He wouldn't hear of it. He had his radio and was determined to get another helicopter. "Promise me," he said, "wait just one more day." We promised, although we knew we couldn't expect the good weather to hold.

John was more confident about helicopters than were Jim and I. We had been on enough rescues where the planes and 'copters didn't make it in and ended up crashing or not making it in at all because of bad weather.

John's hearing wasn't that good, and he started hearing planes and 'copters. "I think I hear a plane," he'd say, but Jim and I couldn't hear it. Pete was eating, not paying any attention.

On the radio, we listened to the rescue effort going on below for Helga Bading. A plane came in at 14,000 feet and lifted her off. The pilot was Don Sheldon, the same guy who had flown us in several days before to 10,000 feet. If we could just get John down to 14,000 feet, we could get him lifted off, too.

The next morning, John informed us that another helicopter was coming. As we were talking, we heard the engine of a fixed-wing plane. Looking up, we saw a small plane do a couple of circles above us and then it just went into a full-power nose dive and *wham!*—hit the mountain about 200 feet from us and burst into flames, sending pieces of Plexiglas and debris flying all over the snow and ice.

We were speechless. John turned white as a ghost and said, "I've been talking on the radio. My son is in Talkeetna and was coming up and I wonder if he hired that plane. Could you guys go and find out who's in it?"

After it cooled down a little, Jim and I searched the wreckage. There were two people in it, just torsos left after the burning. We found a watch, two military rings, and some other items that pretty well ruled out either of them having been John's son. We weren't positive, though, until John made radio contact with his son a short time afterwards.

We later learned that one of the people in the wreck had been a military paramedic and the other a pilot who had volunteered to help. We hadn't found any oxygen in the plane. Knowing that they had to have come in around 20,000 feet, we wondered if the pilot had passed out from oxygen deprivation. Or maybe something had gone wrong with the plane. We never did find out, but the families of the two men sued us. John Day's insurance company settled out of court.

Now Jim and I became adamant. "That's it, John, no more waiting for a plane or a chopper. One way or another, we're responsible for the deaths of those guys. We're dragging you off this mountain." We started packing up our gear and getting John ready for the descent.

Suddenly John heard another helicopter. Jim and I were thinking, for a near-deaf guy, John is really something, and we kidded him about it. Jim and I didn't hear anything, and went about the job of breaking up camp.

Then we heard it. We ran out to the edge of the ridge and, sure enough, there was a little chopper coming up the side of the ridge. When it emerged above the ridge, Jim and I ran over, but the pilot didn't like the landing spot and moved to another. We ran over there. He didn't like that place either, and moved to another. After about four runs, Jim and I were out of breath and finally realized that we'd best wait until the chopper landed for good.

It was just a two-seater Hiller. The pilot, Link Luckett, had removed the doors and the battery to save weight. He told us, "I just want the guy with the two broken legs. No room for more."

That was fine with us. We went back up to John and put him in a sleeping bag to carry him down to the chopper. We strapped him in the seat. We didn't know it at the time, but if Luckett pulled this off, he would make the highest lift in aviation history.

Luckett said, "I need help getting off the ridge." The 'copter was perched on the edge of the 3,000-foot cliff. The blades were still turning, but he needed more air cushion to lift off.

"I want you guys to pick me up and throw me off this cliff." Jim and I looked at each other, incredulously. John turned white, and sputtered, "What, what, what?" The pilot said, "Do it. It's the only way. Lift with all your strength and I'll go full power."

Jim and I grabbed the pontoons of the chopper and lifted the bird as high as we could, just above our shoulders, took a few steps and heaved it off the edge. As it went over, we saw John, clasping his hands above his head like a prizefighter, a gritty grin on his white face. The chopper fell out of sight.

We peered over the edge and, about 1,000 feet down, we saw the chopper and heard its *tut-tut-tut-tut-tut* as it headed out away from the ridge. Jim and I cheered our fool heads off and went running back up to Pete.

We were anxious to get Pete dressed and break camp, but we realized that it was too late. Better to wait another night.

In the morning, as we were finally breaking up camp, we all heard another helicopter. It was Luckett again in his little Hiller, back to pick up Pete. Before we threw them off the cliff, Jim and I told Luckett, "Don't come back for us. We're walking down." Better not push our luck. Luckett happily agreed.

Jim and I were so damn relieved. Both the injured were off the mountain and we were in good shape. All we had to do was pack up and get outta there. We got our gear and packed up the rest of John's and Pete's gear. We took only the best of their stuff, such as down parkas and altimeters. We left the stove and headed out, our packs bigger than when we had started.

We arrived at our third camp at 16,200 feet, chowed down the rest of the good food that Pete hadn't eaten, and hit the sack. The next morning we spotted some rescuers heading our way up a 1,500-

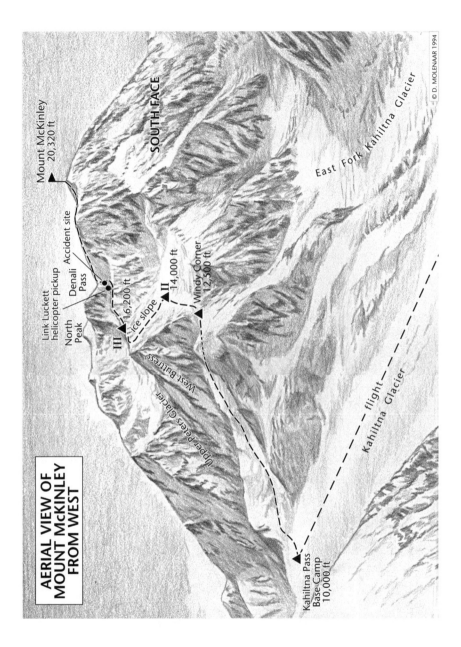

AERIAL VIEW OF MOUNT McKINLEY FROM WEST

Mount McKinley 20,320 ft

SOUTH FACE

© D. MOLENAAR 1994

East Fork Kahiltna Glacier

Link Luckett helicopter pickup

Accident site

Denali Pass

North Peak

III

16,200 ft

Ice slope

II 14,000 ft

Windy Corner 12,500 ft

West Buttress

Upper Peters Glacier

flight

Kahiltna Glacier

Kahiltna Pass Base Camp 10,000 ft

foot wall, using our fixed rope. We rushed to get packed up again and were soon descending with an advance group of our rescuers.

The rescue party had begun their efforts at our first camp, at 10,000 feet. During good weather, they had put up a second, higher camp at a place now called Windy Corner, a pass at 12,500 feet on the route up the West Buttress. As we descended, we noticed that a light storm was moving in. When we got to Windy Corner, we found about fifteen guys among five tents. We recognized some of them as Seattle mountaineers and most of them were hurting. But they cheerfully invited us to stay for tea. It sounded good, so we set up our tent, then crawled inside one of the rescue party's tents to have tea and swap stories.

The storm intensified and turned into a maelstrom of howling 100-mile-an-hour winds that started tearing apart the tents. As the winds slammed against our tent, Jim and I were thinking that maybe a helicopter lift off the mountain wouldn't have been so risky after all. About eighteen of us ended up crammed into a five-person tent that had survived the winds. After three days of good-natured misery, all of us were more than anxious to break free. Lucky for us, the storm had subsided a little, and Jim and I decided to make a go for the lower camp.

I told the rescuers, "We can lead us out of here, you guys. I've got an altimeter and compass, and snowshoes." I had taken azimuth readings with my compass on the way up and now would just use the opposite reading, or "back azimuth," to descend.

Some in the group elected to stay and wait out the storm, but most of them abandoned the lone tent and followed Jim and me in the storm. We kicked loose a few avalanches and watched them slide down the mountain. You can do this safely as long as you know what you're doing, so you don't get caught in them yourself. On most of the route, we used the altimeter and compass to guide us down to 10,000 feet, to the camp where we had started the climb.

On the way down, I had a mysterious experience. Many mountaineers have spoken of the "unseen climber," or the "other presence," a ghostlike entity or comforting presence they've felt or seen when climbing alone or when they've been caught in a threatening situation. Well, I heard music.

I was out ahead, roped to Jim, and suddenly I heard music. At first I thought I must be picking up radio waves off my pack, because the music was faint. Then it got louder. It was the damnedest big choir, like a hundred voices, accompanied by a full orchestra. I stopped and coiled in the rope while Jim caught up to me.

I was embarrassed to ask him, even though I knew him better than anyone, but I didn't want to appear a fool. "Jim, do you hear a big choir and orchestra?"

Jim said, "No," and I didn't press it. We continued down the mountain and I listened to that music for about a half hour. It was classical music, and gave me an uplifting feeling, just as it had when I was a kid, driving to rescues with my mentors, Otto, Max, and Ome.

At the lower camp, the storm was quieter. The rescue party knew we were up on the mountain, but the storm had kept them in their tent. We sneaked up on them in a whiteout blizzard and shouted, "Who the hell is in there?"

There was a great commotion inside the tent until they got the front flap open and saw us. Then a cry, "Yay, Whittakers!" and we had a big reunion with our friends from Seattle, including Dee Molenaar and Max Eckenburg, who had come up to help get us off the mountain.

The storm passed and Don Sheldon flew me out. A helicopter took Jim out and then evacuated the rescuers. Jim and I looked up John in the hospital in Anchorage. He had a broken left leg, a dislocated ankle, and severe frostbite. He was moving his legs and ankles continually. They made odd, clicking noises.

"What are you doing, John?"

"Aw, the doctors say that I might end up with fixed joints, so I'm working them, to keep my flexibility. I know I can do it."

And sure enough, he did keep more than 50 percent mobility. After that, he cross-country skied a lot more than he climbed. He even won some races. The guy was nearly unstoppable.

Pete Schoening ended up losing most of his frostbitten fingers. But that didn't slow him down. He still climbs today.

Right after the climb, Jim and I noticed that when we climbed stairs, we'd miss a step, hit steps in the middle. We went to Dr. Spickard, a fellow mountaineer, who tested our reflexes and informed us that we had nerve damage. He told us, "You keep doing things like that and you'll be old men before you're forty." We learned a heck of a lesson, one that I still teach in my mountaineering school. You never go that high that fast unless you're trying to save a life—and then you'd better be in top shape. You should always take time to acclimatize. The less oxygen, the more damage that occurs. No peak is worth a life.

After the McKinley climb, John Day was motivated to go to Everest, so he invested in the proposed first American ascent of Mount Everest, scheduled for 1963. The climb was funded in part by John, the National Science Foundation, and the National Geographic Society. Both Jim and I had been chosen for the team. John eventually became discouraged with the team leadership. He and Norman Dyrenfurth clashed. Dyrenfurth wanted to have the ultimate say, to which, as team leader, he was entitled. John wanted more autonomy with his dollar investment than he was getting. He was used to doing things his way. He dropped from the team before I did, but remained a strong supporter and good friend until his death in the late eighties of prostate cancer.

John was one good man.

◆ 5 ◆

DECADE OF CHANGE

In the early 1960s, I was all fired up from our success on McKinley and gung-ho to make a career in mountaineering. At the same time, I wanted marriage and a family. What I ended up with, by the beginning of the next decade, was a real education in the difficulties of weaving the two together.

The sixties began with Jim and me being honored to be among the first three or four climbers selected for the American Everest team. The expedition, which would put the first American on top of the highest point on earth, was to begin in February 1963. Several team members were climbers we knew from the Pacific Northwest, including Lute Jerstad, Willi Unsoeld, and Tom Hornbein.

It was only natural that Jim and I would train together for Everest. Nearly twenty years of mountaineering adventures had led us to this goal. We were fully aware of the implications of the climb. Not only might we be among the first Americans to reach the summit of Everest, we also might be the first twins. It would be a unique feat, and one unlikely to be repeated.

Our good-natured competitiveness really came out during our training. Just as we had pushed each other beyond our physical capabilities as kids, we now pushed each other to run faster, carry heavier packs, build more muscle. We even competed at holding our breath, to strengthen our vital capacity. We both had to drive from work to our homes at Lake Sammamish over the Lake Washington bridge, which was connected to Seattle by a tunnel. One night, I called Jim and told him that I had just held my breath all the way through the tunnel on my drive home from work. He said, "That's great! I'll try it tomorrow night."

The next night he called me and said, "Lou, I just held my breath all the way through the tunnel to where the ramp goes down and touches the water."

And I said, "No kidding! I'll try it again tomorrow night." So the next night I called Jim and said, "Jim, I just held my breath through the tunnel and down the ramp to the middle of the bridge where the boats pass through."

The next night Jim called me. "Lou, I held my breath through the tunnel, down the ramp, across the bridge, and all the way to where the bridge leaves the water again on the other side. But we've got to stop doing this."

"Why?"

"The cop said I was doing ninety-two!"

In September 1962, the members of the American Everest team spent ten days on Mount Rainier, honing their techniques for Everest. Rainier was, and is, the best and most accessible training ground for Himalayan expeditions in the United States.

By that winter, I felt the fun and challenge of training for Everest diminishing, due to a growing sense of responsibility to my wife and two children. How could I just take off for four months, with no income coming in? To complicate matters, at the beginning of 1963 the chance arose for me to buy into a sporting-goods store in Tacoma that was going bankrupt. I realized that owning a store might be the opportunity I was looking for, a way to stay in the mountaineering business.

I struggled with my decision to go to Everest. I even wrote up a list of the pros and cons. Pat was supportive and encouraged me to go on the expedition. Mom and Dad also wanted me to go. They always felt more at ease when Jim and I were together in the mountains. They knew we'd watch out for each other.

Having climbed with Jim for twenty years, I had envisioned us summitting Everest together. I felt that Jim and I were probably the strongest climbers on the team. At age thirty-four, we each had as much mountaineering experience as many men twenty years older. I knew that we'd both have a good shot at being chosen for the first summit team. Still, I couldn't help but feel a little selfish when I thought about leaving my family without support for four months.

As the departure date drew nearer, we were informed by the expedition leader, Norman Dyrenfurth, that the first team sent to the summit would consist of one American and one Sherpa, in honor of the Sherpas' contribution to the expedition. That meant that either Jim or I might make the first team, but not both of us. This knowledge, coupled with my commitment to my family, helped me make a very difficult decision.

A few weeks before the team was scheduled to depart for Kathmandu, I informed Jim that I was dropping from the team. Up until then, I hadn't told him that I was even considering it. I didn't want to disrupt his focus on his training. Jim was pissed. He tried every which way to get me to reconsider, but I stood firm.

There were two replacements scheduled for the team and John "Jake" Breitenbach was one of them. He replaced me, and was killed in the Khumbu Icefall on the second day of the climb. A giant block of ice broke lose and buried him. I couldn't help but wonder, would that have been my fate?

After Jim returned from the climb, he told me that he had carried his anger and disappointment at me all the way to Everest Base Camp. But after Jake was killed, Jim said that he was glad I hadn't gone on the expedition, because he knew I'd take care of his family if he also didn't make it back.

The American Everest team departed for the expedition in mid-February. I knew that it would be nearly two months before we'd start getting any climbing news. The team first had to hike 185 miles from Banepa, near Kathmandu, into Everest Base Camp. That alone would take a month.

So I decided to buy a store.

I had worked for Osborn and Ulland since college—my first job had been to put metal edges on skis in the ski repair shop—and I felt an allegiance to them. I had developed a nice relationship with the owners, Scott Osborn, Olaf Ulland, and Hal Kihlman, and with the manager, Yosh Nakagowa. Yosh was my age and had started working nights at the store at the same time as I had, during college. He had worked his way up to retail manager. Later, he became a part owner.

I thought I might strike a deal on the new store in Tacoma with these guys. I made them an offer: "Give me 10 percent ownership in Osborn and Ulland, and let me run this new shop for you." Two of the owners liked the idea, the third didn't. So I told them that I was going to do it on my own. I promised them that I'd never open a shop in Seattle and compete in the same town. In return, they promised never to open a shop in Tacoma.

The next person I approached was Jerry Lynch, who by then had left management of the Paradise Inn to become an attorney. I knew I would need some help with the business end of the deal as well as some cash to help buy inventory. I offered Jerry 10 percent ownership in the store, which was to be called Whittaker's Chalet. It would be a mountaineering and backpacking store in summer, and a ski shop in winter. Jerry agreed to the partnership, and threw in a few thousand dollars. He also knew the bank president in Tacoma, where the store was located. In my mind, this made Jerry an extremely valuable partner!

In the midst of these business dealings, I had received a letter from Jim saying that he and Sherpa Nawang Gombu had been chosen as the first assault team. I knew Jim would succeed, barring bad weather. He had the heart and the will to achieve the goal. As his twin, I knew exactly what he was feeling, and I could easily visualize myself at his side. I kept this vision in my mind as I went about starting my business.

In early May, I was in California on a buying trip for Whittaker's Chalet when I received a call from a news service in Seattle saying that two people on the American expedition had made it to the summit of Everest, but no names had been released. I asked the caller if he could tell me if one of them was a Sherpa. He said, "No, why do you ask?"

I said, "If one is a Sherpa, that will be the first team, with my brother, Jim. If it isn't, that means the second or third or another team made it. The first team was to have included a Sherpa."

The person from the news service said he'd find out and call me back. In the middle of the night, I got another call saying that it was definitely a Sherpa and an American. "Do you know who that would be?"

I said, "I feel 98 percent sure that it's my twin."

About five hours later, the guy called again and verified that

Sherpa Nawang Gombu and American Jim Whittaker had summitted Everest on May 1. I was so proud of Jim, I felt that I had made the summit myself. I phoned the news to Mom and Dad in Seattle right away.

I felt no regrets at not having been on the expedition. Part of that feeling came from being a twin and sharing each other's experiences, even the ones you don't participate in directly. But a bigger part of it came from the fact that, once I make a decision, I tend to take a pretty straight and rapid course toward my new goal. No looking back.

I was waiting at the airport when Jim arrived home from Everest. He had lost fifty pounds and looked terrible. The first thing he said to me was, "Now you know you can do it, Lou." I said, "Great, Jim—now I know I don't have to!"

During the expedition, four other climbers, in two separate teams, had also made the summit a few weeks after Jim and Gombu. Lute Jerstad and Barry Bishop had followed Jim and Gombu's route to the summit, up the South Col. Willi Unsoeld and Tom Hornbein had traversed the summit from the West Ridge, and descended via the South Col.

Norman Dyrenfurth had wanted the Everest success to focus on the team effort, rather than on any one individual. But President Kennedy felt that the United States needed a hero, and Jim became it. From this association with the president, Jim became friendly with the Kennedy family, especially with Bobby and Ethel.

After his Everest success, Jim continued to work at REI and eventually moved up in the management ranks to president. He spent a lot of time with the Kennedys during that period. Pat and I also met the family through Jim, and we'd all often converge in Sun Valley to ski.

After Everest, our twin lives began to take different paths. Jim divorced Blanche, which severed one tie. His affiliation with the Kennedys aroused an interest in politics, which never held any fascination for me. He became active in the Democratic Party and, in the late sixties, ran Bobby Kennedy's campaign for president in Washington State. Between attending to his Everest fame and running REI, Jim didn't have much time to climb. Pat and I had moved to Tacoma to be closer to my work, and I spent nearly all my time building my retail and guiding businesses. Now and then, Jim and I would meet in the mountains on a rescue.

I don't think either of us took conscious note of this separation at the time. In our mid-thirties, it was a natural outgrowth of our maturing lives. Even so, through the years, I don't think we've ever lost our natural feeling of closeness, no matter how long the time span or how wide the physical distance between us.

When Pat and I moved to Tacoma in the spring of 1963, we sold our Lake Sammamish house to the Jesuit Order of Seattle University. We had purchased the house in the mid-fifties for $14,000, remodeled and improved it, then sold it for $28,000. This is when I discovered a great hobby that also has become a source of additional income: construction. A couple of skiing friends were carpenters, and they taught me enough carpentry skills to get started. Another friend was a contractor, and taught me how to pour concrete. So after work I'd tinker around with construction. I'm like my mom—I have a lot of energy, I'm restless and have to keep busy.

In 1965, my namesake and youngest son, Louis Winslow Whittaker Jr., arrived. We decided to call him Win. All the kids picked up our active life-style. They learned to ski as soon as they were walking, and I had them out climbing around on Mount Rainier not long afterwards. Peter first summitted Rainier at age twelve, which set a record at the time in our family. But he wasn't the youngest climber ever to summit Rainier.

Whittaker's Chalet was very successful in its first several years, and absorbed an increasing amount of my time. I had decided to continue to represent a few lines of ski gear, as I had done at Osborn and Ulland, and that kept me on the road during parts of spring and fall, attending different trade shows and selling to other retail accounts. In addition, I was guiding on Mount Rainier during the summers and teaching a climbing course at a nearby college in Bremerton. During the winters, I ran a ski school from Whittaker's Chalet. At its peak, the school generated 1,200 students during a single season.

In addition to being away on road trips, I also continued to participate in rescues. As soon as I'd return from a rescue or a road

Kim Whittaker, age fifteen, on Mount Rainier (Photo: Lou Whittaker)

trip, my busy schedule would immediately resume. This left Pat alone with the kids a good deal of the time. I had grown up in a loving, easygoing household, and had assumed that Pat and I would generate the same type of atmosphere in our home. I hadn't taken into consideration that her childhood had been almost the opposite of mine. Her father was an alcoholic and she and her mother had never gotten along. It became obvious that Pat wasn't that comfortable in the role of mother. We agreed less and less on how the children should be raised, and it wasn't long before our discussions on the matter turned into arguments.

Although our difficulties over the children were slowly pushing us apart, Pat and I did continue to share a love of the ocean. In college, we had discovered a beautiful spot out on the Olympic Peninsula, in the Quinault Indian Reservation. A few years after I had opened Whittaker's Chalet, we happened to be out there on an excursion with the kids, and I met a Native American who told me about some choice oceanfront property that was coming up for sale.

I couldn't afford to buy the entire piece, but I could easily find enough mountaineering friends who wanted some of it. I split up

Win Whittaker, Lou, and Jerry Halsey on Mount Rainier, 1975 (Photo: Ingrid Widmann)

the property into several 100-foot beachfront lots, sold each of my friends a parcel, and gave the owner the price he was asking. As part of the deal, I ended up with a free 200-foot beachfront piece for myself. I built an A-frame cabin on the front of the property, and a cabin for my parents on the back of the lot.

In 1967, Jerry and I decided to open another Whittaker's Chalet near the Tacoma Mall. A second store was a big commitment, both financially and time-wise, but the demand was there. We decided to go for it.

The following year, my guiding business also took a turn for the better. In 1968, the Park Service awarded me the official guide concession in Mount Rainier National Park. As before, when Jim and I were guiding together, my operation would be the sole sanctioned guide service of the park. The designation prompted me to incorporate the guide service. Jerry was my partner in Whittaker's

Chalet, and the guide service enjoyed a clientele generated in part from the store, so it seemed natural for Jerry to become a partner in the guide business. Jerry agreed to start out as a "silent" partner, with most of the income going to me during the first few years, to allow me to devote my time to building the business. So in 1968 Rainier Mountaineering, Inc. (RMI), a full-service, professional guiding operation and climbing school, was born. For me, it was the realization of a lifelong dream and, though I didn't know it at the time, the beginning of a new era in my life.

What I did know was that I was working longer hours than ever before and spending even less time with my family. President Kennedy's emphasis on physical fitness and the advent of "Earth Day" had made the outdoors more popular with college students and the general public. As a result, the backpacking, mountaineering, and skiing business was becoming more competitive. I liked being in sporting goods, but didn't relish the thought of being indoors so much of the time. My heart remained in guiding on Mount Rainier.

My heart has always been a good indicator of the direction my life will follow. Within a year of the incorporation of RMI, my guiding business had taken off and the other parts of my life had started to nosedive. Whenever I took time to guide on Mount Rainier, or go on the road to sell ski gear, the stores would suffer. Both stores were broken into a couple of times, and we were always having to deal with shoplifting. If a customer was spotted walking out the door with stolen merchandise, the salespeople let him go. They didn't have a vested interest in the place, so they didn't give chase.

At home, Kim and Pat were fighting nearly every day. They seemed to have no basis for communication. I'd defend Kim and end up arguing with Pat. I threatened to leave the marriage, and moved out a couple of times before I finally left for good in 1969. I took Kim, who was twelve, and rented an apartment in Tacoma.

Pat agreed to keep Win, who was only four years old at the time. Peter was eleven, and wanted to finish school in Tacoma, so he stayed with Win and his mother.

The divorce was a killer. Going through it was one of the toughest times of my life. It was like everyone says: part of you dies. It was like climbing the worst mountain, steeper than hell, no moments of enjoyment, only heartbreaking struggle. The ties and beliefs that you shared for so long get shot to hell. You end up making decisions that you can only hope are best for your kids and yourself.

That same year, a young woman came to work for me at Whittaker's Chalet. We needed a sales clerk, so I had contracted with a placement agency, Snelling and Snelling. They sent Ingrid Widmann. I liked the idea of a good-looking, dark-haired young girl with a German accent working in a ski and mountaineering shop. She spoke English well and knew how to ski. Later, I taught her to climb.

After I hired Ingrid, I discovered that she was getting out of a bad marriage to a G.I. she had met when she first came to the United States. This was just before I moved out of my marriage. For a year, I never made a pass at Ingrid, but I liked her and watched her. When we finally did get involved, in 1970, I was forty-one, Ingrid was twenty-three. The age difference has never meant anything to either of us. It's as though we were destined to be together.

In our divorce settlement, Pat got our home in Tacoma plus the A-frame and some of the property on the Quinault Reservation. I kept the rest of the Quinault property, which included an island and some mainland property. I asked Pat to transfer my parents' cabin into their names. I wanted to give it to the kids after Mom and Dad were gone. Pat agreed, but she did sell the A-frame.

During the divorce proceedings, Ingrid decided to go back to Germany for about six months, to give me time to get my life sorted out and to give herself time to be sure of what she wanted. I finally wrote and told her that I wasn't going back to Pat and that I wanted her, Ingrid, to come and live with me.

At the same time, I was trying to keep up with a growing guide service. It had become apparent that I could clear more money by guiding than by running two stores. I approached Osborn and Ulland and asked them if they'd like to buy the stores. They could now enter the market in Tacoma, free of competition. They liked the idea, and we struck a deal. It was 1972, and my first step toward being free to head for the mountains and devote my time to guiding.

My partner, Jerry, was all for the move. He hated being a full-time attorney and agreed to become equal partners with me in Rainier Mountaineering, Inc. We made him president and me vice president. Jerry did the paperwork and I did the guiding. He's always been the detail man, I've always been the personality out front, hawking clients and guides. Jerry had faith in me and hung in there. It's been a natural division of labor for us, and a longtime friendship.

By the time Kim turned seventeen, in 1974, I knew she had to find some sort of peace. She was having a tough time in school and she was having a tough time living with me and Ingrid. Kim and I argued frequently, her school grades dropped, and we both were miserable. I contacted a guy I knew who ran a school for troubled children, and arranged for her to live there for a year.

There were about twenty other kids at the school. I took them all on a few climbs, one to Pinnacle Peak in Mount Rainier National Park. We had fun. It was a good time for Kim, she seemed to be gaining more control in her life. After a year at the school, she set out on her own.

A couple of years after Ingrid had returned from Germany to live with me, we relocated to Ashford, a small town at the entrance to Mount Rainier National Park, to be close to the mountain and the guide service. Ingrid had taken on the job of running the office, which included doing the books and managing the cabin girls.

For several years, Ingrid worked as a cabin girl herself, which allowed us to be together on the mountain much of the time. A lot of couples can't handle that type of closeness—running a business and living together. But we thrived on it. I loved having Ingrid on the mountain with me. We got married in Ashford in 1976, and still live there, in an underground house that we designed and built together.

When we married, Ingrid kept her last name and that was fine with me. I think it's an odd practice, to take the woman's name away. Men like to think that they're adding to their property by branding their wives with their last name. Ingrid is not my property, she's a completely unique individual. She and I vowed to share our lives, to be equal. And it has worked out very well that way.

In the late seventies, Pat met a man who wanted to marry her, but didn't want kids as part of the deal. He already had five of his own, but they were grown and out of the house. Pat told me that she wanted to marry this man, but she couldn't keep Win. So in 1977 Win, then twelve, moved in with me and Ingrid.

Just the year before, Peter had finished high school and decided to live out on his own. He had been guiding for me since he was sixteen, so he moved to the thirty-five-acre ranch in Ashford that Jerry Lynch and I had bought as a place for guides to live inexpensively. Peter continued to live there even after he got married, until a few years ago, when he and his wife, Erika, bought a place of their own, a ramshackle sportsman's lodge on the edge of a lake. Peter had learned some carpentry skills while working with me, and he and Erika got to work right away remodeling the place.

By the time Win came to live with me and Ingrid, I was guiding full time during the summers and traveling on business for JanSport, a small and relatively new backpacking equipment and clothing company that had hired me in 1972 as a consultant. Win wasn't happy living with us. He was out in the middle of the country with hardly any other kids around. I was gone a lot of the time and he didn't regard Ingrid as a figure of authority. At the same time, Ingrid didn't see herself as Win's mother. So in 1982, when Win turned seventeen, I asked him if he wanted to live at the ranch with Peter. He'd be close by, and we could still be responsible for him. Of course, Win jumped at the chance. Ingrid and I got the house back to ourselves, which was great for us, and Win got more freedom.

Other Perspectives: Ingrid Widmann

When I was nineteen, I came to the United States to visit my godmother, and I met and married a man in the military. After two years, I knew I had made a big mistake, so I went looking for a job so I could make enough money to leave him. Whittaker's Chalet was about the ninth interview the agency sent me on.

I walked in and saw this big guy in the back of the shop with an apron on, working on bindings. I was almost twenty-two, really shy, and job interviews were the hardest thing for me. I went over to this guy, who I figured just worked there, and said that the agency

"Cabin girls" Marty Hoey, Gertraud Ciesler, and Ingrid Widmann in cook shack, 1972 (Photo: Lou Whittaker)

had sent me for an interview. Could he tell me, where is his boss? He said, "Let's go to the cafeteria next door, where we can talk."

The minute I started talking to Lou, I knew I had found a friend for life. It was just one of those things. We talked about everything. He wanted to know about my life. He was fascinated that I was from Germany because that's where a lot of his old climbing buddies were from.

When I started working at Whittaker's Chalet, I didn't know Lou was having trouble in his marriage. I was the little shop girl and he was like a big brother. Jane, another girl who worked at the shop with me, was also going through a divorce, and we'd talk about our problems with Lou. We'd see him go next door to buy things for his wife. He'd have us wrap them. We'd say to each other, "Wouldn't it be great to be Lou's wife, if he just weren't so ugly?" He had this big nose. He was older. But he was the nicest guy. Now, I think he's so good-looking!

When Lou decided to separate from his wife, he developed a greater interest in me. He asked me to help him with a fashion show that Whittaker's Chalet was putting on in Aberdeen. The girl who had arranged the whole thing had gotten sick and couldn't go. He needed a model, and asked me. I had never been in front of people, and he was asking me to model tennis dresses and stuff like that. He was the boss, so I went. I was scared out of my mind to do all these things I had never done before, but Lou made it seem okay.

On the way back to Tacoma, it started to snow really hard. Lou just loves snow. He gets like a little kid when it snows. Aberdeen is 100 miles or more from Tacoma and we had to drive all the way through this blizzard. It was like a great adventure to Lou, driving me through this snowstorm. By then, I had moved to my own place. When he dropped me off, he kissed me—and that was it. It took a while for both of us to sort out our marriages. We were discreet. Nobody knew me. We were in totally different circles. Mine was the military. Lou's was the country club, parties he really hated. I know he must have hated it, because we've never lived like that.

In the midst of all this, I went back to Germany for several months. It was a tough time for us. Lou didn't want to hurt his wife or the kids. I didn't want to cause a problem. I told him, "When you're free and available, let me know." He did.

Lou is a man who loves women. It used to bother me a lot in the early days. Other people knew who he was and that his brother was famous, but I didn't know anything. The guide service was our life. All the guides were our friends. In the early days, the only guides besides Lou were Joe Horiskey, Eric Simonson, George Dunn, Phil Ershler, and Dan Boyd. We were together all the time. Of course, Lou was their boss and so we had parties with the Ashford locals and all the girls would fight over Lou and nobody would dance with me because the guys were afraid of Lou. I would just cry and cry. I got so I hated parties. But Lou was having a great time. I finally just grew up with it. If I wanted to dance, I just grabbed a guy and danced. But it was hard at first.

Being married to a climber can be hard. There are lots of divorces among climbers. A lot of people think it's like being married to a career soldier who's always out on a high-risk mission, but it's different. If you're married to a policeman or a fireman or a soldier, he's doing a job to make a living. Climbing, for most people, is not a good living. So basically these guys are on vacation, which makes it really hard when the woman is left at home minding the kids and working.

When I came back from Germany, we first lived together in a small apartment in Tacoma. There were people in all directions making noise. Lou had never lived in apartments. He'd always had a house. We started looking for houses in West Seattle, closer to his mother, farther away from Pat. We couldn't afford any of the ones we wanted. One day, when we were in Ashford, I saw this old cabin for sale and suggested that we try it for the summer, to be closer to our guiding. After that summer, we decided to stay there for the winter. It was 1972, and Lou had just started consulting for JanSport, a backpacking equipment company, and either worked on the phone or traveled, so it really didn't matter where we lived.

We bought the cabin for $10,000 and started remodeling it that winter. It was about twenty by twenty-four feet, really old. It took us ten years to pay it off. We were pretty poor in those days. Most of Lou's JanSport salary went to child support, and we lived the rest of the year off three months of guide income.

We'd scavenge materials for remodeling. There was a big old barn across the valley that was falling down. The owners agreed to let us tear down the barn in exchange for the wood. We did the same thing with a burned-out log restaurant, salvaged the logs. Got windows from here and there, some plain, some stained-glass. With really no money at all, we added on to this cabin in all directions. In the seventies, that was kind of a funky thing to do. Lou loves to rip and tear and rebuild, and I got to love it too. We still own the house and rent it out to RMI guides. Everyone now calls the place "the estate."

Win lived with us for five years, from the time he was twelve until Lou returned from Everest in 1982. It was rough at times for all of us. After Everest, Lou asked Win if he wanted to move to the ranch, where Lou and I could still keep an eye on him, but Win would have more space to himself. He's still living there.

Early on, Win didn't want to become a guide. Peter had been involved in an icefall tragedy in 1981, and Win decided that he didn't want to climb. Lou told him, "That's fine. Whatever you want to do, that's fine." Now he's guiding clients on both Rainier and McKinley and, from what we hear, the clients just love him.

Peter used to fight anything that would associate him with Lou. Lou wanted him to help work on the house, to learn construction, and Peter had no interest at all. He rebelled. And now he's exactly like Lou. He'll work for twelve hours straight without stopping for lunch. He's building his own house now and turning out to be so much like his father.

It took Peter and Win a long time to grow up. I think it's an American thing. People are just kids longer over here than they are in Europe. Life is much more easygoing here. In Europe, you go to school and right when you get out of school you get a job and you do that job until you retire. There is just no other way. Everything is very structured and regulated. People don't just take off and "find themselves." It's just not done.

For Peter and Win, having time to find what they want to do has been the best thing that could have happened to them. Lou always encouraged them to do something they liked to do. So far, they both have decided on a life in the mountains.

The kids had a tough time growing up. Especially Kim. Some people go with the flow. Others, like Kim, are always trying to swim upstream. In 1984, she met a nice guy and had a daughter, Kalen, with him. But they split up soon after Kalen was born and Kim moved to Alaska. Over the next few years, Kim's problems with alcohol and instability continued to increase to the point that, despite efforts to help herself and to be an adequate mother, she had to give up Kalen for adoption.

Kim still lives in Alaska, in a remote cabin with a wood stove and no electricity. I hear from her off and on. My granddaughter lives with a good family and seems to be a happy child. It's painful to watch Kim go through so much turmoil, knowing that in some ways I'm responsible, but also knowing that I can't put her life back in order for her.

I don't think it's possible to figure out why people turn out the way they do. Watching my children grow up, I see there is only so much influence a person can exert. We bring down a lot on ourselves. You see lots of people stuck in a program—the death program, the lying program, the alcoholic program, the life-is-misery program. Maybe our programs are all set up in the first five or six years of life, as some psychologists believe.

I believe we have free will to break out of our programs. We first get programmed by our families, by society, by religion. Later, we begin programming ourselves into doing so many mundane things that are so boring and unfulfilling. We get into a life of drudgery and go through it without ever experiencing life. Some people get stuck in this drudgery and see no way out, or don't even look for an opportunity to get out. I've never been able to live that way.

The best you can hope for your children, as they grow older, is that the adversity they face inspires them to break out of their programs and helps them mold the sort of life they envision for themselves. That's the best any of us can expect to do.

The philosophy of life that I developed during the seventies has stuck with me. And it's simply this: You can check out of this life at any time. If you go without having done what you wanted to do, it's your own fault. If you're doing something you don't want to do, you shouldn't be doing it at all.

♦ 6 ♦

K2 1975:
CONFLICT AND CHALLENGE

By 1974, RMI had become established and I felt secure enough financially to commit to a four-month expedition to K2, which had been planned for 1975. Ingrid had a hard time coming to terms with my leaving. She supported my climbing ambitions but, having climbed and guided with me on Rainier for the past few seasons, she also understood the inherent dangers in mountaineering. We were in the early years of getting our lives together and, during the year of planning that led up to the team's departure for Pakistan, she became increasingly concerned that I wouldn't return. We made arrangements to meet in Pakistan at the end of the climb, so that we could reunite as soon as possible.

Ingrid later told me that as soon as I left on the expedition she began to feel better. I had encouraged a few of the RMI guides to stay at the house with Ingrid while I was gone, to keep her company. As it turned out, six of them lived there with her, on and off, and it was like a party every night. She also absorbed herself in

Opposite: *Lou, sixty-five pounds lighter at end of K2 expedition, 1975 (Photo: Jim Wickwire)*

helping Jerry Lynch run the guide service, and she said that helped pass the time.

I was still consulting for JanSport, so when we started planning the expedition, they were considered a natural source for gear. JanSport donated the tents, sleeping bags, and packs for each member of the climb.

On this expedition, for the first time in our lives, Jim and I clashed. We hadn't climbed that much together since Jim's success on Everest in 1963, but I felt that we had remained close. On the K2 climb, however, I lost him as a climbing companion because he brought along his new, second wife, Dianne Roberts, and spent most of his time with her. I never once climbed with Jim on the upper mountain.

Jim was the leader of the expedition, with the goal of getting the first U.S. team to the top of the 28,250-foot peak. The climbing team consisted of me, Jim, Jim Wickwire, Fred Stanley, Fred Dunham, Leif Patterson, Rob Schaller, and Galen Rowell. Steve Marts signed on as cinematographer, but his extensive mountaineering skills would have easily qualified him as a member of the climbing team. Jim's wife, Dianne, was originally designated as a photographer, but she saw herself in a greater role—specifically, as one of the climbing team. This created some problems among the rest of us.

We all had spent about a week on Mount Rainier before the expedition, training for the climb. At the time, Dianne was twenty-six and had done very little climbing. She was still learning basic technique. Before we left for Pakistan, she started telling the media that she planned to climb as high as she could on the mountain. She even had Rob Schaller, who was also the team physician, fit her for an oxygen mask, which meant that she envisioned herself going higher than 23,000 or 24,000 feet.

Jim continually reassured the other climbers on the team, including me, that he would only take Dianne as high as she could safely go, and only when he was carrying loads to higher camps. None of the other climbers would have the responsibility or risk of roping up with her on the upper mountain. We all had varying responses to this decision. Several of us finally agreed that the mountain would ultimately resolve the question of whether Dianne would climb higher than base camp. As it turned out, she made one trip to Camp II at 20,400 feet.

Postcard of K2 expedition team, 1975 (Sketch: Dee Molenaar; photos: Steve Marts)

Things were pretty friendly between me and Jim on the long hike into our base camp at K2. Once there, Jim began spending most of his time with Dianne. We all had to admit that this was natural, because they were newlyweds at the time. On the other hand, we resented the fact that we couldn't easily mingle with our team leader. I don't know if it was this self-imposed isolation, but something caused him to be unusually autocratic and short-tempered.

My temper wasn't much better. Both Galen and Dianne were extremely verbal, headstrong people and not only did they clash with each other, but they both got on my nerves. I clashed with Dianne because she kept interfering with the process of organizing the climb from base camp. Jim and I would disagree on certain things and then Dianne and I would get into it. I'd get mad at Dianne and then Jim would get mad at me for being mad at Dianne. I had Dianne in tears a couple of times at base camp. At one point, she started telling me how much oxygen to use on the upper mountain. I really resented hearing things like this from a novice.

In my estimation, Galen was a disappointment as a member of a climbing team. Many times he refused to carry a pack, so that he'd be free to take photographs. He had joined the expedition as a climber, though, and I felt that he should carry his load, just like the rest of us. Galen boasted about his rock-climbing feats in California so much that, at one point, I said, "I hope you can climb as well as you can talk." Unfortunately, Galen got sick before we started setting up the upper camps and never made it past one trip to Camp II.

With Dianne coming between us, Jim and I generally drew apart. I put all my energies—and frustrations—into the climb. I paired up instead with Jim Wickwire, who was as enthusiastic and motivated to achieve the summit as I was. The only time Wick and I had climbed together before had been on a rescue on Mount Rainier

Jim Wickwire and Lou on K2, 1975 (Team photo)

in 1969. I had a great climb with Wick on K2, and we forged a lasting friendship. It was the most positive outcome of the climb for me.

The others on the climb didn't really see the rift between me and Jim. What they saw, as expressed in Galen Rowell's book about the climb, *In the Throne Room of the Mountain Gods*, was an "us against them" situation. Jim, Wick, and I against the rest. They thought the three of us were determined to reach the summit at all costs, with the others there only to help carry loads so that we could reach our goal.

That wasn't true. What was true was that we had a lot of personality conflicts that came to a head on the six-week trek to base camp that were never really resolved during the climb. Some of these conflicts were fueled by the troubles we had with our porters striking or threatening to abandon the climb. Pakistan had just opened up again to climbing after several years, and most of the porters were untrained and not used to working with expeditions. We had started out with several hundred Pakistani porters, and ended up with fifty by the time we reached base camp. At one point, we threatened to burn the money we carried to pay them, and lit a handful to call their strike bluff. It worked. But we never had the cooperation and skill that you see among the Sherpa of Nepal. The Sherpa are trained climbers and guides, as opposed to porters, whose primary purpose is to carry loads into base camp. Some porters possess the skill to carry loads to higher camps. We had a handful of these on the K2 climb, designated as high-altitude porters, or HAPs.

The problems on the expedition were made worse by illness. A few in the party came down with pneumonia and bronchitis, which meant that the rest of us had to work harder to carry loads and put in the route to the summit. Instead of eight healthy climbers on the team, we ended up with four—five, really, including Steve Marts, the cinematographer. Steve, Jim, Wick, Rob, and I stayed healthy and strong. The others were debilitated by illness as well as the personality conflicts that had arisen among the team. Leif contracted pneumonia, but recovered enough to carry loads to our higher camps and to accompany me and Wick to our high point of the climb.

K2 is the second-highest mountain in the world, but it's rated as more technically difficult than Everest. The peak rises steeply on all sides, like a true pyramid, and is situated at the remote end of the Karakoram Range in Pakistan, about 800 miles west of Everest. Our intent was to follow the unclimbed northwest ridge to the summit.

We were delayed over and over again by storms as the team pushed to establish Camp I at 19,000 feet and Camp II at 20,400. Wick and I spent more than a month at or above Camp II, putting in the route and fixing ropes on a steep, 600-foot ice wall. We were trying to set up more high camps, but we kept getting beaten back by weather and a dwindling supply of human effort. Leif was with us when, at 22,000 feet, we encountered an extremely steep rock and ice ridge that descended more than 6,000 vertical feet from the summit to a col above base camp. Above the ridge, the sharp, pyramidlike peak of K2 rose for more than a vertical mile. When we reached that impassable, knife-edge ridge, we knew the climb was over. To this day, that particular route remains unclimbed.

Living at that altitude for so long really takes a toll on your body. I normally weigh 200 pounds. I left for K2 having beefed up to 215. On the climb, I lost 65 pounds. When I got home, I'd drink tomato juice and look like a thermometer.

You never gain weight at altitude. In fact, you have to eat like a pig and drink water like crazy to survive. You stuff food inside your clothing, under your hat, and eat at every opportunity. On K2, I'd eat 7,000 to 10,000 calories and drink seven liters of liquid each day and still lose weight. On Rainier, I'm always reminding my students to eat and drink at every opportunity. I tell them, "You can't run a bulldozer on a pint of diesel!"

A lot of people wonder what a bunch of guys do for three or four months on an expedition, when they're not climbing. It's not as macho a scene as people might think. You read, keep a journal, tell jokes, and talk about your dreams. And you mostly dream about food. On Jim's 1963 Everest expedition, the National Science Foundation spent thousands of dollars on a study of dreams. Basically what they found out was that, at high altitudes, climbers have very few erotic dreams. Instead of dreaming about sex, they dream about fresh fruit and salad.

The hardest part of an expedition is saying goodbye to your loved ones. Not from a sexual point of view, but from a feeling of "I'm leaving the people I love and I may not come back." It's especially hard on the ones left behind. When Jim came back from Everest, he likened it to going away to war. You're going to war and people might get killed and leave loved ones behind.

So when you say goodbye, it's with the realization that you may never see them again. And then when you're gone, you think about that a lot. You get lots of chances to reflect on your relationships and responsibilities. Am I doing the right thing? If I die, is the house covered? Will the insurance be enough to take care of the wife and kids? When you're climbing, your objective is simple: get to the summit and back, alive. You focus on that, put all your energy into that. Then when you're not climbing—you're on a rest day or holed up in your tent during a storm—all these other thoughts come flooding back.

And you're always dealing with health problems. Some minor, some major. The major ones confine you to camp and to medical treatment. The minor ones usually don't prohibit you from climbing, but they become nagging irritants. At altitude, my lips were always split from fever blisters. In the years since then, we've learned some ways to beat these problems. The newer lip balms have sunblocks that seem to curb blisters and cold sores. Also, the amino acid lysine often deters development of fever blisters.

But on K2, we had to make do with whatever remedies we could rummage from our first-aid kits. One day, my lips were hurting and bleeding so badly that I called our doctor, Rob Schaller, in base camp and asked what I could do. He said, "Look in your first-aid kit. There's a blue tube. Put that stuff on your lips several times a day. Take it to bed with you and put it on during the night as well."

Wickwire, who was with me in the tent, grabbed the radio and said, "Hey, Rob, I've got a problem too. I've never had one before, but I've got a hemorrhoid as big as my thumb. What should I do?"

Rob said, "You know that blue tube I just told Lou about...?"

One high-altitude porter, Akbar, had climbed up to Camp II at 20,400 feet. He became sick with roundworms. Many of the people native to the area suffered from roundworms without ill effects, but Akbar's condition was severe. He was vomiting constantly, which dehydrated him, and passing worms, some up to ten inches long. He was taken back to base camp and treated for perforated intestines until he could be evacuated lower.

In the meantime, Schaller was worried about me and Wick

becoming infected, since we had spent time in the tent with Akbar. Akbar had even drunk from my cup. Rob said that he'd send up some blue pills with instructions for us to take one every hour for five hours, to kill any worms that might be starting to grow inside us.

Wick and I waited eight days for the pills to be carried up. A storm had moved in and left us tent-bound. We kept asking each other, "You feel anything yet?" Thankfully, neither of us became infected.

Most of my health problems on K2 were of the nagging variety that were easily treated with the infamous blue tube or some other all-purpose medication. One of the problems I had actually led to a new business association. One of my toes had started hurting on the mountain, but I ignored it until we had abandoned our hopes of attaining the summit and headed back down to base camp. There, I showed it to Rob. He said that it had been ulcerated to the bone from being confined in socks and boots for so long, and from rubbing up against the toe next to it.

Rob treated the toe and then told me I should air it as much as possible. This meant it would be better if I didn't wear my stiff leather climbing boots. We still had a 40-mile walk ahead of us on the Baltoro Glacier, and then 100 miles along the Braldu River (a tributary of the Indus) before we'd reach a road and transportation. The only other shoes I had with me were a pair of New Balance tennis shoes, so I put those on and wore them all the way out. By the time we reached the roadhead near Skardu, my toe had healed.

When I got home, I wrote to New Balance and complimented them on their tennis shoe. And I suggested that they consider making a tennis-type shoe with a lug sole for light hiking. They took me up on my suggestion and also hired me to consult on the development of a hiking boot called the "Rainier." I've been on a yearly retainer with New Balance ever since.

When the team returned to Rawalpindi, Wickwire and I were met by our wives, Mary Lou and Ingrid, who had flown to Pakistan together. This is how Ingrid describes her reaction to our reunion: "The team looked like Auschwitz survivors. None of them had had a shower yet. They had all lost tremendous amounts of weight. Lou had lost sixty-five pounds. Mary Lou and I were so shocked—they looked like they were going to die, they were so skinny and hairy and dirty. Mary Lou and I both burst into tears.

"The team got cleaned up, and we all flew back to Karachi. Wick, Mary Lou, Lou, and I stayed with an embassy family. The Wickwires had their own bedroom, Lou and I had ours. It was late and time for bed. Mary Lou and I were ready to have some privacy with our guys. And there they were, out in the hallway still saying goodnight.

" 'Lou, come on, what are you guys doing?' I called. They were saying their long farewells. After all, they had shared a tent for nearly four months. They could hardly bear to part."

Not long after we returned home, Jim began planning another attempt on K2. Since he intended to include Dianne on the team again, I agreed to stay home. I had no desire to go through all that dissension again.

In 1978, with Jim as expedition leader, Jim Wickwire finally realized his lifelong dream. With Lou Reichardt, Wick became the first American to summit K2. They followed the Northeast Ridge and the uppermost Abruzzi Ridge, the route pioneered by an Italian team in 1954. Reichardt did it without oxygen. Wick lingered on top too long and had to bivouac just below the summit. He nearly died. He contracted pneumonia and pleurisy, paralyzed his vocal cords and diaphragm, and suffered frostbite. He went home in a wheelchair. But this didn't stop Wick. By 1981, he was ready and willing to join the China–Everest expedition that I planned for 1982.

I came back from K2 in 1975 with this understanding: the measure of a good team is not whether you make the summit, but how well you get along during the climb.

Other Perspectives: Jim Wickwire

K2 was for me the ultimate mountain. It was the shape of it, the history. It is the hardest 8,000-meter peak. If I had to pick a mountain that I'd aspire to climb when I first started to climb, it would be K2 over Everest.

This was the first expedition that had gone into K2 in fifteen years and we had great difficulties with the porters. Few of them had gone up the Baltoro Glacier. Their fathers might have been up there, but most of them hadn't. We had a series of strikes and work stoppages, all the way from the last village to base camp. We'd have two or three days of arguing with the porters through interpreters. More than anything, I think, this is what led to some of the problems that we experienced once we got on the mountain. Everyone was so frustrated with the delays and difficulties we had experienced that, despite the fact that most of us had climbed together in the Cascades and knew each other before the trip, by the time we reached base camp people had already split into factions and there were bad feelings among the team.

Galen Rowell was the only person with whom no one else had climbed. He was basically a Yosemite and Sierra rock climber and had done very little snow and ice climbing prior to this expedition. Jim and I had gotten to know him while serving on the board of directors of the American Alpine Club. We both thought that Galen would be a good addition to the team.

Galen talked a lot. He's very verbal and that got on Lou's nerves and, to some extent, on Jim's nerves. There was a clash in personalities from the outset, particularly between Galen and Lou. I think Jim and Lou both felt that Galen was just there to make sure that he got great photographs. Consequently, there were times when everybody was pitching in with the work of the expedition, packing loads, all the things you do just to get tons of gear from the end of the road to base camp, and Jim and Lou—and even I—felt that Galen was not doing his fair share of the work, and that exacerbated things.

Two groups developed. One was made up of Jim, Dianne, me, and Lou. I think we tended to be more gung-ho, more optimistic, and more positive toward the mountain. The others—Fred Stanley, Fred Dunham, Galen, Leif Patterson, and Rob Schaller—had, I think, a harder time in dealing with the Pakistanis and all the frustrations and delays. Lou and I were so revved up about the climb that we'd work to solve these problems, but we didn't let the problems get us down.

At one point in the expedition, the two Freds decided that they did not want to go up on the mountain. They carried loads and they participated but they were not interested in going higher. I think that attitude was there from early on. Fred Stanley left behind a wife and Fred Dunham left behind a woman that he eventually married after the expedition. Both women were unhappy about the two men going on the climb. I think that had a large bearing on how they were able to perform. If you don't have that support back home, you aren't able to concentrate on the objective, which is to climb this mountain. It just eats at you and leads to a lot of problems. It affects your motivation.

The expedition was troubled by a lot of personal and, sometimes, acrimonious discussions. I don't think that Galen's book about the climb was negative, although some people have said so. I think it was one of the first books to ever lay out openly the conflicts and the real-life story of what goes on in a typical big expedition. I don't think that expedition was unique in the problems it had.

Lou took a dim view of Galen's verbalizing everything, of Galen's performance, of the fact that Galen didn't carry what Lou thought was his fair share of the loads. Some people don't suffer fools gladly, but the Whittakers don't suffer people who are shirkers or people who are weak—not weak physically, but strong people who act in less of a manner than they should.

This was also the first time that Jim and Lou were on a major expedition together, and if Dianne had not come, you would have seen Jim and Lou as a pair. But with Dianne there, it was natural that they would tent together, walk together, and I think that affected Jim's desire to go up on the mountain. He knew he was not going to be out in front, although I think he was quite motivated on the expedition.

I think that led to some problems between Jim and Lou, that they weren't able to have the kind of experience they otherwise might have had if the situation had been different. I guess I was the beneficiary of this in the sense that Lou and I were able to hit it off prior to the expedition and then once we arrived in Pakistan we were inseparable. I think this was a problem for the others in that we were so positive about things and were so, some would say, driven toward getting up the mountain. But I saw it as just two people being committed to the same goal and sharing that commitment.

Lou and I never had an argument the entire expedition. He is one of those few people that I've been with in the mountains who you can be with on a day-to-day basis and be with in the same tent in a storm and never have any problems. Things are always compatible. If you're like that, it's natural that you seek out somebody else who's that way. It's natural that you end up a pair.

I don't know if it had to do with the psychological factor, but Lou and I were lucky enough not to get sick once we were on the mountain. As a consequence, we were doing virtually all of the leading and putting in the route above Camp I, which on the last 700 or 800 feet to our high point at 22,000 feet was quite technical, with very steep ice and some rock. We reached the top of this very steep pinnacle and saw that it was just impossible to go ahead. You might be able to climb along this pinnacled ridge, but it was so technical that it was a real problem in terms of getting loads along it. Even worse, if someone were sick or injured on the far side, getting them back across that stretch of ridge would have been next to impossible. At that point, we realized that the climb was over.

Looking back, I think that maybe we were too motivated, too strong for some of the others, and that turned out to be a problem. And I think the problems are also a function of how you put together these expeditions and who goes on them. Some of the problems we had in 1975 we had again in 1978, when I went back to K2 without Lou. On the two Everest expeditions that Lou led in 1982 and 1984, these types of problems were not experienced.

You kind of have to look at these four expeditions, two K2s on which Jim was the leader, and two Everests on which Lou was the leader, to understand why each of them was so different. Each of them was ultimately successful on the second try, but the two K2 trips were just full of personality clashes and problems, whereas the Everest expeditions were, for the most part, tranquil. I think this has to do with the makeup of the teams.

There's also something about having the two Whittakers together. They are both so strong and such forceful personalities that they're almost more than some of the other expedition members can take, in terms of just reacting to a force. If either Lou or Jim had not gone on K2 in 1975, the end result would have been the same. We wouldn't have gotten any higher. But we probably would have had less serious problems with only one Whittaker. Not that Lou or Jim was causing the problems, but the problems were enhanced by the fact of having both Whittakers together.

On the 1978 expedition, I think both Jim and Lou realized that it did not make a great deal of sense for Lou to go back. Jim put it to Lou in terms of the strong competitiveness between them. Lou criticized Jim for his dictatorial approach to the rest of us and for not involving me more in expedition decision-making, although I felt that Jim did involve me. But I would have been delighted to have gone back with Lou and I think he would have climbed to the summit with me. He was incredibly strong in 1975 and there really wasn't anything to suggest that in three years he would have been less able to climb.

As a climber, I think Lou never fully realized his potential, in the sense of achieving some big climb. He certainly has had the equipment, mental and physical, to achieve some big climbs, but he chose not to follow that course. He emphasized the guide service instead. K2 in 1975 was the expedition that he went to fully poised and ready for a big climb. This was at age forty-six, which is pretty amazing. What would he have been like ten years earlier?

There's absolutely no question that, if Lou had gone to Everest in 1963, he and Jim could have climbed to the summit together. But again, they probably would have been the two strongest guys on the expedition and what would that have meant to that expedition? Believe me, when they are together in the mountains, they are an extremely powerful pair and it is more than just the sum of their parts. Being twins, I think, adds even an extra dimension.

The 1975 K2 expedition caused some ongoing strain in my relationship with Jim. We still respected each other and went on a few rescues together in the following years, but it was obvious that a certain distance had cropped up between us. Part of this was probably caused by the fact that we had been buffeted and shaped by different forces since our mid-thirties. And part of it may have been caused by Jim's commitment to Dianne and my inability, at the time, to accept it. When twins marry, I think they have a harder time switching their allegiance to their spouses than do non-twin siblings. In any case, Jim and I aren't as close as we used to be, and we've never totally resolved the differences that emerged between us on K2.

To say that I still love my brother is too simple a statement. I still regard Jim as the safest guy I could ever tie in with. Our natural bond was forged in the mountains of our childhood and reinforced there during our maturing years. This is a bond that bends and stretches under the weight of differences and disappointments, but never breaks.

The final sad note to our ill-fated 1975 K2 expedition came about a year after we had returned to the United States. Leif Patterson had gone climbing locally with his twelve-year-old son and an eighteen-year-old friend of his son's. According to their rescuers, they either took a rope-team fall or were pulled off in an avalanche. All three were killed.

Leif's son had been a piano virtuoso and had been accepted on scholarship to a musical academy. At the funeral service, they played a tape of the boy's piano recital. It was one of the saddest funerals I've ever gone to.

Leif was a good climber and he loved life. He had been one of the stronger climbers on the expedition and the only one who had kept a neutral position during all the dissent. I'll never forget the photo of him in Galen Rowell's book, standing on a high ridge covered with green grass, the first green grass we'd seen for four months. Leif's arms were outstretched and there was a smile of joy on his face.

Up high, there's just snow, ice, and rock and there are no smells except your own. At the end of a climb, when you come back down and smell the grass and the earth or see your first flower, you feel reborn. You wonder, when you get back home, why the hell did I take so many pictures of that flower?

That flower is life and it's a beauty.

♦ 7 ♦

OF KINGS AND HEROES

There was an article written about me in a small local newspaper in 1989 called "King of the Mountain." I was embarrassed by the title. In my mind, there are no kings of the mountain. No one conquers a mountain. A mountain decides who will climb it and who will not.

Sometimes you feel like a king after you've made an especially hard climb. Most of the time, you feel pretty humble. Most climbers share this feeling. The higher you get, the more insignificant you feel. That's not a bad feeling.

One of the best parts about guiding on Mount Rainier is the opportunity it has given me and Ingrid to meet and climb with so many great climbers. Many have become good friends and some have become good memories.

Willi Unsoeld was a great climber and a great soul. He was my hero. Willi was a happy guy with a generous outlook and incredible spirit. A humble, caring person. He was a hippie in his lifestyle, and taught as a professor of philosophy and religion. When he wasn't teaching, he'd sometimes guide for me in the summers.

Willi also had been a member of the 1963 Everest team. He was on leave from Oregon State University and was working with the Peace Corps in Nepal when he climbed Everest. Willi and Tom Hornbein made the summit three weeks after my twin, Jim, summitted with Gombu. Willi and Hornbein were not only the first in history to go up the West Ridge, but also the first to traverse a major Himalayan peak. They traversed the West Ridge to the summit of Everest, then came down the South Col. Willi lost all of his toes from frostbite on that climb. But he kept on climbing.

After Willi had recovered from losing his toes, he had a pair of custom boots made up. The first time I saw him wearing them, I said they looked awfully short. "Yeah," he said, "and my balance is crummy." He soon went back to wearing a full boot.

About six months later, I saw him and asked how the full boot was working out. "Great!" he said. "I've found another place to put M&M's." He was serious. The guy would stop on the trail, unlace a boot, and dump out a handful of M&M's.

One time, I hired Willi to help me on a five-day climbing seminar. On the third day of the seminar, we had set up a suspension traverse across a crevasse and a top rope on an ice serac for climbing instruction. We taught the students how to clip their harnesses into the pulley attached to the rope suspended between the two walls of the 100-foot-deep crevasse, and then slide across from one side to the other, belayed by another student. And we showed them how to climb up the ice wall by clipping into the rope for protection and using their crampons and ice tools to "claw" their way up the serac.

I was teaching the clawing while Willi ran the traverse. I noticed that almost everyone had done the traverse, so I asked another guide to take over for me on the serac while I climbed up to see how Willi was doing. He was on the other side of the crevasse, preparing to come across, so I turned to talk to a few of the students. Soon I could tell by the looks on their faces that something else had caught their attention. I turned to see Willi halfway across the rope.

Willi had climbed on top of the rope and was now inchworming his way across. Most people in this situation would immediately flip to the underside of the rope and have to traverse the rest of the way hand-over-hand, foot-over-foot, assuming they didn't lose their grip. Not Willi. With incredible balance—and courage—he was sliding his body along the top of the rope. He wasn't clipped to the rope in any way. One slip and he'd have fallen 100 feet to sure death. It was impressive and typical of Willi's self-assurance, but it made the hairs on the back of my neck stand up straight. I told the students, "Willi is demonstrating a technique that *none* of you are to practice."

None of them wanted to, but one of the students did remark, "Now I see how Willi was able to summit Mount Everest."

Eventually Willi's hips gave out, maybe from the imbalance caused by his feet. He had two plastic ball-and-socket hip-joint implants, and kept on climbing. He called it his "bionic approach" to climbing.

Willi and I had a lot of great talks. He was a great philosopher and protector of the wilderness ethic. He liked to lead people in the mountains as much for the thrill and challenge of it as for the opportunity to enhance their appreciation of nature.

In 1977, Willi was co-leader on an expedition to climb the Himalayan peak Nanda Devi. He had named his daughter Devi after that mountain. She was a member of the expedition. She became sick and died in Willi's arms at 23,000 feet, from an acute abdominal disorder complicated by altitude. The loss of his daughter hit Willi hard, but he remained philosophical and optimistic about life. He felt that it was better to experience life than to shy away from it. Willi committed Devi's body to the mountain with the words "Thank you for the world we live in. Thank you for such beauty juxtaposed against such risk...."

By then my son Peter also had decided to take up mountaineering as a profession. In 1975, at age sixteen, he had joined my Rainier Mountaineering guide service. I looked forward to taking him to Everest with me in the future. After hearing about Devi, I started worrying about losing Peter. I told Willi about my fear. He said, "They're going to die someday. You can't protect them from that. But maybe you can teach him a few things and he'll be safer."

In March 1979, Willi died in an avalanche on Mount Rainier. I led the initial rescue effort. Willi had been caught in a storm with twenty-one students from The Evergreen State College in Washington and had decided to take a shortcut back to Camp Muir by going through Cadaver Gap, an avalanche-prone area within sight of Camp Muir, between Gibraltar Rock and Cathedral Rocks. The area got its name following a big accident in 1929, when two climbers were killed during a guided party's fall into a crevasse on the

Willi Unsoeld and Sherpa Nawang Gombu on summit of Mount Rainier, 1971 (Photo: Lou Whittaker)

upper mountain. The bodies were evacuated through the saddle, hence its name.

On this day in 1979, a deep, wind-slab avalanche peeled off and caught Willi and the three students on his rope. Two of the students survived. Willi and the other student, a twenty-one-year-old girl named Janie Diepenbrock, were killed. The storm continued to rage and several more avalanches covered the site where Willi and the girl had fallen. They were taken off the mountain about a week later, after the storm had run out, which storms always do.

I knew that Willi's fate could just as well have been my own. Just six months before, I had triggered an avalanche at another site on the mountain while climbing with my son Peter and a group of clients. We were almost to the top of a corniced ridge on the back of Muir Peak. I suddenly got a bad feeling about our position, but before I could do anything about it, the cornice broke and swept us off the ridge.

Peter and his rope team fell a couple hundred feet before they got hung up on a rock outcropping. I was swept almost 500 feet down the mountain with my rope team, and we just missed going into a bergschrund. No one was hurt, except Peter, who got a badly sprained ankle. We were lucky, Willi wasn't. Willi was playing the odds, but we sometimes do that in climbing.

A couple of days after Willi's accident, I had to fly to New Orleans to give a lecture. I got a cab from the airport, checked into a hotel, and found a square where I could sit in the warm sun. Wearing just a shirt, no parka, I sat surrounded by ornate wrought-iron railings and geraniums blooming and a band playing "When the Saints Go Marching In." I was drinking coffee and eating a croissant and I knew that Willi was still under the snow above Camp Muir, but I swear I could hear him laughing in the empty chair beside me.

Willi called the parts of life that we cannot understand the "mysterium tremendums." He celebrated the joys of the mountain life and he believed in reincarnation. Some of my own philosophy about life developed from my association with Willi. I'm not sure about reincarnation, but it's nice to think that Willi's spirit might return someday. In many ways, I feel that it has never left.

I met Sherpa Nawang Gombu after Jim's Everest climb in 1963. Since Gombu had summitted with Jim, he was chosen to return to the United States with the team. He was honored, along with the rest of the team, by President Kennedy.

Gombu had been on Sir Edmund Hillary's climb in 1953 at the age of seventeen. His uncle was Tenzing Norgay, the Sherpa who had summitted with Hillary. In 1954, Tenzing had helped found the Himalayan Mountaineering Institute in Darjeeling. HMI is a government institute that teaches mountaineering skills mostly to the military and police, although they also train some civilians and college students. Gombu went to work there, too. After Tenzing retired, Gombu became director, and still holds the position today.

After summitting with Jim in 1963, Gombu went back in 1965 with an Indian expedition and summitted Everest again. He became the first person to reach the summit of Everest twice.

Gombu is used to taking care of people, because that's what the top Sherpas do. It's hard to keep him from taking too much care of you. I continually tell my new guides, "If you can just look after the clients half as well as Gombu does, you'll be the best guides in the world."

Sherpas have a high death rate, because so many expeditions use them for the most dangerous parts of a climb. Some Sherpas may lack technique, just from lack of training or exposure, but they're born in the high mountains of Nepal and they have good, basic mountain knowledge.

Jim had written to me from Everest and said that he wanted to teach Gombu some technique, using newer equipment. Gombu, he said, was a real mountain man. He knew how to cook and run a camp, but he had very little exposure to new equipment. When I met Gombu, I was surprised that he spoke English so well, but Jim told me that Gombu had learned a little of several languages from different expeditions. Gombu speaks Hindi, Japanese, English, Tibetan, Nepalese, and, of course, the Sherpa dialect.

I thought it would be great to have Gombu come over and guide with us. Jim was afraid that we would destroy Gombu's uniqueness, but we haven't. He's been here now ten different summers and all the guides love and respect him. To them, he's a living legend. At five feet, he's the shortest of the guides but, as my dad would say, "It's not the size of the guy that counts, it's how tight he's wound."

Gombu is wound very tight. We think he must have two hearts and three lungs because on top of Rainier his resting heartbeat is 38 beats per minute. Most climbers register 180 at that altitude. You'd think Gombu was dead, sitting on that summit. I tell students that Gombu's lungs are so powerful that, when he hikes a trail and takes a deep breath, he sucks up small rocks.

One year Gombu brought his wife, Sita, to the United States with him. We arranged for her to have an operation here to correct her deafness. It was the first time in her life that she could hear. We took her to the ocean and she heard the waves and spent the whole time walking around with a smile on her face. That was Sita's only visit to the United States. She stays home to manage the household. She and Gombu have four children of their own and also adopted another, a girl, from a poor family. Two of his daughters are married. The oldest one, Yangdu, climbs and helped Ingrid arrange preliminary details for a trek to Kangchenjunga in 1989. Gombu's son, Phinjo, guided a couple of years on Rainier for me. Gombu was able to put Phinjo through some good schools and he became a journalist, now living in Montreal.

Gombu's people believe that if you see a yeti you will die in two days. On one of our climbing seminars, I asked him if he believed that and he said, "No, I think it takes seven days."

That same night, during a blizzard, Gombu was telling yeti stories to me and a few other guides in the cook shack at Camp Muir. We all were hunched around Gombu, taking in his every word. It was colder than hell and we were feeling a little jittery. Suddenly we heard pounding on the metal door and we about jumped out of our skins. Gombu's eyes grew wide as he watched me slowly open the door. It was a client from the bunkhouse who needed some aspirin. Couldn't have been better timing.

One of my favorite stories about Gombu involves a reporter who interviewed Jim and Gombu after their Everest climb. The reporter asked Jim to relate what happened when they reached the top. Jim said that first they took pictures of each other and then they had time to reflect. Jim's first thoughts were something like "How strong are the forces of nature and how humble I am. What an incredible, beautiful mountain. For the glory of the United States, we summitted." The reporter then turned to Gombu and asked, "What were your first thoughts upon reaching the summit?" And Gombu said, "How to get back down."

Other Perspectives: Sherpa Nawang Gombu

I was born in Namche Bazaar, Nepal, in 1936, at 12,000 feet. When I was thirteen years old, my father sent me to the Rongbuk Monastery in Tibet, facing Everest, at about 17,000 feet. After one year, I ran away. It was four days' walk across an 18,000-foot pass to get home. All I had to eat was bread and tea.

My father was very mad, and didn't talk to me for four or five days. My mother was happy, though, because I was the eldest. I started climbing then.

My first expedition was with the British in 1953. Tenzing Norgay was my uncle, so I went with him on Sir Edmund Hillary's Everest expedition. I did not summit. I went to Everest again in 1960 with an Indian expedition, but nobody summitted. In 1963, I climbed with Jim. We used oxygen. As we neared the summit, I said to Jim, "You go first." He said, "No, we'll go together." So we did. Two years later, I went back to Everest with an Indian expedition and summitted again. That time, four Sherpas and five Indians summitted. It was the first time so many had summitted at once.

There are only two or three left of the forty-five Sherpas from the 1963 Everest expedition. Four or five have died of sickness, but the others have been killed on mountains—Makalu, Kangchenjunga, Annapurna, Dhaulagiri, Everest. In 1969, nine Sherpas were killed on a Japanese Everest expedition, carrying loads up and down the Khumbu Icefall. They all died the same day, in an avalanche.

People get mixed up about the difference between porters and Sherpas. Porters carry loads and don't go up high. Sherpas carry loads and climb high to help set up camps. Sherpas are a high tribe people from eastern Nepal. Most of the Sherpas mix with the Tibetans, especially those living by the border. Forty years ago, on Hillary and Tenzing's climb, those were true Sherpas. Today, expeditions use Tibetans, thinking they are Sherpas, but they aren't.

Rainier is an amazing mountain, and not a small mountain. For almost forty years, I've been climbing in the Himalaya, Bhutan, India, and Nepal. Many times I've seen storms on Rainier as bad as storms in the Himalaya.

Every year or two, I come to Rainier to work with Lou. I enjoy climbing with him and with so many different types of people. People come from all over the world to climb Rainier.

In 1993, I was in London for the fortieth anniversary celebration of Hillary's Everest climb. We saw the queen again. We had seen her after the Everest climb in 1953, the same year as her coronation. Then, I had asked her secretary, "May I present the queen with a scarf?" He said, "What is this scarf?" I said, "It is a traditional Sherpa and Tibetan scarf. We present it to honor people." The queen told me that she loved the scarf and would keep it. I presented one to

John F. Kennedy, too, in 1963. And to Lou and Ingrid. It is for big people and for friendship.

Dusan Jagersky was an Olympic-status weight lifter from Czechoslovakia who jumped the Iron Curtain and came to the United States in the mid-sixties. He was also a skier and mountain climber.

In 1970, he came to Whittaker's Chalet and asked me for a summer job guiding. I thought, "Well, he doesn't speak English very well, but he looks strong." Top mountaineers don't always make good guides. A good guide has to be patient and not too ego-driven.

I told Dusan that we hired people and tried them out for a few weeks. If they didn't get along with their peers, they were out. He said, "I accept that."

Our one-day climbing schools were designed to check out a person's skills and conditioning. We never took them climbing, we just checked out their basic skills on a hill near the Guide House at Paradise. We gave Dusan a one-day climbing school to guide, and he misunderstood and took them all the way to Camp Muir, a five- to six-hour hike from Paradise. By five o'clock, when the Guide House is supposed to close, we were all wondering where Dusan was, when in he came with the school, having just completed a round-trip climb to Camp Muir. We told Dusan, "You're trying too hard."

Dusan eventually learned the techniques of guiding and became a top guide. Everyone loved him and learned mountaineering technique from him, too. I really enjoyed climbing and skiing with him. We did some great climbs on Rainier together, and also went on some rescues. Each time we'd go out, we'd learn more about each other.

On rescues, you don't have clients, so you don't have to go slow. You have a whole different mentality at work, unless you're stuck with a "green" rescuer. Most of the time, you're with good climbers, and it can be fun. Dusan and I did some fast trips together and that's when I learned how strong he was. He also was a happy guy to be around. Ingrid and I loved to be with him. He loved the mountains as much as we did.

One day I was at Camp Muir getting some clients ready for a

climb. Dusan was up on the mountain, guiding a climbing party. I got a radio call saying that Dusan had fallen and there was a woman injured. Dusan had broken a leg. We usually didn't have radio contact all day long, but for some reason the radio had been on this time. Two other guides were with me—John Rutter, the son of the superintendent of Mount Rainier National Park, and Phursumba, Gombu's brother-in-law. When I got the call on Dusan, I asked, "What do you need?"

They said, "We can use a stretcher and some help, and maybe a helicopter because Dusan is in real pain." I got the break-apart stretcher. I took half and Phursumba took the other half. Rutter was in the middle of our rope. I was leading because I wanted to set the pace and hurry to Dusan's aid.

I took off like a sonofabitch. At first John and Phursumba were keeping up, but pretty soon the rope started to drag and tighten. I dropped the pace slightly. I didn't look back, but I could feel the rope draw tight again. We were about forty-five minutes out and halfway to the top of Disappointment Cleaver, fast time. And then I heard this *chu-chu-chu* and I felt a little tug. I looked back to see that Phursumba had walked up past Rutter and now he was walking up beside me to say, "Lou, it's not me holding back the rope." I said, "Phursumba (huff, huff), I know it isn't (huff, huff). Now get back there." The guy could have gone by me like a train.

We got to the top of the Cleaver and learned that Dusan had gotten pulled off a steep, hard slope while trying to coil in his three clients. He'd broken his leg trying to stop the fall. A rock about the size of a cash register was sticking up on the slope. Dusan fell to one side of it, the rest of the rope team fell to the other side and swung down below Dusan. The injured woman was just bruised and crying, the other two on the rope were okay. If that little rock hadn't been there, they'd all have been killed.

There were two other rope teams up there at the time and the guides had anchored a rope up top so they could drag Dusan back up to a level spot. When we arrived, we used a sled to move Dusan to a place where a helicopter could pick him up. The 'copter lifted off both Dusan and the injured girl.

Later, I visited Dusan at the hospital. He was apologizing and trying to explain that his leg broke in the same place as an old break from skiing that had never healed correctly. He had shown me before where the bone rubbed across his boot. He'd say, "Sometime I should get this fixed." I told him he was lucky to have broken it again in the same place. "This time you'll be in great shape, Dusan."

It took him all winter, but he rehabilitated his leg. I talked to him some about recognizing when to turn around on a climb, and not to press on when danger was imminent.

The following spring, he asked me if I'd go with him on his first climb after his rehabilitation. We got to Camp Muir and he said, "I'm not sleeping in the bunkhouse." He was sweating and scared as hell. I said, "Dusan, don't do the damn thing if you don't want to. But if you're going, you're going with me on my rope."

The next morning, we started out and pretty soon I heard Dusan laughing and yodeling. I turned to look at him. He said, "My God, I'm so happy! I dreaded this all winter and it's so easy I don't know how I could have been afraid."

I figured then that he was all right and wouldn't get pulled off again. But by God, in 1977, on a first ascent of the Fairweather Range in Alaska with Jim Wickwire, Al Givler, and Steve Marts, Dusan got pulled off a wall. Dusan was roped with Al Givler. Wick and Marts were roped together. All four had summitted and were on their way down. Either Dusan or Givler took a fall and pulled the other off the wall.

Wickwire called both Jim and me in on the rescue. Wick was pretty shook up and wanted to confirm beyond a doubt that Dusan and Al were dead. Dusan was strong enough that, if he had been able to hook onto some rocks and hang on the wall, he could have made it, and at first there was some speculation—or hope—that that was what might have happened. Jim and I hiked in about four days later with Wick and found the remains of Dusan and Al. They had fallen about 4,000 feet altogether. We left them there. Dusan's wife, Diane, was in Glacier Bay when we returned with the news.

Ingrid and I had introduced Dusan to Diane. She was a fun-loving outdoorsperson. Dusan had planned to climb all his life, but he felt that he also needed a trade to properly support his new wife. So he had studied to be an electrician. Everything was going right for him when he checked out.

Dusan had guided for me for about six years. He was a top

climber. After he died, I regretted that I hadn't ever let him know how I felt about him, that I respected him as a person and a climber and loved him as a friend. Since then, I've lost a few other friends, but I've tried to be more open and let them know how I feel about them.

I've known Dave Mahre since the mid-fifties when we were on the winter rescue on Rainier with Jim and Dick McGowan. I met Jim Wickwire in 1969 on another rescue. We've become good friends over the years.

Dave has been the mountain manager at the White Pass Ski Area outside Yakima since 1962. Dave and his wife had nine children, including the famous Mahre twins, Steve and Phil. Dave used his twins' natural competitiveness to their advantage. He would clock the boys on a ski course. One would race down the course in great time, then the other would beat that time by a hundredth of a second. The other would go back up to beat that time and on and on they would go, pushing each other. That's how Steve and Phil became Olympic Gold Medal skiers.

Jim Wickwire is an attorney and a climber, a father of five, with a devoted wife, Mary Lou. Wick takes off now and then for three months to climb some major Himalayan peak, then comes home and resumes his law practice and family life. There's a poem by Robert Service that reminds me of Wick:

> There's a race of men that don't fit in,
> A race that can't stand still.
> So they break the hearts of kith and kin,
> And they roam the world at will.
> They range the field and they rove the flood,
> And they climb the mountain's crest;
> Theirs is the curse of the gypsy blood,
> And they don't know how to rest.

In May 1969, when I first met Wick, all three of us ended up on a rescue on Mount Rainier. Dave was already at the accident site with Lee Nelson, a firefighter and a climber from Tacoma, when Wick and I were helicoptered to the summit to lend a hand.

Three climbers had had a rockfall accident on upper Curtis

Above: *Lou, Pat, Blanche, and Jim with Kim, Peter, Barbara, Scott, and Carl, circa 1960 (Photo: Dee Molenaar)*

Below: *Pete Schoening, Lou Whittaker, John Day, and Jim Whittaker on the summit of Mount McKinley, 1960 (Photo courtesy Whittaker family)*

Opposite: *Dusan Jagersky belaying Lou on a direct-aid climb of a serac; Ingraham Glacier, 1971 (Photo: Keith Gunnar)*

Right: *Dusan Jagersky, Ingrid Widmann, and Lou on Mount Rainier, 1971 (Photo: Keith Gunnar)*

Sunrise on Ingraham Flats, Mount Rainier; first rest stop on the way to the summit (Photo: Keith Gunnar)

Lou at 22,000 feet on K2 above tents at Camp III, 1975 (Photo: Jim Wickwire)

Opposite: *Lou demonstrating a suspension traverse, 1972 (Photo: Ingrid Widmann)*

Right: *Marty Hoey, Everest Base Camp, 1982 (Photo: Lou Whittaker)*

Below: *On a carry to Camp II, North Wall of Everest, 1982 (Photo: Lou Whittaker)*

China Everest team in Lhasa, 1982. Left to right (standing): *Nawang Gombu, Dave Mahre, Larry Nielson, Eric Simonsen, Dick Bass, George Dunn, Frank Wells, Tibetan and Chinese staff;* (kneeling): *Dr. Ed Hixson, Marty Hoey, Joe Horiskey, Lou Whittaker, Jim Wickwire;* (kneeling, front): *Tracy Roberts, Dan Boyd;* (sitting): *Gary Isaacs, Phil Ershler (Team photo)*

China Everest team, 1984, first view of Mount Everest. Left to right (back row): *Phil Ershler, Steve Marts, George Dunn, Pete Whittaker, John Roskelley, John Smallich, Dr. Ed Hixon, Carolyn Gunn;* (front row): *Greg Wilson, Dave Mahre, Jim Wickwire, Lou Whittaker (Photo: Ingrid Widmann)*

Kangchenjunga team at base camp, 1989. Left to right (standing): *Skip Yowell, Greg Wilson, Ed Viesturs, Larry Nielson, Jim Hamilton, Craig Van Hoy;* (kneeling): *George Dunn, Robert Link, Lou Whittaker, Phil Ershler, Dr. Howard Putter (Team photo)*

Lou and Ingrid at Kangchenjunga Base Camp, 1989 (Photo: Skip Yowell)

Ridge, an area of mixed rock and ice and one of the steeper routes on Rainier. They had been hit by some rockfall and one of them, George Dockery, had died. Another, Pete Sandstedt, had been seriously injured and was now hanging about seventy-five feet down in an alcove that was undermined. The third man had already been found near the top and rescued.

This was the first time I had climbed with Wick. He and I were helicoptered up to the saddle between Columbia Crest, the highest summit point on Rainier, and Liberty Cap, at about 13,000 feet. As soon as the 'copter landed, Wick jumped out and started running up to the summit, to show me how good he was. So I ran after him and passed him up, to show him how good I was. He told me later that he figured that I had been up the mountain several times already that season and was in tremendous shape. He hadn't been out climbing yet that year and didn't want me to think that he wasn't up to it. I told him that from then on, we could save our strength and didn't have to show each other up.

We got to the summit and discovered that there were already about forty "rescuers" up there, but nobody was doing anything. They were all afraid to go over the Willis Wall. We asked them, "Where's Mahre, where's Nelson?" They told us that they were already down on the wall. Wick said, "What about you guys?"

One of the rescuers, who was obviously in charge, came over and told me, "You realize you're undertaking this whole thing at your own risk. There's a good chance you'll get killed." I said, "What's with you asses? What are you doing up here anyway? Somebody give us a rope."

We knew that Dave and Lee Nelson would need help getting Sandstedt out. It was late, so Wick and I used our headlamps and belayed each other down the face of the Willis Wall.

Sandstedt had hung off the wall for about three days before anyone had sighted him and called for a rescue. He had either dislocated his shoulders or broken his arms—in any case, he couldn't use his arms. About the only thing he could do was get one foot on a rock and balance a little.

Lee and Dave had been helicoptered to the summit several hours before, and had encountered the same gathering of inactive rescuers. It was Dave's first time on the Curtis Ridge, but he and Lee worked together, leapfrogging leads, and belayed each other down an open book of hard rock in the rock band above where Sandstedt was trapped.

They didn't see Sandstedt until they had climbed down below him. The ridge had narrowed and he was hidden under an overhang. Sandstedt saw Lee and Dave first and started screaming, "Don't leave me, don't leave me." Dave later told us that it was the most plaintive cry he had ever heard. They climbed back up to Sandstedt and started getting him stabilized for the rescue.

It was after midnight when Wick and I climbed down. We'd yell to verify our position above them, and then tried not to kick any rocks loose. One good-sized rock did come loose, though, and knocked Dave's pack off the ledge. The pack fell about 2,000 feet down into the dark and landed somewhere on the Carbon Glacier. Dave's an emotional guy, and he started crying, "That was my hard hat, and my favorite down parka." He also had stuffed a borrowed sleeping bag into that pack. I told him, "Don't worry, I'll replace your stuff."

After Lee and Dave had finished getting a little food and water into Sandstedt, we started working to get him out of there. Since he could only use his legs, which were not that steady, we used jumar ascenders, sliding one after the other, to go up the rope. One man went in front of Sandstedt and set the ascenders. Another man went behind and helped Sandstedt place his feet. The other two carried all the gear. It was a vertical push, and nobody up top helped, not even by shining headlamps down to make it easier for us to see the route. When we reached the top, we discovered why. Every one of the so-called rescuers had fallen asleep.

We dragged one guy out of his tent and put Pete Sandstedt in there instead, to rest until daylight, when a 'copter would come to lift him off. It was one of those clear, starry nights on the summit when you can see the lights of the ships out on Puget Sound. Wick, Lee, Dave, and I sat up the rest of the night, shooting the breeze and savoring the fact that we had helped save a life.

In 1966, I took Bob McNamara, then secretary of defense, his wife, Margaret, and his daughter, Kathleen, up Mount Rainier. McNamara was vacationing in the Pacific Northwest and was being

Robert McNamara at Camp Muir, Mount Rainier, 1966 (Photo: Associated Press)

mobbed by reporters questioning him about Vietnam. He had come up to the mountain with a trio of FBI agents.

The FBI agents were supposed to climb with us, but they only made it about twenty minutes out from the Guide House at Paradise before one of the guys started getting red-faced and short of breath. I told him, "You may not make Camp Muir."

He said, "I don't think so."

"You're really a handicap," I said, "and so are those other two guys with you."

"Is there some place we can meet you on the way back down? Our boss will be really mad if we aren't on McNamara." I told them to be in this spot by the trees the next day at around three-thirty in the afternoon. They sneaked off through the trees, then came back the next day and walked down with us so that it looked like they had been part of the group the whole time.

We had a great climb with Mac. We reached Camp Muir that afternoon. Before sunset, we sat out on a ridge above Camp Muir, where you can see about twenty good peaks. McNamara asked, "Lou, what's that peak on the left?"

"That's Mount Adams, 12,307 feet, and there is Pinnacle, and Castle down there, and Mount Hood in the distance," and I gave him the elevations.

Margaret came out of the bunkhouse and climbed up beside us. She asked, "Lou, what's that peak on the left?" Before I could answer, Bob said, "That's Mount Adams, 12,307 feet." And he named the whole range of peaks and their elevations. He was a whiz kid, with an incredible memory. It had taken me about ten years to get all those peaks straight.

That evening, Jim hiked up to Camp Muir to join us for the summit climb the next morning. Bob's physician, Dr. Livingston, had also come with us to Camp Muir. He asked me that evening if I was opposed to sleeping pills. I said, "Yes, I am." He said, "Well, Bob's sleeping pill is a couple shots of bourbon each night." I said, "I like that sleeping pill."

The next day, Bob and his daughter summitted with me and Jim. Bob had climbed the Matterhorn at one time and was in good shape. He was fifty at the time, and had enough energy left when we arrived at the summit to circle the crater rim.

A couple weeks after the climb, Jim and I each received a package from the office of the secretary of defense. Inside, there was a blue chamois bag from Tiffany's with a solid silver box, engraved with an eagle and the emblem of the secretary of defense. The inscription said, "To Lou, a delightful companion and great mountaineer, with my admiration and thanks. Bob McNamara."

Jim and I thought we should send him something, too. We got a rock piton, a basic steel wafer designed to slip between rocks for security. We took that with a snap-link carabiner and had them both plated in gold and engraved: "To Bob, who marches to the beat of a different drum. From the Whittakers."

I've taken a lot of people up Mount Rainier—celebrities, government officials, professional athletes, heads of corporations, disabled people, and everyday people.

A lot of people climb to measure their health or level of fitness. I took a doctor up the mountain who wanted to test how his body functioned in high-altitude conditions. I took Laura Evans. She had just recovered from breast cancer and wanted to see if she had the strength to make it. She did.

I've taken up a priest who wanted to pray and figured he'd be closer to God on the summit.

There was an airplane pilot who wanted to climb to the summit because he had flown by it so many times he wanted to see what it looked like up close.

I led a gay man who wanted to deposit his lover's ashes on the mountain. It's illegal, but I've had the request many times and was moved by the sincerity of the guy. He only got to 12,300 feet, while the rest of the climbing team kept on to the summit. I figured he'd just dump out the ashes, but about three hours later, when I came back down to him, I discovered that he had spread out the ashes in the shape of a beautiful, life-size angel.

I took up Sarah Doherty, an amputee who had lost her right leg at age thirteen. She used special ski-pole crutches all the way up, and a year later became the first amputee to summit Mount McKinley. Handicapped people teach me more about strength, endurance, and determination than I ever teach them.

In the summer of 1981, Jim brought a large group of handicapped people from Colorado to climb Mount Rainier. Seven blind people were included in the group. I spent one day helping train them. I discovered that blind people don't have as much fear of heights as sighted people do. We took them through the training routine, did a suspension traverse. We had a lot of fun.

During the suspension traverse one of the women, who had been blind since birth, exhibited a great sense of humor. She asked me, "Lou, how high up am I?"

"Oh, about 120 feet."

"Okay, I won't look down."

In the evening, we were talking about headlamps because the group would be heading for the summit before dawn. The woman said, "Lou, I don't think I'll need a headlamp."

"My gosh, you're right!"

They were a great bunch of climbers. They made it to the summit that week.

Mount Rainier is a great equalizer. It doesn't matter if you're a blue-collar worker or the head of a big corporation, the mountain treats you the same. I really enjoy taking up corporate executives. Most of them are used to being in control of their environment and working with long-term goals. For them, climbing Rainier can be a short-term goal with immediate, tangible results.

Paul DeLorey, president of JanSport, first attempted to climb Rainier with me and a climbing party in 1984. We were turned back by a bad storm. Paul waited nine years to try it again and summitted in 1993. He told me that he had sensed that it was dangerous the first time, and there were a few years where he didn't think he wanted to try it again. But it had continued to nag him, like unfinished business. "I'm used to usually succeeding at whatever I try," he said.

Paul had some difficulty getting back down to Camp Muir after summitting in 1993. When we arrived at Muir, he sought some time alone in his tent. About an hour later, he came to me and said that he didn't feel cocky, he didn't feel like he had conquered anything. "What I feel is lucky," he said, "just to get up there and back down without getting hurt." He said it was one of the hardest things he had ever done physically, but that it was also just as great a mental challenge.

I never get tired of seeing peoples' faces when we get to the summit, of hearing them shout, or weep, with joy. I can't think of anything more satisfying than helping people overcome self-doubts. It's a hard climb. For some people it's the hardest thing they'll ever do, but their satisfaction is just as great as though they'd reached the summit of Mount Everest.

Climbing mountains takes physical stamina, for sure, but the mind also plays a critical role. The mind can defeat a person, not just in mountaineering, but in life in general. We all have mental obstacles that we come up against one time or another. I call them "Everests of the mind." If you tackle them one step at a time, you can conquer some pretty mind-boggling Everests.

People are always asking, "Why do you climb?" In large part, it *is* "because it's there," and the physical and mental challenge is like no other opportunity in life. Jim Wickwire has said that climbing is an affirmation of life. You appreciate what it means to be alive by putting yourself at risk. Dave Mahre believes that climbing is a great character builder. It gives you the opportunity to see whether you measure up to your own expectations. I enjoy the physical and mental challenge, but also the feeling of being rejuvenated each time I go up high. You gain a greater appreciation for life, for the quality of your life, by putting yourself through a focused challenge that sometimes involves extreme risk.

And there are the aesthetic benefits. My good friend and mentor Ome Daiber said it well after he had become the first to climb Rainier's Liberty Ridge. He offered this description of that accomplishment as explanation for why he climbed:

"The fall atmosphere was hazy from slash burns and every peak up into Canada and down into Oregon was a glorious rose and gold. To the west, you could see the ships on the Sound, to the east there was a great shadow cast by the mountain. It seemed so solid we might have walked on it to the distant horizon. Then the mountain shadow was joined by a thin black line on the eastern horizon. And as we stood there, this thin black line gained height. Only slowly did we realize it was nighttime. It folded over us like the leaves of a book and we were spellbound. It's been our pleasure to see such phenomena and people who don't climb will never see it."

The date of Ome's timeless memory is October 1, 1935.

◆ 8 ◆

Rainier Tragedy

On June 21, 1981, Father's Day, my phone rang at six A.M. I figured some dingbat was calling awfully early. I ignored it and went back to sleep. Twenty minutes later, somebody was banging on my front door. I got up and opened it. It was Bill Briggle, superintendent of Mount Rainier National Park, and I knew something was dreadfully wrong.

"What's wrong?"

"Lou, there's been an accident on the mountain. We think it's a guide party. Can you get dressed and come with me?"

My gear was at Paradise. The superintendent filled me in on the scant details he had during the half-hour drive up to the Guide House.

An ancient wall of ice had heaved down on the so-called "standard route" to the summit of Mount Rainier, a route that leads up the Ingraham Glacier, one of twenty-seven glaciers on the mountain. The fall had caught an RMI guide party, but it was not yet known how many in the party had been injured or killed. While Briggle was filling me in, I suddenly remembered that my son, Peter, was on that climb. I looked at Briggle. "Peter called in the accident," he said, reading my thoughts. Thank God, Peter was alive.

Peter was then twenty-two, and had grown up with the snowfields and glaciers of Mount Rainier as his backyard. He had first

climbed the mountain at age twelve. By age sixteen, he was working for Rainier Mountaineering as a full-fledged guide. His confident, outgoing attitude and athletic ability had made him a natural
for the guide service. Now all I could think was, "What did I get
him into?"

Other Perspectives: Peter Whittaker

*It was spring and we'd been guiding all month and not made the
summit in weeks. The snow buildup was tremendous and we didn't
yet have a route in to the summit. Often by June you have a good trail
beaten in and conditions are pretty stable. Not this year.*

*The icefall occurred on the Ingraham Glacier. The Ingraham
Glacier runs from the summit down into a valley bordered by
several high, craggy ridges—Cathedral Rocks, Disappointment
Cleaver, and Little Tahoma Peak. The Cleaver defines two glaciers:
the Ingraham on one side, the Emmons on the other. The Ingraham
pushes up against the rocks of these ridges.*

*The icefall in this area changes every year, depending on the
amount of glacial activity. The glacier is hundreds of feet thick. In
a bad year, the glacier is pushing up a lot of ice and you have more
calving, bigger break-offs, and more activity. At the beginning of
each season, we go up and assess the situation. Early on, you can get
a pretty good indication as to how things will be throughout the
summer. The weird thing was, this year it really didn't look that bad.*

*No matter how it looks, the area of the icefall is one that we
always move through quickly. We never rest there. There is debris
lying all over, ice blocks that have rolled down from higher up. We
always tell the clients, "This stuff doesn't grow here. Let's move on
through."*

*I don't think anyone ever figured out what actually triggered the
icefall, but some believe that a serac toppled and caused another
section to release. Basically, a whole piece of the mountain came
down. It was the biggest icefall I've ever seen.*

*John Day III, the grandson of the John Day who had climbed
McKinley with my father and uncle in 1960, was leading the climb.
He had been a guide at Rainier Mountaineering, Inc. since 1976.*

Although I was the more experienced guide on the climb, I wasn't leading because I was on what we call a layover. I had been on a trip the day before. We'd had to turn around on the Ingraham Glacier because there was too much snow. We had brought the climbing party back to Camp Muir. I had stayed there to wait for the next party while another guide had taken the climbers back to Paradise.

In addition to me and John Day, the other guides on this trip were Christopher Lynch, the son of my dad's partner, Jerry Lynch, plus Greg Wilson, Mike Target, and Tom O'Brien. We left early in the morning, about three o'clock, and stopped for a break as we usually do, at a place called the Ingraham Flats, a little over an hour out from Camp Muir, on the other side of a ridge called Cathedral Rocks. There, a rope team of three climbers turned back from exhaustion. Chris Lynch led them back to Muir.

One of the four climbers on my rope had wanted to turn around then, too. I had been up here on the route the day before and I knew that there was so much new snow on the mountain that we'd probably turn around soon. We were more concerned about the danger of soft-snow avalanche than we were about an icefall. So I told him, "The chances of our going any higher than Disappointment Cleaver are real slim. Why don't you stay with us? It'll be a beautiful sunrise and a great experience for you." He agreed. He's one of the eleven still up there, buried in the glacier. It took me a long time to get a handle on that. I felt like I had talked someone into making the wrong decision.

After the others headed back to Camp Muir, that left five guides and twenty clients. Since we knew we wouldn't be making a summit attempt, the guides made a joint decision to go far enough to check out Disappointment Cleaver. The Cleaver got its name from an early climbing party on Mount Rainier that, in a storm, thought it had reached the summit when it had only reached the top of the Cleaver at 12,300 feet. Today its name is continually validated, because it's typically a place where people elect to turn around from the effects of exhaustion or altitude.

One by one, walking quickly, our rope teams crossed the icefall area and stacked up against the Cleaver, one group next to the other, to stay away from the debris and to get underneath the shelter of the rock that forms the Cleaver. John continued out onto the steep slope of the Cleaver with his rope team.

I was concerned and yelled up to him, "John, maybe we should put guides on a rope and go out there." Because of the soft snow conditions and steepness of the slope, I felt it would be better for the guides to first check it out. So I made the decision where to stop the group. I didn't want to take the whole party out onto that steep slope when I knew we were going to turn around just above it.

The spot where we stopped was underneath a nearly vertical rock formation and hundreds of feet away from any icefall debris. We were actually tucked under the Cleaver and it felt good. Safe, even.

I told everybody to take it easy. It was Greg Wilson's first day guiding. I asked Greg to unrope his team so that we could use his rope to explore the slope of the Cleaver. Then I untied from the front of my rope, and John and Mike untied from theirs. Greg and Tom stayed with the group. Tom remained roped in to his team.

John, Mike, and I tied in to Greg's rope, with me in front. We told the clients to get comfortable, huddle together, and stay warm. We'd be back in a few minutes. The sun was just coming up. It was a beautiful sunrise.

We went up as far as the spine of the Cleaver. We were about 150 yards from the party, where we could talk among ourselves. We dug a few pits to judge the stability of the snowpack. And we made the formal decision to turn around and not take the party any higher. We agreed it was too steep, the avalanche hazard was too high.

We were just about to start down to the party when we heard a resounding "crack!"—the unmistakable noise of ice break-ing off. To this day, when a jet flies over or if I hear any other noise that is vaguely similar to this "crack!" I can feel the same dreadful sensation I felt at that moment.

We had an excellent view of the Ingraham Glacier and the source of the icefall, at the top of the Cleaver about 1,000 feet up. A couple of the guides and clients later stated that they thought they had seen a big serac collapse, which released a major part of the glacier below. It's hard to remember the minute details when you're witness to such a massive movement of mountain.

Glaciers are just like rivers, and where you have an icefall is the same place you'd have a waterfall in a river. As the glacier expands, it pushes, pushes, and pushes, until a weakness finally occurs and a chunk of ice releases. Sometimes you get a small release. A little debris slides down the slope.

This was a massive release. A huge piece of the mountain pulled away. I remember looking up and my initial thought was, "The clients are in a great spot, tucked underneath those rocks."

We watched the release come down. As it got about halfway to the Flats, I felt a sickening sensation as I began to realize that this thing was more massive than I had thought and that there was a possibility that it could come close to us.

When you're guiding, you always try to be prepared for the worst that could happen, but you never believe that the worst could be this bad. We started yelling at our party to run this way. They heard us and started to move. This thing was so huge and it just kept gaining momentum and the size of it was unbelievable.

Any time there is an avalanche or icefall of this size and going this fast—this one was probably moving about 100 or 120 miles per hour by the time it reached our position—it's preceded by a tremendous air blast. This one was blowing all the new snow on the mountain all over the place. You couldn't see anything. The last thing we guides saw was people reacting to our shouts, standing up and starting to move toward us. They got hit by the air blast and we couldn't see anything else. They had about ten or twelve seconds to react, to begin running. There wasn't much time at all.

Greg Wilson was unroped and sitting with the clients when it happened. Tom O'Brien was roped up with four clients. Greg got up and ran. He later said that he remembered seeing other people ahead of him. He was hit and spun around by the air blast, then slid downhill toward a crevasse. He said that his first thought was, "This is it." Then he got pissed and started ramming his arms up in the air, trying to swim out of the thing, trying to stand up and get out. Somehow he was able to come to the surface. He was lucky.

I kept telling myself, if it had been a normal icefall, or even a large one, we'd have been okay. But the mechanics of this thing… it was literally a piece of the mountain that came down, fell vertically for nearly 1,000 feet, hit the Flats, and fanned out.

As guides, we later asked ourselves over and over again whether we had chosen a good position. We finally agreed that it had been a safe place in any normal situation. This just hadn't been a normal situation.

It was all over in about thirty seconds. It's hard to remember what I was feeling during that time. You're witnessing something you can't even believe. It took a few seconds for the snow blast to settle. We ran back over to the site, trying to get a visual on the situation, taking a head count. How many missing, how many alive and accounted for?

The first thing we needed to do was maintain stability. Take care of the survivors. As a guide, you're in control of the situation, regardless of how bad it gets. You have to be the person in control and give some reassurance to the other survivors. Of course, what you really want to do is let it all out, say, "Fucking-A, Jesus Holy Christ!"—but you can't, your role already has been established. You have to be with your clients. You're the professional. You don't have time for hysteria.

The first thing we did was try to get the survivors away from the area, because they were pretty shook up and disoriented. Oddly enough, those who weren't buried and killed had no major injuries. There were some bruises and scrapes, some bruised ribs, but no major trauma.

First we moved all the survivors farther up under the rocks. Next we went out on the debris and looked for evidence of any other survivors. All this took place within the first few minutes. We scrambled over the rubble of Volkswagen-size blocks of ice. It was rock-hard, blue glacial ice. Not at all like a soft-snow avalanche.

It was hard to walk or stand on these blocks, even in crampons. The chunks were lying every which way. We were looking for ropes, packs, a body. Any indication that someone else might be alive. After walking on top of this thing, we began to understand the scope of the accident. There had been a long crevasse about 100 feet below where we had crossed the Ingraham. It was about 70 feet deep and 60 feet wide. The icefall had stretched about 100 yards wide and 30 or 40 feet high. The edge of it had come right through the middle of the twenty-two people in our group. Eleven had made it to safety.

Eleven had been swept into the crevasse below us, crushed, and buried under tons of rock-hard ice. Killed instantly, no doubt. We lost ten clients and one guide, Tom O'Brien.

There was no evidence on top. Usually there's a little bit of a concave area when an avalanche sweeps into a crevasse, but this thing was so massive that there was buildup instead. It was a workout just to get from one side to the other, to find your way through the rubble.

Because we had to stay with the survivors, our initial search to determine if there were other survivors was hasty. Things were awfully quiet as I got on the radio to call in what was obviously a major accident. I called the Park Service.

"This is Pete Whittaker with Rainier Mountaineering. We've had an accident up here."

"How many people are involved?"

"We're not sure. We think maybe as many as eleven."

There was a silence on the other end. Then, boom—word went out and they were in rescue mode.

Up on the mountain, we were dealing with it the best we could. And the best thing we could do was get these people out of there. Keep moving, keep your mind off the details of what had just happened. We decided that I would lead the survivors back to Paradise. I had the most experience of all the guides present, and I would take Greg Wilson with me. Mike Target and John Day would stay at the accident site.

On the radio, we heard them down below, gearing up for the rescue. They were talking about organizing it from Camp Muir, since there was already a ranger there.

We divided the group. I took five clients, Greg Wilson took five. We tried to concentrate on getting these ten people off the mountain.

I remember leading them away from the accident site. I was on the front of the rope and there was nobody at my side. It was just me and the mountain and everyone else was behind me. I could pretend I was alone. As I walked away from the site, the whole thing hit me at once and I started to cry. I kept thinking about the client I had talked to at our break. He was up here for good now. All four of the people I had been roped in with were gone, within minutes after I had unroped from them.

On the way to Camp Muir, none of us talked. We just moved along. The clients were in shock. So was I. As we approached Camp Muir, I saw Terri Gould, our cabin person at the time. She was roped up with a ranger and a couple of other independent climbers. They were getting ready to head up to the accident site. I pulled Terri aside. "Terri, there's really no need for you to go up there. There are no survivors. We need you here. These people need a hot drink. These are the survivors." That was about all I could say. Just talking to somebody that much was overwhelming.

We stayed at Camp Muir for about an hour. I remember it had been a beautiful sunrise before the accident occurred. After the accident, it was as though a switch had been flipped. The weather deteriorated. Local clouds moved in. A cap formed on the upper mountain. It began to snow. Another storm moved in. Because of the storm, the recovery operation was halted.

The weather was getting worse and worse as we geared up for the trip down to Paradise. Leading the party down the mountain, I got lost! "Son of a bitch," I thought, "don't I have enough to worry about?" Actually, it was a good thing to have happened. It got my mind off the tragedy and made me focus on the problem at hand. Using my compass and altimeter, I got us back on trail and back to the Guide House.

We walked into mass confusion in the Guide House. We were bringing back half the party that we had started with. Nobody knew who had survived and who had not. The families were gathering around. I walked in the Guide House and the first person I saw was my dad. I have so much respect for him. All I could think was, he's going to take care of me and help me get through this.

Before I could talk to my dad, before I even had my pack off, the wife of one of the climbers whom I knew had died up there came up to me, looked me in the eye, and asked me if her husband had made it out alive. I could not answer. Dad was to my right. I looked at him and just said, "Dad...."

The woman burst into tears. Dad comforted her while I disappeared into a back room.

I had only a few minutes alone. Over the next few days, we guides spent hour after hour in the National Park headquarters, giving statements, going over the details again and again.

During the ordeal, my uncle, Jim Whittaker, came up to lend support. And Marty Hoey was there. She was my friend and fellow guide and, at the time, was Mike Target's girlfriend. I looked up to her as much as I did to my father. She was solid in situations like these and I leaned on her as much as I did my family.

The press did a lot of speculating about what happened and how it happened. We guides felt that the facts were being misrepresented and we wanted to speak up, but Jerry Lynch had told us not to discuss anything. An official report was being written up, based on

Icefall area, late summer 1981 (Photo: Lou Whittaker)

our statements, and that would stand as the final word on the accident.

Weeks afterwards, after all our statements had been made and some of the world's best glaciologists had finished their investigation, there was an open "trial" of sorts. All of the information was released to the public. It was determined that the guides had acted in a reasonable manner and that the icefall was an act of God. Not foreseeable, not preventable.

John Day III quit guiding afterwards. It had been Greg Wilson's first day guiding and he figured the odds were in his favor at that point, and he continued guiding. Everyone reacted in a different way.

Dad sat me down and said, "Look, maybe you've been doing this guiding because of me, but please understand that I want you to do whatever you need to do. Make your own decision. You might not want to continue guiding and that's all right. I totally support you in whatever you decide to do."

Mike Target and I took off for a couple of weeks and went down and ran the Colorado River. I came back and jumped right back into guiding. I'd grown up on Mount Rainier. I love the mountains. I love guiding. It was a heck of an education for me. For some reason, I was spared in this tragedy. It wasn't my time. As a result, I gained a renewed interest in the quality of my life. I gained more respect for the mountains. I think the experience made me a better guide.

When you take civilization out of the picture and just look at nature, you realize how black and white it all is. Death is part of life.

Twelve years after the icefall tragedy, on a cold day in early spring, I was working outside my house, which sits in a clearing in the woods above a lake. The lake had recently thawed from the winter's freeze. I noticed a young deer on the other side of the lake. It entered the water and started swimming toward the shore by my house. As it neared the shore, it started struggling. It couldn't get up the bank and out of the water.

I ran down behind some trees, where the deer couldn't see me. Should I get involved, should I interfere with nature? The deer kept sliding back into the water and was obviously losing strength. It couldn't keep its head above water. I couldn't stand to watch it drown, so I dove in and swam out to it. I held up its head and dragged it back to shore. I tried to revive it, but it died, right there on the shore.

I went back to my house, stripped off my wet clothes, and huddled by my wood stove. I felt it was unfair that the deer had swum all the way across the lake, only to drown. Was it predestined to drown? By all the laws of nature, apparently so. But I can't bring myself to believe that my clients were predestined to die in the icefall.

In May 1980, a year before the icefall occurred on Rainier, Mount St. Helens erupted and covered Rainier in black ash. That winter there was minimal snowfall. As a consequence, the mountain's glaciers absorbed more heat than usual the next summer and there was an abnormal amount of glacial melt. I've always felt that this aberration contributed to the abnormal size of the icefall in 1981.

We never recovered the bodies of the eleven who were swept into the crevasse. They were buried under tons of ice and snow. I've had a reunion lunch or dinner with their families almost every year since the accident. When the *Time* magazine article came out in 1992 about the man who had been found frozen in ice in the Alps for 4,000 years, it revived concern among the families of the lost climbers. Now they all want to know when the climbers will come out. They want to prepare the relatives for the press when the climbers emerge from the glacier.

Glaciers move about a foot or a foot and a half a day. The glaciologist who investigated the icefall said that it was the worst in hundreds of years and that it might be another few hundred years before one of that magnitude happens again. But no one can be sure.

What really ticks me off is people who say, after accidents like this, "At least he or she died doing something they loved." No way! You don't want to die in the mountains. You want to live so you can enjoy the mountains another day. I don't want to die from an accident in the mountains. I want to die of old age, in my bed with the television on.

◆ 9 ◆

BASIC SURVIVAL

Mountaineering can be a fairly safe sport if it's done with judgment and a sound knowledge of basic technique. When I learned climbing as a kid, I didn't see it as a high-risk sport. But now I see, after losing about thirty friends in the mountains over the years, that there's quite a risk factor involved. There are hazards that you can't do anything about, such as avalanches and icefalls. These hazards are difficult, sometimes even impossible, to predict. After many years in the mountains, you develop an instinct for danger and, after a few near-misses, you learn to listen to that instinct.

Each year, over the more than forty years I've guided and instructed climbers on Mount Rainier, I invariably get a novice climber who says to me, "I'm afraid of heights." I always reply, "I am, too. That's why I'm still alive."

Over the years I've developed a sense of premonition in potentially dangerous situations. I felt the hairs stand up on the back of my neck and got a sort of funny feeling in the pit of my stomach— like an alarm going off—before the avalanche with Peter in 1978. Same thing happened on Everest in 1984, when I was leading up a steep slope in deep snow, trying to establish a high camp. We were up on the North Col at about 24,000 feet, on a fixed rope that we'd installed earlier. It was after a big storm and we were going to make a carry with about eight of us. I was kicking steps, pulling the fixed rope out of a two-foot cover of fresh snow and looking at indicators peeling off out on the ridge. I was thinking, "We're sticking our necks out here."

John Roskelley, a good friend and one of the United States' world-class mountaineers, was right behind me when I said that we'd best turn back. He said, "I've been waiting for you to say that."

"Why didn't you say something?"

John replied, "I didn't want to be the first one to say anything."

Peter was on our rope too. He said, "Dad, let's keep going. We're so close."

"Pete," I said, "I've got the same feeling I did when you and I got caught in that avalanche on Muir Peak."

Pete quickly added, "I'm willing to turn around."

Even with luck and instinct on my side, I don't consider mountaineering to be a gift. I wasn't born a mountaineer. I'm as dumb as the next guy and I've screwed up in the mountains. I've been in three big avalanches and gotten into some pretty hairy situations. I've been lost without food when I was a kid. That's scary. Food is important when you're expending so much energy. Food is also a psychological crutch. If you have food, you figure you can last for a few days until you can get out.

I have a friend who carries a can of dog food with him as emergency rations. I told him, "Jeez, I think I'd rather carry a couple of candy bars. Something that tastes better." He said, "That's the point—you'd eat those before you ever got lost or in trouble. I wouldn't eat that dog food unless I was absolutely desperate."

A lot of hot-shot rock climbers come to Mount Rainier, and many of them come unprepared. They haven't studied the routes, they're unfamiliar with glaciers, they've never seen a crevasse. They have little or no judgment. If they survive some of their mistakes, they begin to develop judgment.

Some of them don't survive. In 1979, there was a book published called *Fifty Classic Climbs of North America*. It listed Liberty Ridge on Rainier as one of those climbs. For several years after that, we had a rash of deaths on Liberty Ridge. We'd find a copy of that book in the dead climber's pack nearly every time. Now, whenever we get called out to help somebody who's gotten in trouble on Liberty Ridge, we know the first place to look. When they fall, they all funnel down a few thousand feet and stack up in the same place. The deaths were not caused by that book, or any other, but by inexperienced climbers seeking the glory of doing a "classic" climb.

I've learned a lot through my mistakes, as well as through witnessing the mistakes of others. As they say, experience is a great teacher. I feel that I'm a better guide and climber because of these mistakes.

I often illustrate my teaching with stories about mistakes. For instance, a friend of mine took a spill on Mount St. Helens on a training climb. He somersaulted over his ice axe, which was attached to his arm by a wrist loop. Instead of falling free of his axe, he fell on it and punctured his lung on the pick. He was breathing through a hole in his chest for awhile, but we put a patch over the wound and carried him out. My friend is alive and still climbing, but you can bet he doesn't wear the wrist loop anymore.

Same sort of thing happened to a bellhop at the Paradise Inn who fell and punctured his temporal artery with his ice axe. We climbed up to help him out. He was sitting there with his hand against the puncture to stop the blood. There was blood all over the snow. I asked him, "Do you think it's stopped bleeding?" He said, "I don't know," and took his hand away from his head, and the thing started spurting a good three feet. So I tied a few knots in a bandana and tightened it over the wound, applying direct pressure to stop the bleeding. Then we walked him down the mountain.

I used to wear the wrist loop to my ice axe. Now I rarely do. If I'm climbing vertical ice, I'll wear the loop. Otherwise, I don't. I've never lost an axe. I tend to grip the shaft tighter when I feel like I'm going to slip or fall. I guess some people just let go of it. I tell clients that it's a judgment call, but I also advise them to start out without the loop on their wrists.

Today we use at least two guides on a climb, even if we're leading only two or three other clients. Up until the late 1970s, the guide service was small and there often was only one guide leading a party.

It was during this time that I was running a five-day school on the mountain. I had seven clients. On the first day, I had checked them out and they seemed pretty healthy. A couple of them were military sergeants who had been working out of Fort Lewis. They were in good shape. We had hiked to Camp Muir on Monday and done some training in self-arrest and cramponing on Tuesday. It had stormed on and off both days. Usually I'd have conducted crevasse rescue and ice climbing on Wednesday, then made the summit attempt Thursday morning. But another storm was moving in and due by late Wednesday.

This climbing party looked pretty motivated, so I decided to go for the summit Wednesday morning and beat the weather. We started out a little after one in the morning. It was windy, clear, and cold as heck. We were going up the Gibraltar route, a route that Jim and I had used exclusively when we guided together in the early fifties. It was still a good winter route, very direct, but by midsummer there was lots of loose rock. It wasn't a good route for larger parties—those with more than ten climbers—due to some bottlenecks, including a ledge with a twenty-foot dropoff that made it a little tricky to negotiate your move to the next ledge.

By the time we got to 11,000 feet, we had to put on face masks to protect us from the wind. I had put three of the party on my rope and three on another rope with one of the sergeants leading it. He looked strong. The wind was blowing hard, the ropes were stretched out as we headed up the Cowlitz Glacier. As we got to about 13,000 feet, I was kicking steps and all of a sudden I felt weightless. Visibility had been dimmed from the blowing snow, and I sensed that it was getting even darker. I felt the rope tighten around my waist and suddenly realized that I'd fallen into a crevasse.

It took me a few seconds to figure out what had actually happened. The crevasse was more than 100 feet deep, with a 20-foot hidden snow bridge across it. I had stepped on a real thin part and broken through. A big chunk of ice had broken off with me and floated down into the crevasse right below me, giving me the sensation of being on a descending elevator. The rope stopped me at about 20 feet down, while the ice block kept falling. I thought, "Jeez, that was something." Usually, when you fall into a crevasse, it's a pretty abrupt fall.

I was hanging there in semidarkness on a swami belt, which is a simple harness that consists of a strap of webbed nylon worn around the waist. You can tie in with your rope and attach hardware to it, but because it doesn't have leg loops to help support your weight, it's not something you want to hang from for too long.

I shouted to the others that I was okay. I was happy that I'd taught them self-arrest. I was assuming that the guy who was behind me on the rope had gone into self-arrest when he saw me go out of sight. I looked up and discovered that each side of the crevasse was overhung so far that I was dangling in the middle of the crevasse. I still had my ice axe, and I tried penduluming my body, hoping to catch one of the walls so that I could use my crampons and ice axe to climb out. I couldn't reach either wall, so I tried the next alternative.

I always carry ascenders in the outside pocket of my pack. I took my pack off my back, swung it around to the front, and clipped it to my swami belt with a carabiner. I opened the outside pockets to get my ascenders and they weren't there! What the heck? Then I remembered that I had loaned the ascenders to someone and must have forgotten to put them back.

About ten minutes had passed. It was cold down in the crevasse and I knew it was even colder up top, where the wind was blowing. I thought about dropping off the rope and then trying to crawl along the bottom of the crevasse to the end, where it wedged. I thought maybe I could climb out there.

That was assuming that I didn't break a leg falling to the bottom of the crevasse, which looked to be nearly 100 feet below me, and that it was not a false floor. You can usually tell by the shape of the floor whether or not it's false. If it's convex, or comes up in an "A" shape, it's probably a false floor. If it's concave, or a "V" shape, it has probably narrowed down to the bottom. But if it's a really long, deep crevasse, you can't be sure of anything. This one was too deep to take the chance.

On my pack, there was a cord that closed the top hatch. I decided to pull that out and use it to tie a prusik knot onto my rope. A prusik knot can be made out of any rope or cord, but preferably one that is smaller in diameter than your climbing rope. First, tie the cord in a loop and attach it to a vertical rope with a couple of ring knots. Then use the loop as a foothold. The prusik can be slid easily up the rope, but won't slip down when you step in it. I wanted to shift my weight to the foothold, to take the pressure off my waist.

Just then, the sergeant leaned over the edge of the crevasse and yelled down, "Are you all right?"

"Yeah. Are you guys all right?"

"I think so. What should we do?"

I thought for a couple of seconds before I replied, "Untie your rope and throw it down to me." Quickly I added, "But hold on to the other end."

By the time he had done that, I had one knee in the loop I'd made with the cord and had taken some of the pressure off my swami belt. I took the new rope, slid it through the swami belt, made a loop and stepped in it. This method would be even quicker than using the prusik knot.

I shouted for them to take in the slack on the rope so I could stand in it, and to give me some slack in the rope I was tied to so that I could make a loop in it for my other foot. As I lifted one leg, they pulled up the slack in that rope. Then I lifted the other leg as they pulled in the slack on it, and it was left, right, left, right, until I literally stepped up and out of the crevasse. This is called the "bilgiri" technique.

When I emerged up top, about forty-five minutes after having fallen in, these guys were looking scared to death. "Great job!" I told them. "I owe you guys some beers when we get back down to Paradise."

They said, "But what are we going to do now?"

"We're going to go on up." They were cold as hell, but I knew they'd warm up as soon as we started walking. We took a different route, around the crevasse, and made it to the summit. I figured they learned a lot that day. I sure did—I've never loaned out my ascenders since, and now when I'm on a glacier I always wear at least one on my harness.

To teach someone to climb safely, I start with a rope. Forget the harness and hardware, at least at the beginning. I believe that climbers should first understand what their own weight or the weight

Opposite: *Lou in a hasty rappel, 1971 (Photo: Ingrid Widmann)*

of another person feels like and how to safely hold that weight using their own body.

So many climbers get into hardware right away and get a false sense of security. You need to get familiar with the dynamics of holding another person's weight, or how far someone can fall safely without pulling you off balance. You can fall out of a seat harness. If I tie you into a rope, you're not going to fall out of it.

It's true that, when you use only a rope, you don't get support under the legs. When all the liability suits popped up during the "sue you, sue me" 1980s, we had been talking about going back to using ropes instead of harnesses. But we figured, because of the common knowledge that a seat harness offers more support, if a person fell and broke his back, we'd probably have a lawsuit on our hands from not using harnesses. When you're talking about liability, it's one of those no-win situations. And that problem stems from people not wanting to take responsibility for their actions, even when they make a clear choice to risk their lives doing a sport such as mountain climbing.

There are often natural and semi-natural aids on the mountain that can help you out of tight spots. For example, one of the best semi-natural anchors is called a bollard, which can be made by digging a fairly large horseshoe-shaped groove in the snow using hands, a foot, or an ice axe to form a short, thick mound of hard snow or ice that a rope can be looped around. This mound—or bollard—will hold the rope that you use to go over the side of a crevasse or cliff to rescue a fallen climber. We know of rescue attempts in snow where the rescuers had a rope, but couldn't figure out how to anchor it in the snow without hardware. If they had known how to make a bollard, they'd have been able to complete the rescue.

When I'm climbing up a steep slope, I always look for natural protection, such as rocks or projections of ice, that I might use in case of a fall. I select my route above these points of protection in what is called a contour line, on a right angle to the fall line or vertical line of a slope. Many climbers have been saved when their rope falls over one of these natural anchors and catches them.

The more hardware you carry, the bigger and heavier your pack is and the more complicated your climbing becomes. I've got nothing against hardware, I use it myself. I just hate to see climbers relying on it so much before they've mastered the basics. I've heard guys say, "I can't rappel, I don't have a figure eight." You can rappel with a friction wrap or by using a carabiner with a friction wrap.

We often teach the "dulfersitz" and "suspender sitz" as techniques for rappeling. These are European terms for friction wraps without devices. I can rappel carrying a person on my shoulders, if I have to, using a dulfersitz. In a dulfersitz, the rope runs from the anchor in front of you, between your legs, around a hip to the front, and over the opposite shoulder and into that hand. In a suspender sitz, the rope is doubled and split behind you, with each rope piece going in front to opposite shoulders and one hand. These techniques allow you to get down a mountain in a simple way.

First master the basics, then get into hardware. That's what I tell my guides and my students. You can run out of hardware on a mountain, or lose it if a pack falls off a cliff. Then knowledge of basic technique becomes good backup.

I consider a compass and an altimeter to be basic essentials. I always carry a compass and an altimeter with me on Mount Rainier, no matter what the weather or time of year. I've climbed up to Camp Muir hundreds of times, but in a whiteout blizzard with three-foot visibility, I still can't do it without a compass and an altimeter.

I always run a back azimuth as I'm coming up a slope. Then if I get caught in a whiteout storm, I can descend using my compass and altimeter and the back azimuth readings. This is what I did on McKinley with John Day. In a whiteout blizzard, you can't tell where holes or cliffs are, you sometimes don't even know if you're going up, down, or sideways. Without a compass and an altimeter, you're lost right out of the gate.

Above timberline, we stick wands in the snow to mark our route. In a whiteout, once we've located one wand, we send the front end of our rope team ahead to find the next one, while the end person waits at the wand we just located. We try not to move from that wand until the next one is found. By using our altimeter and compass in conjunction with wands, we can work our way up or down a mountain in a storm.

I always tell clients, "Don't depend solely on your guide. Memorize the route on your way up. Look back and memorize every route change, every landmark. Try to keep the person in front of you in your sight." Never depend on your footprints being in the snow on your way down. The wind can wipe them out and the snow fill them in no time. It's like marking a trail with bread crumbs, like Hansel and Gretel did in the fairy tale. You come back and discover that the birds have eaten the crumbs.

Many people get lost because they don't pay attention to the terrain. Maybe they're used to hiking on marked trails. They get lost and tired, and some of them just lie down and wait to die.

Some people are more resourceful. We've found some who have fallen in crevasses and lived for several days. On one rescue in 1967, there were two boys and an uncle of one who had fallen in a crevasse and had been in there for a couple of days. We were told that one of them was a bit retarded. As it turned out, he was the one who lived. He told us, "I got cold so I walked around." His friend had just given up and sat down with his uncle on a ledge and froze to death. The surviving young man had concentrated on keeping warm by moving around. His simple mind had saved him, while his friend and the uncle had been overwhelmed by what they had perceived to be insurmountable obstacles.

With a rope, a compass, an altimeter, an ice axe, and a good pair of boots, you can go almost anywhere in the mountains. Add crampons to the list and you can walk on icy terrain. I also like to carry ski poles with me when I'm on a trail and carrying a big pack. They're good for sniffing around for holes and cornices and also help save my knees going downhill.

In winter we carry snowshoes with us, because the snow can drift so deep that we're in danger of sinking so deeply we can't keep moving. Usually we look for a firm, wind-packed ridge to walk on and avoid the softer snows of the valleys. The ridges may be steeper and technically more difficult, but we don't get bogged down. We see a lot of fox and coyote footprints on the ridges. The animals usually know where to walk safely, but I have found them occasionally in old avalanches.

I've come upon independent climbers in storms who are floundering around, lost. They hear us approaching and say, "Where are you? We need help." They follow us down. I always ask them why they didn't turn around when they saw signs of a storm coming in. A lot of people don't realize that the best thing to do in an approaching storm is to turn around, unless you are an experienced climber and are prepared for it. It doesn't take long to get wet in a storm. You lose your visibility. You can end up in a crevasse, where no one would find you. You can run out of food and freeze to death. It's just not worth the risk when the mountain tells you "no." There's nothing wrong with turning around on a mountain. It will be there the next day. So I say, to hell with ego!

When we're leading clients on a summit climb and we know we're going to be turning around, we have to get the timing just right. Otherwise some of the clients will argue with us. They don't have the judgment, they're still warm and not yet tired, and they're motivated by the fact that they came all the way to Mount Rainier or Mount McKinley and, by God, they're going to climb it even if it kills them, which it can do and sometimes does. As a guide, you know that no mountain is worth a life, so you don't allow these egos to get in the way of your decisions.

What I like to do is call a rest break at the turnaround point, where the clients can watch the weather develop, feel the nip of the wind's cold teeth. "See that lenticular cloud, rotating around the summit?" I say. "Hear the wind? Doesn't it sound like a freight train coming off the summit? Could be blowing sixty to eighty miles an hour up there. It'll blow you off your feet." After ten or fifteen minutes spent waiting for the lower rope teams to reach us, everyone is cold and shivering and the reality of the situation has set in. I usually ask the most macho of the bunch, "What do you think about turning around here? You've all done a great job, but the mountain is getting tough." By then the entire group is cold, ready, willing, and feeling great about turning around.

It's different on rescues. We go out in all sorts of weather. And it's different for guides. I ask my guides to go out in weather as a learning experience. As long as the people in the group are dressed properly, have the right gear, and someone in the group has knowledge and judgment, it can be an excellent learning experience for a guide who has to be prepared for the worst.

On a guided client climb, we start out from the Guide House at

Paradise in all weather conditions because the clients are committed to a date. And we don't know what the weather will be later in the day or the next day, despite reports from the National Weather Service. Mount Rainier makes its own weather. It might be pouring rain or snowing at Paradise, but we'll start out anyway. If it gets worse as we go up, then we make the decision to push on or turn around. Lots of times we get up around 8,000 or 9,000 feet and the sun breaks through. I've spent a whole week in the sun up at Camp Muir when it's been raining down at Paradise the entire time.

I once hired a couple of climbers who said they didn't care about being paid, they just wanted to learn to guide. I told them, "Okay, let's try it." After a couple of weeks of guiding in the rain, they were suddenly not too anxious to head out of the Guide House when it was raining. They said, "I'd just as soon not go out today. I'm not getting paid, you know." They cut their guiding career short. A guide has to be willing and able to handle weather. Nowadays if a guide isn't on the payroll, he doesn't guide.

When you go out in weather, you learn about your body and how to listen to it. A lot of people get cold or thirsty and ignore their body's signals. On a mountain, you have to drink liquids. Your body is continually dehydrated from the altitude. We often feel like we're teaching people how to breathe and walk and take moisture for the first time, in order to stay alive on the mountain.

In our climbing school, we teach pressure breathing and a type of walking called the "rest step." These two techniques allow you to cover steep terrain at altitude by maximizing your energy output. Pressure breathing begins with a loud exhalation of breath, to empty your lungs and make room for more air when you inhale. We tell people to "make noise" when they exhale. Purse your lips as you would to whistle and force as much air as possible out of your lungs. Then take in a full breath. At really high altitude, we sometimes take several breaths like this between each step. On Everest, my summit climbers took up to eight pressure breaths between each step as they neared the summit. If you pressure breathe at sea level, you'll hyperventilate. At high altitude, you can't hyperventilate—the atmospheric pressure is too low.

Climbing on Mount Rainier is a lot like climbing stairs. It involves going straight up the fall line, as well as switchbacking, to the top. In this situation, a technique called the "rest step" becomes vital in helping sustain energy. To do the rest step, as soon as you've swung your front leg forward and put it down with no weight on it, straighten the rear leg so that the bones are in vertical alignment by locking the knee. Rest your weight on that leg. Then step off the back leg and place it in front with no weight on it for a moment, while the new back leg is locked again.

To gain solid footing, you kick the toe of your boot into the snow or into the step that has been kicked by the climber before you. Each time you straighten your leg and shift your weight onto that leg, it has the effect of transferring your body weight off your muscles and onto your skeletal structure. The second or two involved in making this shift from muscle to bone support gives your leg muscles a rest. Do this in conjunction with pressure breathing and you've got a really efficient machine at work.

These two techniques have gotten many of my guides and clients to the summits of mountains all over the world, from Rainier and McKinley to Himalayan beauties such as K2, Kangchenjunga, and Everest.

Climbers who sign up for our summit climb are usually coming up from sea level in Seattle to 10,000 feet at Camp Muir on the first day. This is more than any elevation gain a climber will experience on Everest in a single day. For some people, this is the toughest part of the climb. The second day, their packs are lighter after they've dumped their sleeping bags, pads, and extra clothing in the bunkhouse.

As you acclimatize, you build up a higher blood hemoglobin count, which means that your body can carry more oxygen to the muscles. At 10,000 feet the atmospheric pressure is about a third less than it is at sea level. At Everest base camp, at about 16,900 feet, the atmospheric pressure is about half as much. The result is a shortness of breath or a winded feeling. You feel like you can't get enough air. Some people get altitude sickness as low as 10,000 feet. Some get it higher. Some don't get it at all.

Your body can acclimatize to living at 18,000 feet. Above that, you die a little each day. Symptoms of altitude sickness include headache, nausea, vomiting, and, in extreme cases, cerebral edema or pulmonary edema. We sometimes see edema on Rainier, but it is more likely to occur on higher mountains. The best antidote for altitude sickness is to turn around and go back down. The best preventive measures are to acclimatize slowly and drink lots of water so that your body stays hydrated. Just being at high altitude dehydrates your body.

On our five- and six-day seminars, we spend a couple days between 10,000 and 11,000 feet, practicing technique and acclimatizing before we go for the 14,410-foot summit. On the two-day summit climb, we hike to Camp Muir the first day, go to bed early, get up at midnight or one o'clock the next morning, and head for the summit. We come all the way back down to Paradise that same day. For some people, this is too grueling. They're better off on a five- or six-day seminar.

In a five- or six-day climbing school, we can teach enough basics to get somebody started climbing on their own. We can tell right away those who are at ease with themselves and those who aren't. Lots of people fight instruction. Their egos get in the way. It takes them longer to learn.

We can also spot those who have been in scouting or who have been outdoors regularly. They're a little more attuned to reacting quicker, they're more alert to weather changes and possible dangers. They're also more likely to be in better physical condition, which always helps.

There are certain "standard rules" in climbing, and all of them get tweaked at one time or another. Today we see more people going solo, whether it's rock climbing, mountain climbing, or even Himalayan mountaineering. In earlier days we'd always say that a three-person team was safest. If one got hurt, one could go for help and one could stay with the injured person. Some felt four people, roped together as two teams of two, was safer. If one got hurt, one stayed with that person and the other two went down, to help each other.

I've soloed Mount Rainier and I've done it with just one other person. It's a judgment call based on your level of experience and the experience of your fellow climbers. I'd rope up with my brother Jim anywhere, because I know that either of us could get the other out of almost any situation.

It's not too smart to go solo in a glaciated area because you can never see all the holes in the snow. A Japanese guy who was climbing solo on McKinley was killed, even though he was carrying a long pole tied to himself in case he fell into a crevasse. He fell in all right, but the pole wasn't long enough to span the crevasse and he couldn't get out by himself.

Even today we see independent climbers walking out unroped on the Cowlitz Glacier on Rainier, just above Camp Muir. They're strictly playing Russian roulette. They're walking on stuff with hundreds of holes in it. Every year people drop through. Some live, some die. But the basics never change. Always rope up on a glacier or accept a higher risk.

Lots of experienced mountaineers take chances and make mistakes. Most of them don't make mistakes out of ignorance. They know what the consequences of their actions might be. They take a calculated risk and play the odds. Climbing Everest without oxygen is far more dangerous than climbing with it. Climbing solo without backup and no equipment except two water bottles is sticking your neck way out. Some people like the added thrill of burning their bridges behind them. I call that dumb mountaineering. Some of these climbers eventually end up in a bivouac, which I call a French term for "mistake," and they do serious damage to themselves, or they die. To me, there are enough risks out there already: lightning, storms, rock- and icefalls, avalanches, earthquakes, snow blindness, equipment failures, high-elevation sickness, frostbite, and sunburn. Why manufacture more?

Other Perspectives: Ingrid Widmann

Lou has this thing about RMI employees not needing outside help. We're all supposed to take care of ourselves and each other. It's a matter of pride to him and I think he sometimes goes a little overboard with it.

One time we were on the summit of Mount Rainier with a seminar group when my hip gave out on me. It was so painful I could not put any weight on my left leg at all. I would put my left foot down for one second and twist my body so that my right leg swung forward, and that way I hobbled all the way back down to Camp Muir.

We had to jump a crevasse on the way down and I just started

Ingrid climbing a serac using direct aid, 1971 (Photo: Lou Whittaker)

crying because I thought there was no way I could make it to the other side with only one good leg.

I told Lou, "I can't do it."

He yelled at me, "Yes, you can! You have to jump!"

It took about ten minutes for me to get mad enough at him to give me the adrenaline to make it across. It hurt, but I did it.

When we got back to Camp Muir, I just collapsed on a bunk in the hut and I thought I had it made. I cried and begged Lou to let me stay overnight and descend to Paradise the next day, after a good rest. But he would not hear of it. "Nope," he said, "we're going all the way down the mountain. You can make it."

He did not even offer me an aspirin for the pain. I was so out of it, I did not even think to ask for one.

Two clients took pity on me and helped me down the snowfield. I slung an arm over each of their shoulders and they practically dragged me down the mountain. I got madder with every hop, and by the time we reached Paradise four miles later, I hated Lou with all my heart.

"I did that on purpose," Lou told me, finally all sweet and caring. "I knew if you got mad, you'd have the strength to keep moving and get down off the mountain. If you had stayed at Muir overnight, the hip would have stiffened up and we would have had to bring you down in a stretcher." And that was something he wanted to avoid at all cost!

I think he considers all of us, the guides and cabin persons, to be an extension of himself, and he doesn't want to lose face in front of clients and the rangers.

He was probably right about my hip. The next day, the doctor told me I had a really bad case of bursitis that required a cortisone shot into the joint to enable me to walk again.

People are always asking about the best clothing system, the right sleeping bag, pack, and tent to use. There are lots of options, but here are some basic guidelines.

First of all, understand that cotton kills. On a hot summer day, there is nothing cooler than a cotton T-shirt. It gets wet with per-spiration and then keeps you cool and ventilated, and that's great.

But if the weather should cool off or the wind come up and all you have is that wet cotton T-shirt, even under a jacket, you're in trouble. Then cotton can be dangerous, even fatal.

Cotton takes forever to dry. You can die of hypothermia because you can't get warm and dry in a wet cotton T-shirt or pants. Not too many years ago, we recovered the bodies of a couple who had died of hypothermia. They were wearing cotton clothes under expensive, state-of-the-art jackets and bib pants. They got caught in a storm while hiking and froze to death because the cotton they wore was wet from sweat and they couldn't get dry. Marty Hoey, one of my senior guides, had encountered them on the mountain and advised them to turn around, but they decided not to. Once again, ego got in the way of better judgment.

Hypothermia can overtake you very quickly when you stop moving and are no longer generating body heat through muscle movement. Your core temperature drops rapidly. In wet clothing, the process is accelerated and death can come very quickly. There's nothing wrong with climbing in a cotton T-shirt and shorts on a hot day. But also take along a shirt and pants of wool or synthetic fabric, such as knit nylon or polyester or one of the "moisture management" fabrics—Capilene, Thermax, Coolmax, Polartec, polypropylene—and change into these when the weather changes.

Layering systems work best in the mountains. Start with a lightweight synthetic top and bottom next to your skin. The next layer should be wool or polyester pile, such as Synchilla or Polartec. On top of this, wear a nylon or polyester shell jacket and pants that are treated for water- and wind-resistance. As the temperature cools down or warms up, add or take off layers as necessary.

We also advise climbers on Rainier to pack a down-insulated parka and hood for extra protection. When we get near the summit, or get hit by a hard wind off an icy glacier, things can cool down pretty quickly. I keep my jacket in my pack until a rest or "maintenance" break. Then, after I coil in the climber behind me, I take off my pack, put on my jacket, check my crampons, harness, and other gear, then eat and drink something. When the break is over, I take off the jacket and put it back in my pack, knowing that I'll be moving and staying warm.

I always take an extra pair of gloves or mittens and an extra hat, because these little things can get easily blown away when you're rummaging in your pack. For gloves, I use a system similar to the clothing layering system: a synthetic knit liner, a pile or wool overmitt or glove, and a shell on top of that to block wind and snow. On warm days, I wear nothing on my hands or just a liner for protection in case of a fall on snow or ice. If I lose my gloves, I can use a pair of socks for backup.

I was once on a rescue on Rainier with a ranger, looking for a guy who was lost somewhere out on the Ingraham Flats. The ranger and I roped up before we started out onto the Cowlitz Glacier. The wind was blowing about fifty to sixty miles per hour. Before we started up the ridge to the Flats, the ranger decided to put on his gloves. He pulled them out of his pack and the wind ripped them right out of his hands. Over the ridge they went, out of sight. I said, "Where's your extra pair?"

"I don't have an extra pair," he said. I gave him an extra pair of my glove liners and an extra pair of socks to use. He put them on, but pretty soon he said, "Boy, I don't like this. I can't hold my ice axe right." We were on hard ice. "Jeez, I'm sorry, Lou. The rescue's off." Just like that. A pair of gloves blew away and the rescue was called off.

When we got back to Paradise, we found out that the guy we had gone to look for was dead, anyway. Even so, I hate to see a simple mistake like that made on a rescue.

Socks are part of your survival kit because they help keep your feet warm and prevent frostbite. Even with gaiters over your boots to keep snow out, your socks can get wet from perspiration. Take along an extra pair or two to change into. They're especially nice at night, when you're no longer generating any body heat and your extremities start to feel the cold. I never use cotton socks on a cold climb, only wool and synthetic blends.

Most sleeping bags come with temperature ratings, and most of those ratings are somewhat bogus because of different factors that come into consideration: Will you be sleeping in a tent or outside? Will you be using a ground pad? Do you tend to sleep warm or cold? Do you get cold easily? Did you eat a good meal before

bedtime? In general, if you're planning to do winter climbing or summer climbing on a glaciated mountain, get a bag rated at least 20 degrees warmer than you think you need.

For our regular summer climbing seminars, when we know the clients will be sleeping inside the bunkhouse at Camp Muir, we recommend a bag rated to only 10 or 20 degrees. If the client is going out on an expedition seminar, where he or she will be sleeping out on the mountain inside a tent, we recommend a bag rated to 0 degrees. We recommend bags filled with either down or synthetic insulation. Synthetic bags do dry out faster and will still keep you somewhat warm if they get wet. But down is still the best insulator—unless it gets wet from snow, rain, or condensation. Then it bunches up and loses its insulating value. With a little care, down will stay dry and work great for cold climbs.

We supply tents on our seminars for clients who want the experience of sleeping outside in the snow. To clients who want to bring their own tents, we recommend an "expedition-style" tent, one with reinforced poles and heavier nylon fabric than the usual backpacking tent. It has to be able to withstand high winds, ice, and snow loads, even in the summer months. The tent should not be too light. It's the same theory as saving weight by drilling holes in a spoon. It's lighter but it doesn't work very well.

In a tent out on Mount Rainier during a blizzard, in summer or winter, you can learn a lot about basic survival. For example, do not seal up the tent and then light a stove to melt snow for drinking water. We've found people who have done that and died from carbon monoxide poisoning. To prevent this sort of mishap, most expedition-style tents made today have a ventilation flap built into the tent.

Here in the Pacific Northwest, the snow is wet and heavy. Tents collapse easily under the weight of wet snow, so it's important to try to keep the snow from building up too much on the outside of the tent. It's also important to keep snow out of the inside of the

Opposite: *Lou rescuing a client's sleeping bag during crevasse rescue instruction, 1971 (Photo: Keith Gunnar)*

tent. Otherwise it melts and your gear gets wet. It's easy to get soaking wet just trying to accomplish these preventive measures. If your tent finally collapses because you're forced to stay inside to keep from getting wet, how are you going to light a stove to melt snow to keep yourself hydrated? You could dig a snow cave and hope that you don't get all wet doing that, because it's hard to get warm and dry afterwards inside that cave, with the wind blowing all around you and the snow drifting in.

It is possible to stay inside a collapsed tent for a little while. Keep it pushed up a little, move around, and form an air pocket. Stay that way until morning or until a break in the storm occurs, then push your way out and get out of there. Of course, if you're prone to claustrophobia, this won't work.

I've been in storms that crushed and demolished our tents, until we got the design right on a tent made specifically for us for the China–Everest climb in 1982. When that tent was tied down properly, winds of 100 miles an hour or stronger didn't faze it. A free-standing tent can become a hang glider in high winds. I've chased a tent with two climbers in it a half mile across a frozen lake in Japan as the two men inside tried to self-arrest through the floor of the tent.

The danger is worse if you're near a crevasse or cliff. On the 1962 Everest tryouts on Mount Rainier, tents were torn off Camp Muir. On the 1963 Everest expedition, high winds almost blew two climbers in their tent off the mountain at around 27,000 feet. When you see a storm coming, the best approach is to turn around. Head for the summit another day.

We use both external- and internal-frame packs on major mountains all over the world. An external-frame pack is one with a frame made of lightweight aluminum tubing—early models were made of wood—and a sack made of heavy-duty nylon attached to it at various points. The rigid frame helps keep the load distributed in the pack sack. It's best to carry a load high and close to your back with the weight spread up and down instead of projecting out behind your back.

Some internal-frame packs are also called "soft packs" or "rucksacks." They have little or no frame or rigidity. The pack is an empty sack that you stuff gear into. Larger, more expensive internal-frame packs usually have some sort of internal support built into the back, either through aluminum stays that adjust to the curve of the back or a sheet of some type of pliable material to give the pack some form. An internal-frame pack fits close to the body and therefore allows better balance, if packed correctly, with the weight close to the body's center of gravity.

When I'm just carrying a heavy load and not worried about balance, I use an external-frame pack. If I need balance and want to look like a hot-dog climber, I go for an internal-frame pack. I like a straightforward design without a lot of gimmicky pockets and extra straps. (A pack should have enough straps to tie on gear such as crampons and ice axe.) Some internal-frame packs also have slots for carrying skis.

I usually carry a load high. With an external-frame pack, I can put the heaviest part of a load up high, from my shoulder blades on up, and the pack doesn't feel like it's pulling me over backwards. Years of carrying big loads up mountains probably accounts for why doctors now tell me that my lumbar vertebrae are getting pretty close together.

It didn't help my back much when I carried Larry Nielson off Everest in 1982 after his feet were too frostbitten to walk on. I strapped him to an empty external-frame pack and carried him on my back. I thought about starving Larry until we could carry him out, to make him lighter, but he wouldn't go for it.

Packs change your center of gravity. An internal-frame pack or rucksack loaded with fifty pounds of gear can pull you back if loaded incorrectly. If the load is carried in the middle of your back, it's going to pull you backwards. Coming downhill, it doesn't matter that much. Usually you're carrying the biggest loads uphill to your destination. We often use external-frame packs to carry big loads up the mountain, then switch to internal-frame packs for climbing.

Mount Rainier has its own microclimate, as do many big mountains. Certain big peaks have specific indicators that signal approaching bad weather. When we're in unfamiliar territory, we first ask the local inhabitants what the weather patterns look like. That's a regular practice in the Himalaya.

RMI-guided party heading for Camp Muir, mid-1970s (Photo: Keith Gunnar)

On Rainier, we can often see the dark cloud mass of an approaching storm moving in. One of our best indicators is the lenticular cloud cap that forms on the summit. When we see that cap forming, we know there are high winds up there and more weather on the way. I've been at Camp Muir in the summer when it's sunny and 80 degrees out and I look up and see a mean cloud cap swirling around the summit. By nightfall, we're holed up in the hut at Camp Muir, waiting out a big storm.

When I was called in on the Willi Unsoeld rescue, a big storm had settled in on the mountain. The twenty college students who had survived the avalanche had made it back down to the bunkhouse at Camp Muir but were trapped there. The Park Service had called me and told me they had a chopper ready. They thought they could get me to Camp Muir.

We flew up and encountered sixty-mile-per-hour winds scouring the sides of the bunkhouse. "I'll chance it," I shouted to the pilot. "I won't," he said, and we flew back to Paradise.

At Paradise, I learned that there was a ground party bivouacked at Panorama Point. They had made it only about a half hour out from Paradise before the storm had shut them down. I radioed to tell them to come back down to the Guide House and wait until morning. No use in camping that close to a warm building.

The next morning it was still storming, but I met with the rescue team in the day-use building. A ranger was there who was planning to accompany us. I asked him, "What have you done lately?" He said, "I've been going to Camp Muir, so I'm in pretty good shape."

"Good thing," I said, "because we're going to go fast." Phil Ershler, one of my top guides, was going with me.

The ranger said, "You know, when we get up there, I'd like you to wait outside while we interview the students."

"Pardon me?"

"The Park Service would prefer that the rescue team didn't listen in on the interview."

"You sonofabitch. You think I'm going to lead you up there in a storm and then wait outside and let you interview those kids? We're taking them out of there as soon as we get there and we're bringing them back down here. Their families are waiting for them."

That ranger has since quit the Park Service. I know he was only trying to follow orders, but I have a hard time with some of these guys, whose last assignment was the Washington Monument or some place where they've never set foot on a mountain or been involved in a mountain rescue.

Phil and I led the rescue team up the mountain by compass and altimeter. We used wands to mark our route, but we ran out of them about 800 feet from Camp Muir. We could only see a few feet in front of us, so I relied on the compass and altimeter. As soon as we reached an altitude of 10,000 feet, where the Camp Muir bunkhouse is located, Phil and I each ran contour azimuths. I went east, he went west, sniffing for landmarks in the storm. In about 150 feet I ran into the Butler shelter, the rangers' quarters that sits on a rise above the bunkhouse. I retraced my steps to Phil and yelled in his ear, "I've got it!"

The students started cheering and crying when they heard us beat on the door to the bunkhouse. They'd been singing a song they had composed about Willi while waiting to be rescued. We spent a few minutes talking with them, checking them out. They were in good shape, physically, so Phil and I tied in all of them to a 160-foot rope and got ready to head back to Paradise. I led, Phil took up the rear. We all were wearing snowshoes.

We knew we had about 800 feet to go before we'd hit a wand. It was still snowing and blowing. The windchill factor was keeping the temperature down around 50 below. I got my bearings and walked down 800 feet. By God, what luck! I stepped right on the last wand we had placed. Our steps leading to the next wand were gone, of course, erased by the wind. I coiled in the rope, got everyone grouped around, and asked Ershler to stay on that wand while we went on ahead and looked for the next one. We did that for a few thousand feet, then suddenly emerged from the clouds above Panorama Point.

Another ranger was waiting for us there, along with Willi's son, Krag. "There are forty reporters milling around the Guide Hut, waiting for you," said the ranger. "Could you lead them in a different way?" Willi's climbing exploits were legendary, even before he summitted Everest in 1963, and his death had really brought out the press vultures.

In snowshoes and still almost waist-deep in snow, we sneaked in on another route that leads to the back of the day-use building, but a few of the reporters had staked that out, too. As soon as I saw them, I said to the students, "Okay, ignore these guys and just sing that song about Willi that you were singing when Phil and I arrived."

The lyrics they had composed for Willi were something like "You can't kill a spirit, it goes on and on." We sang that as we walked into the day-use building and announced that the rescue was over.

◆ 10 ◆

THE MAKING OF A GUIDE

It takes about three years to become a full-fledged guide with Rainier Mountaineering. It takes at least that long to experience Mount Rainier's unique microclimate and to learn about avalanche-prone areas, the characteristics of the glaciers, the various weather patterns of the Northwest.

Developing "people skills" is as important as mountaineering skills. We emphasize both. We've found that it also takes at least three years to develop the familiarity and judgment needed to handle both yourself and clients on this mountain.

We sometimes get experienced rock climbers trying out for the guide service. Rock is a more stable element than ice and a person can become pretty good at rock climbing in a year or so. It takes longer to become a good ice climber because there are so many textures of snow and ice. Our guides have to be good on both rock and ice. That's why we have a mentor system, where we have a new guide learn the ropes from a couple of experienced guides. If new guides don't progress during their first season, they aren't hired for the following spring. If they do progress, they work in this system for three years before they become qualified to lead a party up a mountain.

An apprentice guide can lead a rope of four or five clients, but cannot be in charge of a whole climbing party. We currently have nearly thirty guides who are qualified to lead parties anywhere on the mountain, or on any mountain in the world for that matter. These guides form the core of our operation. The newer guides learn technique from them.

During the three years of a guide's apprenticeship, he or she gets assigned all the crummy jobs, just as in boot camp in the army. They have to clean the cook pots, keep the outhouse clean, coil the ropes at the end of the day, then lay them out for the next day. And they have to shovel snow to melt water for cooking and drinking.

The only water we have at 10,000-foot Camp Muir is from snow and ice, which we melt into fifty-five-gallon drums using propane gas. The guides siphon the melted water from one tank to another, and haul propane tanks up to the melting barrel from the cook shack, where we dump the tanks by helicopter each spring and fall.

For many years, all supplies for Camp Muir had to be carried up on foot or on horseback. Sometimes we'd hire an airplane to crisscross the Muir Snowfield below Camp Muir and drop food in gunny sacks. We did it this way for several seasons, until one day when the plane accidentally skip-bombed the cook shack with about eight huge cans of ravioli. It took about five years to get the ravioli stains off the rock walls. Then the Park Service got worried that this method might end up beaning an independent climber. So we switched to over-the-snow vehicles.

These vehicles had a big flatbed on which we could load hundreds of pounds of provisions. We found that we could drive from Paradise to Camp Muir by getting on the Mazama Ridge, going up over Panorama Point and working our way over Pebble Creek, then going on up to Camp Muir from there. Eventually the Park Service decided that it didn't like this method either, because it left tracks in the snow. We'd do this in March, with twenty feet of snow yet to fall before the summer season!

One time, when we were still using an over-the-snow vehicle, Jerry Lynch, another guide, and I started out for Camp Muir and promptly encountered a fifty-foot-high snowbank. Jerry said, "Well, we can wrap it up for today." I thought we could do it. We rammed that vehicle into the snowbank again and again, and eventually plowed through it. I winched onto trees to help pull the truck through in some places. I just couldn't give up once we cleared that snowbank.

In 1970, we built the bunkhouse at Camp Muir, a prefabricated wood structure about fifteen by forty feet with two rooms, one for clients and one for guides, which also has room for storage. We had it helicoptered up the mountain piece by piece. I had kept complaining to the Park Service that we needed a shelter to which we could bring rescue victims. They finally let us build the bunk-house as a "temporary shelter." It's been standing for nearly twenty-five years. It used to shake a lot in storms. We have it anchored now, with steel cables that run deep into the rockslides that surround it.

Since the bunkhouse was built, we've also been using helicopters to supply Camp Muir with propane and food staples. The helicopter also performs another important service: hauling away trash and human waste. We call these lifts "anti-pollution runs."

The rangers use post-hole diggers to empty the waste from the outhouses into fifty-five-gallon drums, which we fondly call "honey buckets." The drums are rolled over to the helicopter pad and then lifted off by a private helicopter, which is hired by the Park Service. The chopper doesn't land, it just hovers above the drums while somebody takes a cable, attaches it to a drum, then stands on top of the drum and hooks it to the belly of the chopper.

One day I was the somebody in charge of hooking the cable to the chopper. After I had hooked it, the pilot pulled out too low, caught the bucket in the snow, and crashed. Jet fuel spilled out all over the snow but, luckily, it doesn't explode fast like gasoline, so I was able to approach the crash site quickly.

From a distance, I could see the pilot hanging upside down, unconscious, about six feet above the ground, still strapped into his seat. As I got closer, I saw him come to a little and begin to struggle with his seat harness. The only thing on his mind was getting out of that wreck.

He managed to release the seat harness, but he fell out of his seat, slammed against the hard snow, and passed out again. I got to him, dragged him out away from the wreck, and stopped to take a couple of pictures for the record as the chopper burned. I radioed for another chopper to pick up the pilot. He was going into shock, so I gave him my down parka. This was the best down parka I'd ever owned or ever will own. It was the parka I had lived in for three months on K2 in 1975, and it was my favorite. But this guy needed it now, so I loaned it to him.

He was lifted off the mountain. A couple of days later, I went to the hospital to see how he was doing, but he had already been discharged. I checked the helicopter service and found out that he'd been fired. He disappeared and I never got my parka back. I'm still ticked at him for that.

Another time, we were trying out some experimental propane toilets at Camp Muir. These were supposed to cook human waste into ash for easy disposal. As it turned out, the toilet ended up parboiling at best. One day, the chopper got in trouble bringing up one of the toilets and had to jettison it to keep from crashing. It just missed me and a climbing party I was leading down from the summit. I could imagine the headlines: "RAINIER CLIMBING PARTY WIPED OUT BY FALLING TOILET."

Helicopter burning on Muir Snowfield, 1976 (Photo: Lou Whittaker)

Apprentice guides have their hands full just learning the basics and keeping up with the daily routine. An apprentice is in charge of cleaning out the bunkhouse after a climb—most of the guides learn to encourage the clients to help—and then he or she is usually the last one off the mountain after a climb, unless it's socked in. An apprentice usually lacks the training to go down on his or her own in a storm. New guides get a lot of static, just like they would in army boot camp. After the first year, the grunt work lets up a little, as new apprentice guides are hired.

We watch new guides closely to see how they get along with the other guides and with clients. Just asking a client on the five- to six-hour climb to Camp Muir "How are you doing?" too many times can build self-doubt in a client and hurt his or her performance. During the climb to Muir, we learn the clients' names and begin to evaluate who may have to stay at Muir on the day of the summit climb. We watch how they walk, how comfortable they are on the permanent snowfields going into Camp Muir. Some may have passed the one-day school on a marginal basis, so we work with them closer on pressure breathing and rest stepping. Along the way, we also teach the new guides how to do this evaluation.

There are many good climbers, but very few climbing guides. It takes a certain personality to be a good guide. A lot of good climbers just don't have the patience and empathy to teach or to care for other people. When you're a guide, there's no room for one-upsmanship. A guide is there to instruct and to encourage, to be understanding of other people's limitations and of other people's egos. As a guide, you meet a wide range of personality types and learn a lot about the human race. You also learn about yourself in the process.

Other Perspectives: Win Whittaker

I don't remember actually learning how to climb or ski. All of us kids started learning to ski at age two and then began climbing not long after that. So I'd never really gone through a learning process. Skiing and climbing just came naturally.

When I started guiding at age eighteen, I did it because it was easy work. I lived in Ashford, that's what my dad and brother did, so I did it too. It was something I didn't give much thought to.

I liked the mountains. But I would at any opportunity request a turnaround on a climb if there were people who couldn't go on, because I just really wasn't into it. I was actually known for that among the guides, for spinning on those climbs. I was often impatient with the clients. I'd think, "Jeez, these guys just don't get it!"

When I was twenty, I hurt my knee up at Crystal Mountain Ski Resort while working there in the spring as a lift operator. I wasn't able to guide that summer, and I really enjoyed the time off. I had never done anything else but work in the snow year-round— Rainier in summers and Crystal Mountain in winters.

I went to the beach, relaxed, and enjoyed myself. My brother, Peter, had just gotten into windsurfing and it looked like fun. I decided to teach myself and took a board out one day and floundered around on Alder Lake, near Ashford. After about four times, I was hooked.

I was also frustrated. Windsurfing was something completely new and humbling. Here were all these people, including women, doing circles around me. That had never happened to me before. That's when I began to realize that the clients I guided on the mountain were probably as frustrated trying to learn climbing technique as I was trying to learn windsurfing. I hadn't been able to relate to the fact that the clients were often coming into a completely alien and intimidating environment. With this new realization, I started guiding again part-time and found that I enjoyed it more.

I even got into guiding on McKinley. On big trips like McKinley, I learn a lot about people and it inspires me musically. I write a lot of songs when I climb.

I realize that we've grown up in a society that's very used to comfort. And if we lose a little bit of that comfort, we don't like it. During the last couple of years, I've concentrated on convincing clients that it's okay to be uncomfortable. It's going to happen, it's also going to end.

As guides, we can only do so much. It's still up to the clients to take care of themselves. We give them pointers. Every time I do a climb and people come back down and say "Thanks," it's hard for me to say "You're welcome," because they're the ones who did it. We help show the way, but I think they should give themselves a little more credit.

Guiding is not a high-paying job, but the rewards are great. We pay each guide a salary and provide lodging plus meals while they're on the mountain. The guides who come back year after year do so for four main reasons: when they get out on the mountain, they are their own boss, they get so damned healthy, they have a good time, and they get a great tan. How many jobs offer these benefits?

It's been a great satisfaction to me to see my guides excel, to form their own guiding companies, to lead expeditions, to summit Mount Everest. To date, only two Americans have summitted Everest without the use of supplemental oxygen: Larry Nielson and Ed Viesturs. They both learned their skills as guides in the RMI guide service.

We encourage our guides to develop their own guiding services outside the Rainier season. This not only allows them to make a living in a mountaineering life-style, it also keeps them around. Jerry and I don't want to have to hire a new crew every year. Our most senior guides—Joe Horiskey, Phil Ershler, Eric Simonson, and George Dunn—have each been here twenty years or longer. In the climbing community, that type of continuity is pretty rare. These guys are good, they've climbed all over the world, and they have formed a nucleus that has added strength to RMI over the years.

There's no better training ground for Everest than Mount Rainier. Climbers come here from all over the United States to train for big climbs. There are twenty-seven glaciers on Rainier, and the weather can drop to 50 below in the winter. Geologists call Mount Rainier an arctic island in the middle of a temperate zone. The snow and ice of Rainier is a perfect place in which to prepare for the two or three months that climbers will spend in the lifeless blue and white environment of Everest or other Himalayan peaks.

Rainier is also an intriguing mountain in itself. In 1954, Jim and

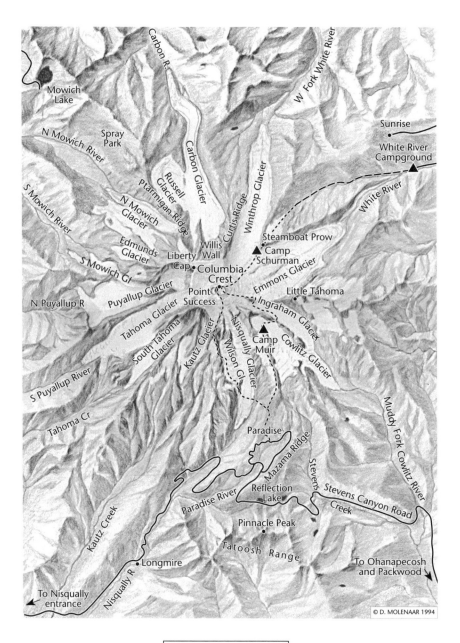

MOUNT RAINIER

© D. MOLENAAR 1994

I had done a preliminary investigation of the steam vents, or fumaroles, on the summit. In 1970 I finally got an opportunity to explore the vents with Lee Nelson. Lee sometimes guided for me and had been just as curious about the steam vents as I. Since he also worked as a fireman, he was able to bring oxygen rebreather units for us to wear inside the vents.

We used strong headlamps with willow wands wrapped in aluminum foil to reflect our light. Our plan was to traverse the crater through the steam vents. There was a network of caves in the crater that had been formed by the escaping steam of the volcano. The steam had formed ceilings and walls of ice in the caves beneath the snow that had accumulated in the crater.

We had a climbing party with us, and we all camped at the summit rim. The party waited outside the vents while Lee and I entered. From the outside, the crater rim is only about a quarter mile across, but the steam vents led us down about a thirty-degree slope to a point about 400 feet below the roof of the crater, then back up. It took us about an hour to go all the way across. We did find a small lake but, to my disappointment, no mermaids, as I had envisioned back in 1954. Halfway through the caves, Lee took off his rebreather unit and said, "Lou, the air is sweet. It seems okay."

The scalloped ice ceilings of the caves were sixty to seventy feet high in places, and in other places we had to duck to get through. Steam hissed from between rocks on the floor of the caves and reminded me of the descriptions of Dante's *Inferno*. It was pitch black. As we ascended, we'd switch off our headlamps now and then to look for signs of light. We finally saw blue ice up ahead and used our ice axes to chop our way out. When we climbed out, we saw that we had emerged on the other side of the crater. The climbers we had left on the other side cheered. It was the first time anyone had "threaded the needle," and the local papers played it up.

We've since led a few parties through the vents, including several geologists. It's a tough excursion for most people, because they first have to climb to the summit before they can begin exploring the steam vents. By then, most people are exhausted and ready to head back down.

Several years ago, a small plane crashed in the crater. Now when you go into one of the vents, you can see the wing of the plane protruding through the ceiling. It's a pretty eerie feeling.

As a guide, your level of fitness generally exceeds that of your client. You know you could be down off the mountain in two or three hours, having a beer or meeting your girlfriend. With your client, it's going to take six or eight hours and it's going to take patience to climb that slowly.

A guide learns to recognize the limitations of the clients. Often, the guide picks up signals before the clients do or before they're willing to admit it. Good technique is holding the rope behind you in order to feel the next climber on the rope. You can see the climber in front of you. If I see you holding your rope with your arm hanging loosely behind you, I know you're relaxed. An arm held at or above the waist is a sign of tension.

Some people go like gangbusters, then suddenly give out. Others fade slowly. The best kind are those who get worse slowly, because we can usually see it coming. With the others, we get no indicators. I've been with clients who are looking strong, sounding strong, then suddenly they're throwing up and freezing when they shouldn't be that cold. Then I feel I've read the climber wrong and I should have stopped sooner. I have to decide if I can send the climber down with another guide or leave him or her in a sleeping bag while I take the rest of the party to the summit.

We'll send people back down off Rainier with a guide as close as a half hour from the summit. When you're done, you're done. In good weather, if a climber runs out of gas, we put him or her in a warm sleeping bag, then pick him or her up on the way down from the summit. Each rest stop has a place to leave climbers, or we can dig a secure spot to anchor the sleeping bag.

Opposite: *JanSport dealer seminar participants training in a crevasse on Cowlitz Glacier, Mount Rainier (Photo: Keith Gunnar)*

We assign clients to different rope teams before we head to the summit. We try not to put husbands and wives on the same rope, to keep them from being either over-protective or argumentative, and we mix strong climbers with weaker ones. I always tell the clients who they'll be roped up with for the summit attempt, and I ask them to let me know if they have any problems with our selections. Occasionally, some do.

On one climb, a client came up to me after I had assigned him to a rope that was to be led by one of my best guides, Leonard Faulk. Leonard worked for me for three seasons before he quit to become a sales rep for Kelty Packs. The client told me that he'd like to be put on a different rope team. His accent revealed that he was from the Deep South. Since Leonard was black, I figured I had a prejudice problem on my hands, so I asked the guy, "What seems to be the problem?"

"Well, there's a Japanese climber on the same rope, and I think he's been really clumsy and I just don't feel safe on the same rope with him."

I was still suspicious of the guy's motives, so I said, "How about if I move the Japanese guy to my rope and leave you on Leonard's rope? Will that be okay?" The guy agreed.

The next day, as we climbed to the summit, I'll be damned if the Japanese guy didn't stumble or fall about eight times.

All RMI guides can count on getting involved in rescues at one time or another. Our concession permit with the Park Service requires that we participate in rescues. If we're with clients at the time a rescue operation begins, some of the guides go to the rescue and the others stay with the clients. Generally, we find that the people in trouble are in non-guided parties. Apprentice guides don't get involved in rescues until they've become proficient in the techniques of ice and snow climbing, learned the terrain and weather patterns of the mountain, and developed a working knowledge of rescue methods.

In 1981, I happened to be with a group of clients at Camp Muir when I got a call from the ranger at Paradise telling me that there was a "Jesus freak" holed up in a steam cave in the summit crater. He'd been there for three days, a storm was coming in, and his parents were worried that he'd die. The Park Service was going to send up a helicopter. They wanted me to get the guy out of the steam vent and over to the chopper site.

After we summitted with our climbing party, I left the clients with another guide and traversed the rim, looking in several different steam vents before I found the guy. He said, "I'm here to talk to God. Leave me alone."

"Why did you pick a mountain in a national park?" I said. "God is on other mountains, you know. Now you've got the Park Service involved and your folks are down below and they're really afraid for your life."

"I don't talk to my folks anymore."

"If you're not talking to your folks, seems like you'd have a hard time talking to God. Your folks brought you into the world, which gives them a connection with God, don't you think? You'd better follow me."

By this time, I'd climbed down into the vent next to the guy. I was prepared to knock him out if I had to and carry him out. But I wanted to first try to reach him with basic appeal. His sleeping bag was wet, he wasn't dressed or prepared for a storm. He looked miserable. I knew he'd die when the storm hit. He finally agreed to follow me out of the crater. The chopper was landing just a little ways away. He heard it and started to move away. I said, "That's for you," and took hold of his arm.

Two rangers wearing pistols jumped out of the chopper. "What's the matter?" the guy asked, trying to pull away.

"It's okay. They won't hurt you. They just want you to go with them."

"Where can I go to talk to God?"

"There's a great mountain not too far from here, Mount Baker. It's not in a national park and you can talk to God there as long as you want."

He got in the chopper and I went back to my clients with a great story. I felt bad about the effect the rangers' guns had on the guy, but rangers are required to carry guns nowadays. I never found out if the guy went to Mount Baker.

In 1990 my son Peter and I plus three recovery personnel hired by an insurance company were helicoptered to a point just below the summit of Rainier where five people had died in the crash of a light plane. We climbed down to the site in crampons. We were at about 13,600 feet and it was the first time these recovery guys had ever used crampons or ice axes. They were wearing blue jeans and weren't at all dressed for mountain weather. I wasn't too worried. I figured we'd be out of there in an hour. My mistake.

Sure enough, after an hour the recovery guys had finished their investigation and we were ready to leave. I radioed for the chopper to return. He told me he couldn't fly. He was about a half hour away with a few clouds surrounding him. I said, "I can see the clouds you're in. The peaks are all out, it's clear up here. Can't you try anyway?"

He said, "I don't have a penetrator. The FAA says it's illegal to go through the fog."

"If I'm radioing you and I know where you are in those clouds, I can tell you that there's nothing above you. Just come straight up. There are a hundred places to land when you go back."

"I can't. It's illegal."

"You've got guys in danger up here. We have about one day's food and a storm is coming in."

"Sorry, can't do it."

That left me and Peter stuck with these recovery guys. We camped out on the mountain as best we could. We had a stove, fuel, the lunches we had packed for the day, a few packets of soup, and a tent. Peter and I rarely go out on any type of recovery or rescue work without some basic supplies.

We were on a rock ridge beside the Kautz Glacier. The lenticular cloud cap was forming above the summit and I knew we were in for a good storm. We cooked a light meal but melted lots of snow for water for the descent the next day. We tried to save fuel and ration food for the possible long sit, should the storm run through for a few days.

Peter and I awakened everyone at four the next morning. It was already snowing, but we thought we could get down the mountain before conditions got worse. The other three guys had never climbed in their lives and now I was asking them to descend a mountain in a snowstorm. The Kautz Route was too dangerous, so we first had to climb back up to the summit, then head down our regular route. One of the guys was big and overweight and Peter didn't want to tie in with him for fear he'd not be able to hold him if he fell. I put the guy on my rope. We took them up over the summit and down the other side. By the time we got down to Paradise, these guys were freezing and hurting, but they made it in one piece. They were great. It's amazing what people can do when they have to.

I hope that's the last time I get stuck like that, relying on a helicopter. They're great and they're fast, when they're able to fly.

Since 1988, I've guided climbs on Rainier during the summer to raise funds for the American Lung Association for a program called "Kids with Asthma." We take corporate personnel from the state of Washington up the mountain, charge each of them $5,000, and donate it to the American Lung Association. The first few times, we raised $50,000 to $60,000 on each climb.

Then the recession hit and it became harder to find companies willing to participate. Even with only five or six climbers turning out, the money still helps the cause. As the economy improves, we expect the number of participants to increase again. We now plan to open the climb to corporate personnel from all states, not just Washington.

I've taken a lot of corporate groups up the mountain, such as employees from Boeing and Weyerhaeuser. In the summer of 1993, I took up a team of Microsoft employees. They surprised me by serving me with a "COMPLAINT FOR DAMAGES" after we summitted. It was typed on legal stationery and read:

CAUSE OF ACTION: On or about the 2nd day of September 1993, on Rainier Mountain, Pierce County, Washington, the defendant did intentionally, gratuitously, and most gracefully, and with great fanfare (and without much whining), escort the plaintiffs, a motley crew of Microlimp employees, and others, on a moonlit walk up through the heavens to a most awesome place, to wit: the highest point in this great state.

WHEREFORE, upon reaching said peak, the parties aforesaid did bask in the sun and thoroughly enjoyed said awesome view.

DAMAGES: As a direct and proximate result of the conduct of the defendant … the plaintiffs did suffer the following damages:

Burning thighs, parched throats, sunburnt proboscis, chapped lips, and shortness of breath.

WHEREFORE, the plaintiffs pray for the following relief:

a. An easy walk down said mountain;

b. Copious quantities of brew upon reaching Paradise Inn; and

c. Such other and further relief as the court deems just and equitable.

On that climb, we were blessed with sunny weather the whole time. They had a easy walk down the mountain and, indeed, drank copious quantities of brew in the Glacier Room, the watering hole at the Paradise Inn and often the first stop for climbers exiting the mountain. It's also the place where the psychologists in a climbing party call the beer and good mood a "celebration of life." I think it's just being down off the mountain, feeling damn tired, and having a lot more oxygen to breathe. People actually wait on you, the room has electric lights, heat, and cold beer!

After Bobby Kennedy was assassinated in 1968, Jim and I went back to Virginia to visit Ethel and her eleven kids. I was getting ready to hire some new guides for the 1970 summer season and I asked seventeen-year-old Joe Jr., Ethel's oldest child, if he would be interested in a summer job. He jumped at the chance.

I decided that Joe's mentor guide would be Gombu's brother-in-law, Phursumba, a Sherpa from Darjeeling, India. Phursumba was a strong, experienced climber and an excellent guide.

The first time Joe climbed Rainier, he did a good job. He was hurting a little, but no more than any new guide who has never been on the mountain. He was treated like any other apprentice guide, and pitched right in on the grunt work. He got along real well with the rest of the guides, too. We tried to keep a lid on the

Lou and Joe Kennedy Jr. at Paradise, 1970 (Photo courtesy Whittaker family)

fact that he was working for the guide service, but reporters eventually found out. They hounded him so badly, wrote down every word he said, took photos like crazy. Luckily, he could escape up on the mountain. None of the reporters was fit enough to follow him.

During that time, Ingrid took a short trip to Germany to visit her family and found out that she was famous. Apparently an

American news service had sent out a photo of her with Joe Jr. and a German magazine had picked it up. There were also photos of Joe with a couple of other girls he had met while he was working on Rainier. But according to this German magazine, all of the girls were Ingrid Widmann of Munich, the local girl who had met a Kennedy. It was a big deal in Germany.

One day, after Joe had been working for a few weeks, Ingrid and I went by the Guide House to see how he was getting along. We were told that he was out climbing with Phursumba, who was teaching him some rock-climbing technique at Pinnacle Peak. About the same time, a car drove up and a guy hopped out and ran up to us, saying that he just saw somebody fall off Pinnacle Peak.

"Did you go up there, is he alive?"

"No. I ran down the trail for help instead."

While the rangers started organizing a rescue party, Ingrid and I took off in our car. We drove the three miles to the trailhead. I got out and ran up the trail, pressure breathing and doing whatever tricks I could muster to get myself up there fast. All the time I was thinking, jeez, hasn't Ethel had enough to deal with?

As I was climbing up the rockslide below the peak's west face, I was wondering what Joe and Phursumba would have been doing on this side. It was about an 800-foot vertical cliff, with a steep rockslide and boulders as big as cars. Not the best side to climb on. We have some granite on Rainier, but since the mountain is a volcanic peak, most of the rock is igneous. It's unstable, creating what I call "portable handholds."

Soon I saw the blue, yellow, and red colors of an RMI guide sweater lying among some large boulders about fifty feet from the wall. I got there quickly, checked out the climber, and knew right away that he was dead. His face had been deformed from the fall, so I wasn't sure who it was. He had a good physique, like Joe. His hair was similar to Joe's. I was in tears as I searched his pockets for identification. I found a pack of cigarettes. Joe was smoking cigarettes at the time, but so was another guide, Eric Weigel. Just then I heard a call from the other side of the peak. It was Phursumba, with Joe. So I'd found Eric. Not Joe. I was relieved and distressed at the same time.

I picked up Eric and started carrying him back down. Ingrid met me on the trail. She saw that I was crying and started crying too. We decided to wait there with Eric instead of trying to carry him over the rockslide. Soon the rangers arrived with a stretcher and we carried him down.

Later, I found out that it was Eric's day off and he had hoped to go climbing with Marty Hoey that day on a route on Rainier's Mowich Face. But Marty had already made plans to go climbing with another Eric on the staff, Eric Reynolds. Eric Weigel got pissed and went off climbing by himself on the West Face of Pinnacle Peak.

I was shook up. We rarely lose a guide. When we do, I feel as though I've lost a child.

That same summer, we had a dope scare. I got a tip from one of the rangers that one of the cabin girls had been caught outside the park smoking marijuana. The ranger had heard that they were going to bring in dogs and sniff out the guide quarters, which at that time were inside the park at Paradise.

I was at Camp Muir with a climbing party when I heard about the planned "invasion." It was the afternoon of the day before our planned summit climb. I gathered the guides together—six of them—and told them, "Okay, you guys. I just got a tip that they're going to bring in dogs to search the guide quarters for dope. If you're involved, you're going to have to go down and clean out the place. Take everything out of there. If you're ever caught, you're out of here in a minute. I've told you this before and I mean it. It could cost me the guide service."

They started mumbling among themselves. I overheard one of them say, "Yeah, mine is in the drawer beside the pillow," so I interrupted: "Wait a minute. It's each person's responsibility to take care of his or her own stuff. If you're involved, you go down there and clean it up. Don't send somebody else to do your dirty work."

I added, "And I want your asses back up here tonight, ready to leave for the summit climb in the morning."

I couldn't believe it. All six of them got up and left. I was left there all alone while my sterling, all-American guides went down the mountain to dispose of their dope.

The rangers never showed up with the dogs.

Rainier Mountaineering, Inc. has enjoyed an affiliation with JanSport since the early 1970s. I met Skip Yowell, one of the founders of JanSport, in the late 1960s. Skip and his cousin, Murray Pletz, had started a small backpacking equipment company in 1967 and got me to buy some backpacks and tents from them for Whittaker's Chalet. In 1972, I joined JanSport as a product consultant after having guided Skip and Murray on a winter seminar the year before.

Since then, JanSport has been the major sponsor of all my expeditions—four to the Himalaya and one to Peru. In 1973, RMI began conducting five-day climbing seminars each June for JanSport retailers, who fly in from all over the country to climb Mount Rainier with me, Skip, and several RMI guides. Skip and I and our wives also have found time to take some great trips together, to Greece, New Zealand, and Africa. That's our idea of a stimulating vacation—to go experience the outdoors in another part of the world.

Some of the best parties I've ever been to have been the ones following a week-long JanSport dealer seminar on Mount Rainier. When we come down off the mountain, we always go to the Glacier Room at the Paradise Inn for beers with clients. On the JanSport dealer seminar, the group stays overnight at a rustic motel called the Gateway Inn, in Ashford just outside Mount Rainier National Park. There, we hold a dinner, an awards ceremony for the retailers on the climb, and a party.

In the early years, we got a little wild at times, and the party at the Gateway Inn sometimes migrated to the hot tub at my house, about ten minutes away. We've tempered our parties some since then. But one year, we got thirty-eight guides and JanSport dealers in the hot tub at one time. Set a record. We'd never have made it if we'd been wearing bathing suits.

People might wonder why all of us guides are so willing to jump out of our clothes. Part of the reason is because we're in good shape and not ashamed of our bodies. But there's a more important reason, one that all high-altitude climbers understand. You spend a couple of months on a climb, wearing the same clothes, the same long underwear, day after day, night after night. When you finally get someplace where it's warm enough to strip down and there's warm water for a shower, you feel like you never want to put clothes on again. One of the greatest feelings in the world is to feel fresh air and warm water on your bare skin.

I always kid people who are a little hesitant about going nude in a hot tub. I say, "If God had meant for people to go nude, they would have been born that way."

There used to be a trampoline by my hot tub. One night, we were partying in the tub—again, after a JanSport dealer seminar—and this beautiful Hawaiian girl who worked for the guide service was jumping up and down on the trampoline. She was naked, of course.

This guy from Southern California climbed out of the tub and started bouncing with her. He slipped, bounced off, and smashed his nose against the springs of the trampoline. He started bleeding profusely. We carried him over to the guest house near the tub and stopped the bleeding. He was feeling no pain from all the alcohol he'd consumed, so we left him there to sleep for the night. Needless to say, the party was over.

The next morning, he looked pretty bad. His eyes were black, he couldn't breathe through his nostrils. I told him, "I've cleaned up the blood, but I think you'd better get to a hospital and have them look at you."

He decided that he'd rather get home and have his own doctor take care of him. He made the flight okay, but when he went to the doctor's office they told him, "You should be in intensive care."

They found bone fragments everywhere, some even near his brain. After an operation and during his recovery, he met and fell in love with one of the nurses. A week later they got married. He called me and said, "Lou, it was worth every minute!"

When my son Peter was younger, he brought a first date over to the house with the intention of using the hot tub. He didn't realize that Ingrid and I were home—and that we were already in the tub. "That's okay," we told him, "come join us."

The girl, a beautiful eighteen-year-old, went in the guest house to change out of her clothes. She emerged without a towel and slipped into the tub, casual as hell, talking to me and Ingrid. Meanwhile, Peter was still trying to figure out how to get in the tub with his date. He finally got over to the tub wearing only his jeans, turned his back to us, quickly pulled off his jeans, and slid into the water.

I said to Peter, "I gotta tell you, when I was eighteen, if I had seen either of my parents naked, I'd have died. If my parents had ever seen my girlfriend and me naked, they'd have died, too. It's a new world, thank God."

Pete learned more about anatomy at hot-tub parties than I ever did in four years of biology at Seattle University.

In 1987, on one of the JanSport dealer seminars, we held a wedding at Camp Muir. JanSport sales representative Larry Harrison and his fiancee, Carol, hiked up to the bunkhouse for the ceremony. I had the honor of giving the bride away. She and I walked through a tunnel formed by guides and climbers standing on each side, holding crossed ice axes above us. Jim Thomsen, another JanSport sales rep who is also an ordained minister, conducted the ceremony. After the climb, the couple consummated their marriage at the Gateway Inn in Ashford. They say that their first child was conceived that night. I was a little disappointed that they didn't name it after me.

The only living thing that's been named after me, other than my youngest son, is one of Iditarod champion Susan Butcher's sled dogs. My twin and I met Susan at a gathering of conservation-minded outdoor people a few years ago and we hit it off. A few months later, she sent me a photo of herself holding a couple of puppies, which she had named "Lou" and "Jim."

Each year I travel around the country making appearances, giving talks and slide shows for JanSport at college bookstores, outdoor stores, and various industry trade shows. One year, at a ski industry trade show in New York City, we were all staying at a big hotel and I was having a great time. I was doing what has become fondly remembered as "stemming the hallways." I'd lie down in a hallway, place my hands against one wall and my feet against the other, then walk up the walls to the ceiling, same way I'd do to stem a crevasse. I'd get above a person's room and call to him. He'd walk out, look around, see no one, then jump like a rabbit when I'd call down from above.

It was just a way to have fun in the city.

We have more fun in the mountains. When the guides aren't guiding, they're often out climbing, skiing, riding mountain bikes, hiking—or hot tubbing. We all live an active outdoor life-style.

There's an exclusive club on Mount Rainier called the Rim Club. It's made up of guys who have made love to a woman on the summit of Mount Rainier. I know that several of my guides, including my sons, are members. The guides are pretty healthy and they like to take girlfriends to the summit. The nights up there are incredible. On a clear night, you can see the ferryboats going across Puget Sound and planes landing at SeaTac airport. Members of the Rim Club are inducted on their word. It's not something we feel we need to witness.

We were holding new guide tryouts on Rainier on a clear day in May 1980 when Mount St. Helens erupted. St. Helens is only about forty miles from Rainier as the crow flies. Huge clouds and lightning flashes filled the sky. The sky began to darken and the white snow and ice of Rainier was soon covered in black ash. Within a few hours, the sky was pitch dark and we had trouble driving down the mountain, even with our headlights on. When Ingrid and I got home to Ashford, our house and cats were covered in ash. The roads were closed for several weeks. We had to show proof that we lived in the area to go in or out.

Mount St. Helens blew 1,300 feet off of her top and killed a total of fifty-eight people. I had been up to that summit many times on rescues and ski ascents. The eruption was an awesome sight. You can see St. Helens from Camp Muir. Now, whenever I look at that blown-out peak, I feel like I've outlived a mountain.

◆ 11 ◆

EVEREST 1982: CHOMOLUNGMA, GODDESS MOTHER OF THE WORLD

The Chinese call Mount Everest "Chomolungma," which means "Goddess Mother of the World." There is no higher place on earth and none so spellbinding as this magnificent peak that straddles the borders of Nepal and Tibet.

The Chinese occupied Tibet in 1950. The harsh repression that followed forced their leader, the Dalai Lama, to leave the country. In 1980, after thirty years, the Chinese opened Tibet again to mountaineering. Like many mountaineers, I had read a lot about the country and had dreamed of seeing the rolling brown plains of Tibet and the holy city of Lhasa. Anybody would want go there just to see the country. But to go to Tibet and also climb the world's highest mountain would be, in my mind, the ultimate adventure.

Ever since my brother Jim's success on the south side of Everest, I thought that if I ever went there, I would set my sights on a different route, one that led up the north side of the mountain. Two

Opposite: *Marty Hoey on icy wall near 26,000 feet, just before her fall; Everest, 1982 (Photo: Jim Wickwire)*

British climbers, George Mallory and Andrew Irvine, had attempted the summit from that side in the 1920s, and I had read of their exploits. Both Mallory and Irvine perished on Everest during a summit attempt in 1924. It has never been determined whether they died going up or on their way down after summitting. Consequently, their climb is not recorded as a successful summit.

Over the years, nearly 2,000 mountaineers had tested themselves against Mount Everest. For every ten who had tried, only one had succeeded. For every ten who had succeeded, three had died in the attempt.

The Chinese had climbed to the summit of Everest via the north side in 1960, and in 1980 the famous Italian climber Reinhold Messner summitted via the North Col. But a U.S. team had never made a successful assault of the mountain from that side. And no team had ever attempted the summit from the route that we intended to follow, one that led up the Great Couloir, the center gully that begins at 20,000 feet at the Rongbuk Glacier and runs to the summit peak at 29,028 feet.

In 1979, Chris Kerrebrock, an energetic twenty-three-year-old graduate student at Columbia University who guided for RMI during the summers, began working on securing a permit from China to climb Everest. Chris had an "in" through his father, a professor of aeronautical engineering at MIT who had professional contacts within the Chinese government. He helped Chris obtain the permit. Chris asked me to lead the expedition, and we planned it for the spring of 1982.

The Mazama Club, a climbing club based in Portland, Oregon, of which I am an honorary member, became the official sponsor of the climb. JanSport agreed to be the major sponsor and source of equipment and clothing. As primary suppliers of raw materials to JanSport, both DuPont and Allied Fibers signed on as cosponsors. We also received support from C. Itoh & Co./Toray. They donated cash and supplied JanSport with a waterproof/breathable fabric called Entrant for our jackets and bib pants. New Balance gave a cash donation and shoes for the team, Coleman supplied stoves, Quaker Oats donated oatmeal, and General Foods sent Tang.

General Foods shipped us a truckload of Tang. A forty-foot semi backed into my driveway one day and dumped off enough pallets of the drink mix to quench the thirst of an army, let alone an expedition. I gave away a lot of it to Ashford residents. Not too long ago, one of my friends told me that he still had a couple of boxes left. He had been rationing it for more than ten years.

On all of our expeditions, we also raise money by selling commemorative T-shirts, sweatshirts, and postcards signed by the expedition members. We take the postcards with us and mail them back to the United States during the climb.

Rainier Beer donated $5,000 to the climb and asked us to take a cold-pack of beer to Everest. They wanted an endorsement photo of me with a brew at base camp. Five years before, they had asked me to make a commercial. At the time I wasn't sure that I wanted to promote alcohol, so I asked my mother how she felt about it. Even at age forty-five, I felt I needed her permission. She told me to go ahead.

In the commercial, one of my RMI guides, Marty Hoey, threw me the beer. I caught it and said, "Some think I like the name because I'm called Rainier Lou. Huh-uh! When you get the mountain thirst, you want the mountain fresh. Took it with me to the Himalaaayaaas." It took twenty-eight takes for us to get it right. The commercial aired on television for six weeks. For a long time afterwards, I couldn't go into a McDonald's and get a Big Mac without twenty kids asking me for my autograph. Of course, my twin was approached as well and, at one time, suggested that we split the residuals!

Since the 1975 K2 expedition, we had carried out all our own garbage on climbs, including some from other expeditions. You try to go on an expedition fully funded by your sponsoring companies. Part of the funding goes to disposal of garbage. We pay porters to come in and assist us.

Sponsoring companies not only get the exposure and prestige from being part of an Everest expedition, their products also are subjected to one of the most rigorous testing grounds in the world. We never wait to test any product for the first time on the actual expedition, in case it should fail in a life-threatening situation. Instead, as guides, we test products on Mount Rainier as part of our daily routine. One summer of product use by a guide is equivalent to about ten years of normal consumer use.

It wasn't hard to select a team for the 1982 expedition. I had many seasoned RMI guides who were ready and more than willing to go. The nine finally chosen for the team were in their mid- to late twenties or early thirties: Eric Simonson, Dan Boyd, Marty Hoey, Phil Ershler, George Dunn, Joe Horiskey, Gary Isaacs, Larry Nielson, and Tracy Roberts.

I also invited Jim Wickwire, then forty-one, to join us. People have asked me, "Why would you want to climb with an attorney?" I tell them, on a cold mountain like Rainier or Everest, it's the only time you'll see an attorney with his hands in his own pockets.

Dr. Ed Hixson, age forty, from Lake Placid, New York, agreed to be the team physician. He had been an RMI client on both Rainier and Mount McKinley. I called him one night and said that I had a peak that I thought he'd like to climb and, I added, this time I wouldn't charge him. He asked me, "Which peak?"

I said, "It'll take about three months—Everest."

The phone line was dead for almost a minute, then Ed let out a whoop and said, "I'm going!"

Steve Marts, age forty-four, the cinematographer/climber who had been on our 1975 K2 expedition, came on board again as cinematographer as well as still photographer. Afterwards, with Pal Productions in Seattle, he created an award-winning video documentary of the climb called "Everest North Wall," narrated by Robert Redford.

I also asked my old friends Dave Mahre and Nawang Gombu to join the team. At fifty-four, forty-six, and fifty-three, respectively, Mahre, Gombu, and I would be the oldest climbers on the team.

As expedition leader, I had no aspirations to be part of the first summit team. But if we nailed the summit and if there was still time, then I hoped to make my bid. Like the rest of the team, I'd help carry loads to high camps. In addition, I would be responsible for logistics and for keeping the team intact and operating as a team.

I knew that I could count on Mahre and Gombu to give 100 percent to the climb. Either of them could do the job of a man half his age, and both had incredible mountain knowledge. Gombu's experience on Everest and in the Himalaya in general was invaluable. Mahre, a devout climber and just as devout a family man, had passed up many chances to go on big climbs because of family obligations. Now that most of his kids were grown, he and his wife decided that he should take the opportunity. Going to Everest had been a lifelong dream of Dave's.

At the time we were forming the team, there were two men attempting to be the first to climb the highest peak on each of the seven continents. Everest, of course, was one of their goals. They contacted me through Marty Hoey, asking to be part of the team. They were wealthy men and offered to buy into the climb with a sizable chunk of cash. This is how Dick Bass, developer of the Snowbird Ski Resort in Utah, and Frank Wells, vice chairman of Warner Brothers, also became members of the 1982 American China–Everest Expedition. With their donation, the expedition took a giant leap from scrounging for cash sponsors to being fully funded.

Bass and Wells actually did well on the mountain. Wells made it to 24,000 feet and Bass to 25,000. It took Bass four other expeditions, but he eventually summitted Everest and also reached his goal of becoming the first person to climb each of the seven summits. The story of his adventure with Wells is told in his book *Seven Summits*, co-authored by Rick Ridgeway.

Marty Hoey was responsible for bringing Bass and Wells into the expedition. She had been on ski patrol at Snowbird during the winter and had gotten to know Dick Bass pretty well. She had guided him on Rainier and McKinley, and had gone with Bass and Wells to Argentina's Aconcagua, at 23,085 feet the highest mountain in the Western Hemisphere and the highest peak in South America. They had honed their skills on these mountains in preparation for Everest.

The 1963 American Everest Expedition had consisted of 19 team members, plus 850 porters, 45 Sherpas, and twenty-eight tons of equipment and food. Our 1982 expedition was made up of 17 team members and two and a half tons of gear and food. The 1963 climb had a budget of $400,000, which would be equal to about $1 million in 1982. Our budget was under $200,000.

Even so, our actual climbing team was considered large by modern standards because we had decided not to use Sherpas or Tibetan porters to help carry loads, as is common on most expeditions. We felt it would be a more satisfying experience to rely on our own resources. As we later discovered, hauling loads day after day to the upper camps on the mountain eventually takes its toll on your climbing team.

The plan was to leave on March 1, fly from Seattle to Beijing, train to Chengdu, fly to Lhasa, then travel by truck to road's end at the head of the Rongbuk Glacier at 16,900 feet. From that point, we would use nearly forty yaks, the traditional Tibetan beast of burden, each carrying about 110 pounds of gear, to ferry our equipment to advanced base camp at 18,400 feet. From there, we'd ascend the mountain on foot in waves, with alternate teams of climbers carrying supplies to higher camps until we had our last camp in place for the summit attempt. While the first team tried for the summit, the second team would move into place, and a third team would rest up below. If the summit team failed, they'd return to a lower camp, rest, then move up into position again, until the summit was achieved.

We went to Everest feeling like a real hotshot team. We had underestimated the actual hardships awaiting us, the real difficulty of the route we had chosen, the weather, the cold, the wind, the illnesses and accidents that occur up high. You hear about all these things from climbers who have gone before, but it's not until you actually experience them yourself that reality sets in.

The Goddess Mother threw everything she had at us on this expedition. And we suffered. It was a real heartbreaker.

The first tragedy struck the year before we ever left for Everest. In 1981, Jim Wickwire and Chris Kerrebrock went to Mount McKinley for a training climb. On their approach to the upper mountain, roped together and with a 200-pound sled of provisions between them, Chris suddenly plunged into a crevasse. He went in head first, the sled went in on top of him, and Wick fell on top of both of them. The rope between them had been only twenty feet long, too short when you're traveling on a glacier. A longer rope gives you more time to self-arrest and stop a fall.

The crevasse had been bridged and hidden on top. It was about three feet wide and grew narrower as it deepened. Chris had plunged through the snow bridge and fallen about twenty-five feet

*Chris Kerrebrock,
1980 (Photo: Dr. Ed
Hixson)*

to where the crevasse was about eighteen inches wide. He got wedged in real tight. Wick broke his shoulder in the fall, which hampered his efforts to get Chris out. Wick struggled for hours with his ice hammer, he fixed a rope and tried to pull Chris out, but the ice wouldn't loosen its hold. It took Chris ten hours to die of exposure. Music had been one of Chris's many talents. He played classical horn. Toward the end, Wick later told us, Chris was singing.

Before he died, Chris gave Wick farewell messages for his parents and for me and Ingrid, and asked Wick to take the mouthpiece from his horn and place it on the summit of Everest.

It took Wick almost two weeks longer to get off McKinley. He managed to salvage some jam, honey, and crackers from the sled, and this sustained him until he was finally rescued, near death himself.

Chris's body was later recovered by a rescue team. He was flown back to his family. I went to the funeral and gave the eulogy. The loss of Chris was a huge blow to the expedition, but we made a joint decision to go on in memory of Chris.

At one point, Wick had decided to quit the expedition. I asked him if he would at least go on the protocol trip with me to China in October 1981. As an attorney, Wick had been in charge of our expedition correspondence, and I needed him to continue to be our contact man with the Chinese. I also had an ulterior motive— I thought he'd change his mind once we got him headed in the direction of the climb.

After the protocol trip to China, we exited China through Hong Kong. While there, Wick met with Peter Goodwin, a retired British Army officer whose brother, Eric, we had met in Rawalpindi on the way in to K2 in 1975. Afterwards Wick said, "Lou, Peter told me to go on the climb. I'll have to talk to Mary Lou and my kids first, but I think I'll do it."

There's an incredible amount of work involved in organizing a major expedition to a foreign country. You don't just decide to go, gather a bunch of climbers, and take off. Securing a permit takes a mountain of correspondence in itself. Then you have to select the right team. Then there are the visas and passports and immunization certificates and gear, food, and clothing to arrange. Protocol trips are required to climb in China, which brings politics into the picture. If you want the mountain badly enough, you jump through the hoops and try to have a good time in the process.

Once we arrived in China for the expedition, it took us about ten days to get to the end of the road and the beginning of the climb. In Beijing, we toured the Forbidden City, built during the Ming Dynasty. It's now called The People's Museum. We were struck by the contrast between the subdued dress and regimentation of the people and the beautiful, incredible architecture that mirrored the culture of the past forty centuries.

The visit to the Great Wall of China was another highlight of the trip for most of us. The fascination of seeing a part of the world that had been closed to Westerners for a couple of decades was great. And I think the feeling among the native people was mutual.

The best part of traveling through third-world countries such as Nepal and Tibet is meeting the people of the various villages. After a smile, a touch, a laugh, you realize that people are people wherever you go. You begin to understand that most of the evils of the world are usually the result of the actions of a handful of politicians.

The team spent three days in Lhasa, the capital of Tibet. Flying from Chengdu at 1,000 feet to Lhasa at 12,500 feet required a few days of acclimatization.

At such high altitude and surrounded by rugged mountains, Lhasa is the most isolated city in the world. It is the religious heart of Tibet, and the people practice an intense form of Buddhism. We were careful to observe religious customs, such as walking only clockwise around prayer stones and stupas.

I carried a Polaroid camera so that I could hand out pictures to the villagers. Most of these people had never seen a picture of themselves. The children enjoyed having their pictures taken. Whenever I could, I took photos of families together, so they'd have some record of their family history.

Most of the villagers you meet are friendly and open to visiting climbers, and I try to treat them likewise. A lot of climbers have a hard time being around the people of third-world villages. The villagers are poor and their hygiene is not up to Western standards. Their lives are incredibly hard, by our standards, and some of the ailments and diseases they suffer could be easily controlled or even obliterated by modern medicine. In fact, many expedition doctors spend a great deal of their time on treks into base camp administering to porters and villagers along the way.

By the time we had boarded a rickety bus for the dusty, three-day drive to the Rongbuk Glacier, we all were consumed by our own thoughts. I thought back to a conversation I had had only a few months before with Sir Edmund Hillary, who in 1953 had become the first man to climb Mount Everest. I had asked him about weather and the timing of the climb, about the mountain in general. Sir Edmund had been very encouraging. "I know you'll get the summit," he had said. The excitement of just being in his presence had been extremely motivating for me.

As the bus drew nearer to the great peaks of the Himalaya, I finally caught a glimpse of Everest, Chomolungma, Goddess

Mother of the World, and my motivation was tinged with another familiar yet exciting sensation: awe.

By mid-March, we arrived at the Rongbuk Glacier. We established base camp and began organizing and transferring supplies to yaks for the carry to advanced base camp at 18,400 feet. There we ran into a British climbing team led by premier British climber Chris Bonington. Bonington's group was going to attempt an untried route on the East Ridge of Everest. They planned to mount an alpine-style climb, a quick assault and retreat, using only six climbers. Bonington and his team joined us for tea and we swapped stories, then they continued on to their destination.

Our route up the Great Couloir was also an untried route. With no information from previous climbs to rely on, you have the added challenge of plotting your course by observing from below and by scouting to determine the route of your climb and the position of the higher camps on the mountain.

We began the enormous daily task of sorting and carrying food and supplies up the mountain. Camp I was established on April 1 at 18,800 feet. Only two days later, we had set up Camp II at 20,300 feet, at the base of the couloir. It had been only a two- or three-hour walk from Camp I, and would serve as our principal base of operations.

Camp III, at 22,300 feet, was essentially another walk from Camp II. Everyone on the team carried loads up the mountain, sometimes for ten and twelve days in a row. The rapid stocking of these upper camps was an outstanding example of teamwork.

A steep snow-and-ice face above Camp III necessitated putting in fixed ropes. It took the team four days to put in the route and, because of the difficult terrain, Camp IV ended up only 1,400 feet above Camp III, at 23,700 feet. At that point we realized that we'd need a total of six camps, instead of the five that we had originally planned.

The distances the team could travel in one day began to shorten. At high altitude, the body doesn't absorb nutrition properly and endurance is limited. We each had to maintain a daily intake of at least 6,000 calories and six quarts of water to prevent our muscles from deteriorating. It was very difficult to get up and get going in the morning. It took two or three hours to get dressed, get through breakfast, put on crampons and packs, and get roped up. We worked until late in the day and sometimes didn't make it back down to camp until dark. I set up a rotation schedule so that each climber could regularly descend below 20,000 feet, to diminish the effects of altitude and intense cold.

To get the most out of a team, I feel it's important to give each climber as much freedom as possible. Each must do a certain amount of leading on each new route on the mountain, in addition to a certain amount of load carrying. By the time the team has followed the rotation, put in the route, and carried loads to the upper camps, the selection of who is most qualified to be first to try for the summit often becomes obvious.

Even so, that selection is the most difficult decision that the team leader has to make. Each team member has his or her own opinion of who has performed well and who has not. The larger the group, the more difficult the decision becomes. As leader, I had the authority to make the final decision, but I liked to feel that the team was in agreement, or at least understood my reasoning.

It fell to Marty Hoey, Larry Neilson, and Jim Wickwire to make the first summit attempt up the Great Couloir. They were chosen for their strength, experience, and performance on the mountain to date. They would immediately move up to Camp V, spend the night, set up Camp VI around 26,500 feet the next day, then go for the top the following day. Dave Mahre would go in support and help break trail above Camp V.

As the only woman on the expedition, and one of a small circle of high-altitude female mountaineers, Marty Hoey was fully aware of the notoriety that her success on Everest could bring. In fact, before we had left on the expedition, she had admitted to me that she was a little concerned about the hoopla that could result. She wasn't seeking fame and fortune through her climbing. She climbed for the challenge and the joy it brought her. I climbed for the same reasons. That's why we had become soulmates.

Marty Hoey was a free spirit and, in her own way, had become the heart of the guide service. She was from a small town on the Kitsap Peninsula in Washington. She had come to Rainier right out of high school in 1969. She knew how to ski but was just getting started in the mountains.

Marty went to work as a cabin girl, but before I knew it she was climbing as well as cooking and doing other cabin-girl chores. She stood about five feet seven and had strong legs. We used to call her "Thunder Thighs," her legs were so muscular. She had no trouble carrying a big pack up the mountain. In 1973 Marty said to me, "I want to guide. You know I can do it." She was right. We relieved her of her cabin-girl duties and promoted her to guide. She turned out to be one of the finest climbers and guides, male or female, who ever worked at RMI. After a dozen years in the guide service, she had been a natural choice for the Everest team.

Marty was quietly competitive. She had great stamina and could climb as well as, if not better than, any of the guides, and would often challenge them. You wouldn't know it until you started walking uphill, then you'd notice that the pace had picked up a bit, then you'd notice that the pace had picked up a hell of a lot, and before you knew it you'd be in a race for some nearby peak or for the summit.

She was never competitive with clients. She had compassion and patience to spare, and all of the clients came back raving about Marty—except for one guy, who felt that Marty had dropped him in a crevasse too fast during a crevasse rescue practice. Marty had told him that we always drop clients that fast. But he had broken his ankle in the drop and took her to court. The judge was a climber. He told the guy, "If you don't think there's risk involved in climbing, you shouldn't be doing it," and threw the case out.

Marty was one hell of a package. She lived at the ranch in Ashford with the other guides. There she could keep and train a horse, which, along with climbing, was one of her passions. She had other interests too.

When Marty wanted to be attractive to someone, she could be very attractive. She went through the guides like wildfire. Every climbing season she'd pick a new lover. The guy would never see it coming, then *boom!* He was head-over-heels in love with Marty. Marty's life-style was a switch on the old rooster-in-the-henhouse story. At first I was concerned because she'd always pick my best guides. I thought jealousy alone would wreck the guide service.

But Marty handled her affairs skillfully and remained friends with all her lovers.

Marty had become best friends with both me and Ingrid. I think she viewed me as more of a father figure and Ingrid as more of a confidante. In any case, we three had shared many years of adventures together on Mount Rainier. It had been fun watching Marty mature from a young high school graduate into a mature young woman and full-fledged mountain guide.

It got to be amusing to me and Ingrid, figuring out who would be Marty's next "victim." We could spot the guy right away and we'd tell him, "Watch out, you're next." He'd say, "No way, not me." Then before you knew it, he was struck. Married or single, Marty wasn't particular. At one time or another, she had been involved with some of the greatest names in the American climbing community and turned down marriage proposals from several of them.

I had purchased a $100,000 life insurance policy on each climber on the 1982 Everest expedition. As her beneficiaries, Marty had listed ten RMI guides. To our great and everlasting sorrow, they all collected.

Late in the afternoon on the day of the summit attempt, we hadn't heard from the first team at the prearranged time and I started feeling that something had gone wrong. I finally got a call on the radio from Wick about seven o'clock that night. Marty was dead. She had somehow come out of her harness at 26,000 feet and fallen to her death.

Dave had paired up with Larry, and Wick and Marty had roped up together, to climb above Camp V and establish Camp VI. Larry and Dave had started out, fixing rope on the route up the steep ice slope above Camp V. They had stopped a little above 26,000 feet at a rock that was sticking out of the ice about waist high. Some of the equipment that had been carried up that high by other teams had been cached behind and on top of the rock. Dave and Larry picked up one spool of rope and started fixing line from that point up.

By the time Dave and Larry had climbed up about another 200 feet, Wick and Marty also had reached the rock. Dave called down for more rope. There was another spool of rope at the rock that had come unraveled and was a mess. Marty and Wick began to straighten it out. To save time, instead of unsnarling the tangled parts, they just cut them and retied the ends.

Dave told me later what happened next: "The wind was blowing spindrift and obliterating our visibility. Most of the time, we couldn't even see Marty and Wick. All of a sudden, we heard Wick yelling, but we couldn't make out what he was saying, the wind was blowing too hard. Then the wind quieted down and we heard him: 'Marty's gone, Marty's gone!' "

Larry and Dave pounded pickets into the snow to secure their gear, then descended to Wick. He was extremely emotional, blaming himself, but there was nothing he could have done. He wanted to go down and try to find Marty.

As the three men descended the fixed rope they could see, every 70 or 100 feet, a depression in the snow or ice where Marty had hit. At first it was just a polished spot and then later there were some blood stains, but farther down they lost all visible signs of where she had fallen.

It was a slow process to descend the Great Couloir. The ice there is extremely hard at the end of the pre-monsoon season. At about 24,000 feet, there is an ice cliff that Marty went over and dropped about 300 feet before she hit the slope again. In all, she fell about 6,000 feet to the bottom of the couloir, right down to the glacier.

Other Perspectives: Jim Wickwire

I wanted to get to know Dick Bass and Frank Wells better before we took off for Everest, so in January 1982 I joined a climb of Aconcagua in Argentina with them and one of my partners, Chuck Goldmark. Marty Hoey and George Dunn, who were also slated for the Everest expedition, came with me to guide the three inexperienced climbers.

I was really impressed with Marty. The six of us had been trying to reach the summit from 20,000 feet. Frank Wells began to have problems just walking on this not-too-steep ice and I said, "Let's get off the ice and go over here on the rocks and size this up." Marty turned to George and said, "Well, George, let's go for a little walk."

I told them I was going to lead everybody else back down to camp. Goldmark, Wells, Bass, and I returned to our camp while Marty and George took their "little walk." Late that afternoon, Marty and George came in looking beat but flushed with victory. They had made the summit.

The next morning, Bass and I headed up the Polish Glacier and had a marvelous climb to the summit. It was one of my best days in the mountains.

On Everest, I ended up pairing with Marty. She was very strong as a climber, physically strong and highly motivated. She was looked up to by everyone as being not just a woman, the only woman member of the team, but an equal partner, and she was actually stronger than several of the other team members.

She was clearly going strong enough to be considered for one of the summit teams. The first team ended up being me and Marty and Larry Nielson and Dave Mahre. Dave was supposedly there as support, but I think he was very ambitious for the summit and, had Marty's accident not occurred, it's quite likely that the four of us would have made a try for the summit the next day.

Marty got along with everybody. She was a good listener and she participated in the group discussions that Lou held in a way that allowed for everyone's view to come out and for everyone to feel like they had been able to participate in the decision making. She was one of a kind and really the glue of the expedition. She was instrumental, along with Lou, in sorting out any difficulties that arose among the team members.

After Camp V was established at 25,000 feet, Lou sent the first team up to try for the summit. The plan was to put in Camp VI, then continue to the summit the following day.

Late in the day, Marty and I had stopped to wait on a large rock on the forty-five-degree ice slope in the Great Couloir. We were probably at about 26,200 feet. Dave and Larry were a couple hundred feet above us, looking for a good site for Camp VI. Visibility was poor up above, but we heard them yell down for more rope.

There was a spool of fixed rope attached to the ice-screw anchor just above the rock. But it was snarled up and I had to do some cutting to get it ready. Marty had come up last. We had alternated *leads during the day. I figured it was her turn to go through, so I asked, "Do you want to take the rope up to them?" She said, "No, why don't you? It'll be faster."*

I started to put on my pack and Marty said, "Let me get out of your way." Then I heard a snap! and looked over to see her falling backwards.

I instantly yelled, "Grab the rope!" She was going down head first on her back and fumbled for the rope, which went directly down the fall line for about thirty feet before angling toward the side of the gully. She couldn't grab the rope. Once she was past that thirty feet of opportunity, she was gone. It was an absolute shock.

I looked back to my left and there was her ice axe and harness. The harness was lying there, open and attached to the fixed rope.

We hadn't been roped together, but had been tied in to the fixed rope. Apparently Marty had neglected to loop her harness belt back through the buckle, which would have prevented the belt from slipping out of the buckle. When she leaned back, it simply came undone.

After the expedition, we looked at several slides of Marty and noticed that in some of them she had doubled back her harness belt and in others she hadn't. She hadn't been consistent. About a week before the accident, she also had cut the leg loops off her harness because she felt that they weren't tight enough anyway and were just hanging there in the way. If she had left those on, those leg loops probably would have hung her up. It wouldn't have been this clean break where once you're loose you're gone.

I did a stupid thing at that point. Dave and Larry came down and they walked down the fixed rope, looking for signs of Marty. I walked right down the fall line, straight down, without being tied in. I found one of Marty's crampons and knew she was gone.

At the time of Marty's death, the team was isolated in small groups in different camps. We had radios, but only turned them on at designated times of the day to conserve the batteries. When I got the news about Marty, I was able to notify half the team right away. I couldn't reach the others until our prearranged radio call the following morning.

My message to the team members that night was to back off the climb. It was over.

The next morning, I led a team of climbers to the bergschrund at the bottom of the couloir to make sure that Marty wasn't lying out in sight. We figured she had gone into the 'schrund at the bottom of the wall. Before the climb we all had agreed that, if anything happened, we wanted to be left on the mountain. We left Marty there, at the base of Mount Everest.

After the rage came the disappointment, sadness, and incredible loneliness. I felt like the heart of the expedition had stopped beating. Many of us questioned whether mountaineering was something that we would follow in the future.

Dave Mahre was particularly despondent. He told me that, as an experienced guide, he felt that he, Larry, and Wick had overlooked their responsibility to check each other out. That was part of our regular routine on Rainier: double-check each other about locking your harnesses; check the webbing and make sure you ran it back through the buckle to safeguard yourself. Dave said to me, "We somehow forgot or overlooked our buddy system and Marty paid the price." Dave was being too hard on himself. This was not a summit climb on Rainier. We were pushing 26,000 feet on uncharted ground on Mount Everest. The Goddess Mother was granting us no slack.

That first night I lay awake in my sleeping bag, imagining the details of Marty's accident, replaying scenes of our trip through China and Tibet, replaying scenes of times with Marty on Rainier. I decided to quit climbing a dozen times, and decided to continue a dozen times more. I had called off the climb, then decided to go ahead with it, then called it off again. I thought of Ingrid and how the news would devastate her, and how I wouldn't be there to comfort her or to be comforted by her. None of the rescues I had been on, none of the deaths I had witnessed up to this moment had prepared me for the powerless, hollow feeling that overcame me when I realized that Marty Hoey was gone.

Morning brought the cold, clear realization that, at least for this moment, my life was going to continue. I was the leader of this expedition and I had to get on with my responsibilities. On Everest in 1963, after Jake Breitenbach died in the Khumbu Icefall on the second day of the climb, the team regrouped and went on to summit the mountain. I realized that I had a responsibility to the other climbers on this team. If they wanted to go on, they would have the chance.

I also realized this truth: Marty would want us to try again. I announced to the team that the climb was still on.

That day, Dave accompanied Wick down from Camp V. Larry waited there as Eric Simonson and George Dunn, the second summit team, made their way up from Camp IV to join him.

Eric, George, and Larry had to spend most of the next day trying to push above 26,000 feet to establish Camp VI. They got a late start and, at twilight, found themselves up fairly high when Eric got hit by a rock. It put a hole in his knee. He was hurting pretty badly, but they pushed on a little farther.

They found a shallow crack, a crevasse up high in a steep slope, and crawled into it. By then it was almost nine o'clock at night. Instead of setting up a tent, they huddled in their sleeping bags around a couple of stoves, melting snow for water and drinking liquids most of the night.

The next morning they started out for the summit. Larry led the rope, followed by Eric and George. Within a short time, Eric told Larry that he was not going to be able to go on. His knee was hurting badly and he was afraid that he was not going to be able to get back down on it. You've always got to be aware of that when you're up high in the mountains—will you be able to get down safely, or have you burnt all your bridges?

Eric and George decided to stop, but Larry unroped from them and headed out of the main couloir and into the rocks. He got to a ledge at about 27,500 feet and decided that the chances of falling were too great. He decided to descend. Later he told us that he had been overwhelmed at that point with thoughts of his family.

In the meantime, George and Eric had holed up again in the crack to rehydrate and rest Eric's knee before starting back down. Larry appeared shortly and said, "I've got to get down, my fingers are numb."

They descended together to Camp V. Eric and George decided to spend the night there. Eric was having a hard time walking and couldn't descend any farther. Larry, concerned about his fingers,

Lou and Chris Bonington at Everest Base Camp, 1982 (Photo: Jim Wickwire)

felt his way down the fixed ropes in total darkness. He descended a total of 4,200 feet to Camp III. There we discovered that both his hands and feet were severely frostbitten. He was also dehydrated from the long descent. His condition worsened and he eventually had to be evacuated on a sled to base camp.

The monsoon season was setting in and time was running out. A slight break in the weather gave us a final chance at the summit. Wick decided to try again, with George Dunn and Dave Mahre.

By then we had discovered that the British climb being led by Chris Bonington had turned back short of the summit after two of their team, Joe Tasker and Peter Boardman, had disappeared and were presumed dead. This news made me doubly anxious about my own climbers as they approached 24,000 feet and encountered severe weather.

I called Wick on the radio: "Jim, I've made a decision down here that I can live with and be real happy with. I hope you make the same one up there."

Wick replied: "The decision is probably easy to make. It's just that we all feel so goddamn much effort has gone into this thing. We also all want to come back alive, regretting the loss of one dear person."

"Your choice, whatever it is, is my choice."

I could feel the strain and emotion in Wick's voice, as he came back on the radio: "We'll turn our back on the summit of this mountain, knowing that seventeen gave it their best."

Although the dream of reaching the top had ended, there was a great feeling of relief that the struggle finally had come to an end.

Before we left Everest we built a memorial cairn to Marty, facing the mountains she had loved.

"When we lost Marty, we lost a lot of our spirit," I said at the memorial service we held before our departure. "Marty will always be remembered as a beautiful young person. She left us that way. The rest of us will age and sicken, but Marty will remain healthy and young in our minds, just as she was, a very strong, lively woman who gave our team the spirit and cohesiveness that it needed. We'll always think of Everest and Marty as well."

Other Perspectives: Eric Simonson

We were so young and so green on that 1982 trip. God, we worked hard on that climb. I swear I took only a handful of rest days over two months. I mean, we beat ourselves to a pulp. By the end of that trip, everybody had lost twenty, thirty pounds.

I was twenty-six then and I didn't know diddley-shit. All I knew was that Mount Everest is what I lived for. I thought this was the one and only shot that I'd ever get and I've gotta make it. Death or glory. Now, after having gone back three times in the past ten years, I've gained a better perspective.

There were a lot of expectations wrapped up in that climb. A lot

Lou carving Marty's memorial; Everest, 1982 (Photo: Jim Wickwire)

of media hype, with Bass and Wells involved. The melodrama of Marty's death. It was the first time that most of us had really dealt with any of this. It was a very broadening experience for me to come in contact with all these people, things, ideas. And then not to make the summit and go through the emotion of that and the emotion of losing Marty. It was a wrenching experience. It took a while afterwards to rationalize the defeat and the death. I had known Marty well.

When I first heard about Marty's death, I remember distinctly not being grieved or sad. George and I were at Camp IV, planning to move to Camp V the next day, work on setting up Camp VI, and then go for the summit. The news about Marty just didn't sink in until about a week later, down at base camp where we had our memorial service. There it finally just hit me, out of the blue, and I cried.

I went back to Everest in 1987 and camped there at the bottom of the North Wall, the same place I had been in 1982. I wondered if I'd be visited by Marty's spirit. I remember lying there several nights in the tent, willing myself into an open state of consciousness, making myself receptive and wondering, "Is she out there, is she out there?" Nothing happened. Not one iota of spiritual or otherworldly experience. I was very disappointed.

Lou and I clashed some on the 1982 trip. I was young and pretty hotheaded. In retrospect, I think he did a good job. I've since taken on the role of leading major expeditions myself and managing a bunch of egos and trying to juggle everything, and I have a lot more respect for Lou now.

I was always in awe of Lou. The first time I met him, I was in eighth grade. He sold me my first pair of skis, from Whittaker's Chalet. I broke my leg in those skis.

I first climbed Mount Rainier when I was fifteen and it was a life experience. I tried out for the guide service the summer I turned eighteen. In 1973, I was hired as an apprentice guide. I went to college and earned a master's degree, then worked as a geologist for a while. Eventually I came around to climbing and guiding full-time. I've been on about fifty expeditions and have led most of them myself.

Lou has been as much of a role model to me as my father. From the beginning, I was totally enamored of the freedom of Lou's life-style, of doing what you want, of not having to punch a clock every day, of being able to make a living mountaineering.

Lou's ability to change hats is incredible. He goes from being Ashford's good ol' boy one day to negotiating with the corporate types, to giving a lecture to a bunch of college kids in Memphis, to organizing a major expedition, to dealing with the guides. And then to having a private life with Ingrid. As I do more and more of the same in my own career, I realize how hard it sometimes is to switch gears.

Where Lou's strength lies is in organization and communication. On those expeditions, he didn't need to be out front leading because he had a bunch of dumb knuckleheads like me and the other guides who were more than willing. At the same time, to be able to stay in touch with what's going on and to manage the egos and to give people a sense of direction—I think he did a really good job.

When I finally summitted Everest in 1991 I felt, "Thank God, now I can get on with my life." Up until then, I damn near kicked every step of every trip I was ever on. I always felt the need to be out front and be super-much a part of every climb. In 1993, on an expedition I led to Shisha Pangma, another 8,000-meter peak in the Himalaya, I realized that I was perfectly happy to orchestrate the whole thing. It didn't really matter if I summitted myself. I enjoyed making contacts within the industry for sponsorship, arranging for the permit, dealing with the Chinese, the Sherpas, the guides. I loved the details and got a real kick out of watching the chaos of the trip come together into an organized plan. I realized then that Lou probably feels a similar satisfaction.

Commercial mountaineering trips such as those I lead nowadays to Everest and other choice peaks in the world are more common and pretty much set in routine. But those first Everest trips that Lou organized weren't commercial in the same sense. He had to start from the ground up and sell his vision. He's always been good at doing that. I think he deserves a lot of credit for elevating what we do to a more professional level.

◆ 12 ◆

EVEREST 1984:
CLOSING THE CIRCLE

O ne of the hardest things to contend with on an expedition, besides the deaths of expedition members, is the lack of communication with the outside world. Some of the more recent, highly
publicized expeditions have been able to afford high-tech communication equipment that has allowed them to place phone calls and
send faxes from their base camps. For example, in 1990 my brother
Jim led a generously funded "Peace Climb" to Everest that consisted of climbers from the United States, China, and Russia. As
soon as the climbers reached the summit, Jim placed a phone call
from Everest Base Camp to President Bush to deliver the news.

This is the exception rather than the rule. Most expeditions are
minimally funded and can only afford mail runs. Mail runs are no
small thing. They are among the most anxiously awaited events on
an expedition.

On the 1982 Everest trip, we had scheduled only two mail de-
liveries during the two months we were on the mountain. It was

Opposite: *Wind whipping across the ridge at 25,000 feet, above Camp
IV, where Lou's eyeballs froze (Team photo)*

a three-day drive by jeep to get to the north side of Everest from the nearest airport. The rent of the vehicle alone cost nearly $1,000, which pushed the total cost of each run to nearly $2,000.

In an emergency, we could send word out by jeep from base camp. That's what we did when Marty died. Unfortunately, the Chinese leaked the telegram I had composed to Marty's mother to Reuters news service and they put it out on the wire immediately. A neighbor heard the news and told Mrs. Hoey before she received my telegram. Later I confronted the Chinese and they denied having done it, although they added that it would never happen again.

The day I sent the telegram happened to coincide with a mail run. I received about eight letters from Ingrid and one from my mother. Mom told me that my father had died and that the funeral was over. When I had left for Everest, Dad had been in a nursing home, dying of cancer, but we had thought he'd hold on for another few months at least. He was almost ninety years old when he died.

In her letters, Ingrid sounded a little upset with me for having left her with so many responsibilities. In one letter, I learned that Win had totaled our new Chevy truck. He had come out of the wreck okay, but the truck was gone. In another letter, she informed me that we had made a mistake calculating our income tax and we now owed the IRS $7,000. The next letter from her, which I hesitated to open, told me that a friend of ours had committed suicide.

I read all this bad news and thought, "What the hell has gone wrong with my life?" After first losing Chris, then losing Marty, then not making the summit, then having a couple of climbers get hurt, and then receiving those letters, I wondered if all this was really worth it. It was the worst day of my life.

What we needed on that expedition was some comic relief. And Larry Nielson became the man who inadvertently provided it.

Larry was in such bad shape from the frostbite on his fingers and feet that he had to be carried off the mountain. After the numbness of frostbite wears off, horrendous pain follows, along with the danger of gangrene forming in the damaged tissue. Larry was lucky—he avoided gangrene, but he did lose some tissue after we returned to the United States.

We had a hell of a time getting Larry off the mountain. First we lowered him down to Camp I in a sled. Then we transferred him

*Lou carrying
Larry Nielson
off Everest,
1982 (Photo:
Jim Wickwire)*

to an empty frame pack and four of us took turns carrying him over the rocky scree from Camp I to advanced base camp. I carried him high, with most of his weight on my shoulders, and it scared him to death. When Gombu carried him, Larry's heels dragged on the ground. Gombu just walked happily along, singing a Tibetan song.

We finally ended up tying Larry to a yak. There was no saddle, so we used one-inch nylon tubing to strap Larry onto the animal. When we finished tying him down, we let go of the yak and it took off, madder than hell! The only way you can steer a yak is to throw rocks at it. So of course we all threw rocks, and most of them hit

Larry instead of the yak. Everyone was swearing, especially Larry, who got really ticked.

We gave up trying to catch the runaway yak, and went back for our packs, figuring that the yak would stop at the bottom of the hill. It took us about two hours to hike down. And there was the yak, grazing calmly, with Larry still aboard. He couldn't untie himself because his hands were so damaged, but he could be one mad guy. We rescued him from the yak.

Later Larry told us that the damn yak ride had been scarier than hanging off a ledge at 27,000 feet on Everest. All of us, including Larry, had a much-needed laugh over this escapade.

Larry Nielson showing frostbitten fingers and toes (Photo: Lou Whittaker)

In 1983, Larry went back to Everest and summitted without using supplemental oxygen. He became the first American mountaineer to do so. But the mountain had not given in easily. Larry lost thirty-five pounds, one of his toes ulcerated so badly that the bone was showing, he developed a clotting in his throat, he broke two ribs from coughing, and he got a pulmonary embolism just below the summit, where he threw up some blood. Larry is one tenacious guy, and he made it despite the heavy hand of Mother Nature.

Some people might say that men like Larry take unnecessary risks. Unnecessary to whom? Not to Larry. He chooses to live close to the edge, and he accepts the risks involved.

The members of the 1982 Everest climb had skirted the edge. Most of us had survived and went on to climb another day. A couple of the team members were so devastated by the experience that they quit climbing altogether. I think all of us were compelled afterwards to redefine our boundaries of risk.

Helen Keller said that avoiding danger is no safer in the long run than outright exposure to it. I believe that we all develop our own boundaries of risk. When you experience a tragedy, your first instinct is to draw back from that boundary, to protect yourself. But eventually your instinct draws you back out and determines when and where you will begin to risk yourself again, and how far you will reach beyond that boundary into the unknown. If you don't reach out, you stop learning and growing.

I knew that I would always mourn the loss of Chris and Marty, just as I would mourn the loss of all the people I had loved who had gone before me. At the same time, my instinct told me to go back. Everest was unfinished business.

Other Perspectives: George Dunn

It's odd to try to ascribe meaning to mountaineering. It's kind of a worthless endeavor when you think about it, hiking up and down a mountain and trying not to die. But to me, mountaineering is addicting. I've experienced such mental and physical highs and lows in the mountains that I know I could never follow a normal, mainstream life-style.

*Losing Marty in 1982 was really shattering to me. Her person-
ality was such a force in the guide service. I felt that the guide service
was altered after she was killed. It was never quite the same. Marty
used to say that she would never live beyond thirty. I knew she was
kidding. Her brother and sister had both died just before reaching
thirty. Marty died only a few days before her thirty-first birthday.
Some people think that she had a premonition of death when she
went on Everest, but I know she loved life and she certainly wasn't
seeking death.*

*I think she had a feeling that she was living life to the fullest and
she didn't know how she could continue it in her later years. She
used to joke with another cabin person, Darcy, about when all the
guides got old they'd retire in Italy and live together as friends, get
fat, and just be happy. I think she wondered, as we all do, what she
would do in her later years.*

*I plan to continue guiding and climbing as long as I am able.
Mountaineering gives my life meaning. You plan and live for some
goal in the future. And then when you get back from some huge
endeavor just physically and mentally wasted, life seems so great.*

*I give every climb the best effort I can and go as high as it is
possibly safe to go. On Everest in 1987, Eric Simonson, Ed Viesturs,
Greg Wilson, and I pushed it about as far to the limit as we could.
Eric and Ed got within 300 feet of the summit. They turned around
because they didn't feel like they could down-climb the last bit. We
had no regrets about turning around. How do you have regrets
about not dying?*

About a year after our return from the 1982 expedition, I began
to plan the 1984 American China–Everest Expedition. Once again
I secured a permit through the Mazama Club, this time for fall 1984.
We could only get a permit for the post-monsoon season, which
meant that there would be more snow on the mountain and less
rock and ice exposed on the route. The trade-off would come in
increased avalanche danger.

This time I selected a smaller team. There were seven of us from
the 1982 expedition: me, Phil Ershler, Jim Wickwire, George Dunn,
Dave Mahre, Ed Hixson, and Steve Marts.

On Wick's recommendation, I also invited John Roskelley, one of the world's most respected high-altitude climbers. At age thirty-five, John had already climbed three 8,000-meter Himalayan peaks—K2, Makalu, and Dhaulagiri—and had pioneered technically difficult routes on several other Himalayan mountains. John had a reputation as being fiercely independent and outspoken. On this climb he showed his strength as a great team player.

RMI guides Greg Wilson, age twenty-seven, John Smolich, age thirty-five, and my oldest son, Peter, rounded out the team of eleven climbers. At twenty-five, Peter had accumulated more mountaineering experience than I had at the same age. He was a strong, mature climber, but he'd had no experience in the Himalaya. I was looking forward to watching him cut his teeth on Everest.

Carolyn Gunn was hired as camp manager. She had worked for RMI as a cabin girl, she climbed, she worked as a veterinarian, she lived an all-around outdoor life-style. It would be her job to coordinate all our supplies at base camp, plan and oversee meals, and supervise the general well-being of the team.

We had many of the same sponsors as in 1982, and also picked up Wrangler, *Outside* magazine, Sweet Springs Press, and Shaklee. Shaklee donated vitamins.

We arrived at Everest Base Camp in September, accompanied by a trek that included my wife, Ingrid, Skip Yowell from JanSport, author Peter Jenkins, and Dan McConnell, who had done public relations for the team. They stayed at base camp for about a week, at which point our team began to move to the upper mountain. While the climb took place, Peter Jenkins traveled through China and afterwards wrote a book, *Across China*, that chronicled both the expedition and his adventures among the peoples of China.

We planned to follow the same route that we had attempted in 1982, up the Great Couloir. We were delayed for weeks in establishing our higher camps because of avalanche danger and winds. The video documentary produced after this climb by Steve Marts and Pal Productions, and narrated by John Denver, was aptly called "The Winds of Everest." We encountered incredibly harsh winds, worse than I had ever seen. At times you had to lie down in the snow to keep from getting blown off your feet by winds that would gust to more than 100 miles an hour. It sounded like a train was going to run over you.

One day we were at 24,800 feet, struggling up a steep ridge in

Lou and Ingrid saying goodbye at base camp; Everest, 1984 (Team photo)

the wind to carry supplies to Camp V, which we had established on October 8 at 25,000 feet. It was a clear, sunny day, but with the high winds we were getting tremendous, swirling ground storms. The blowing snow would whip across your face and obstruct your vision.

I was wearing sunglasses with goggles over them, but I began having trouble seeing. It finally got so bad that I couldn't see at all. At first I thought that my glasses had iced over. I lifted them and looked out and still couldn't see anything. I stopped on the ridge and coiled in the rope until Dave Mahre reached me. I asked him to look at my eyes. He said, "My God, they're frozen white."

Expending so much energy at that altitude and not using supplemental oxygen, my body temperature had dropped and, with the wind lashing at my face, my damn eyeballs had frozen! I had no choice but to descend to Camp IV. Greg Wilson and Dave helped me down. I called Ed Hixson on the radio to explain my condition. He said, "Lou, your *eye*balls are the second worst thing to freeze on the mountain!"

Then he added, "I think you're going to be all right. In Lake Placid, I had a drunk break the windshield out of his car and drive eight miles in 40-below weather. He froze his eyes and came out of it pretty well, although he later died of cirrhosis of the liver. Just take some painkillers so you can get some rest tonight."

I reminded Ed that I was in a tent at 23,000 feet without a first-aid kit. He said, "Well, Lou, you're going to have a tough night." He wasn't kidding. The pain was unbelievable, the worst I have ever experienced.

The next morning, I told Greg and Dave to head back up the mountain. I would just follow the fixed ropes down to Camp III and have somebody meet me there to lead me across the glacier. I bandaged my eyes and started down the rope. I had to rappel on the way down, but I was used to doing that. I fell a few times, but since my ascender was attached to the rope, I could hang from it until I regained my footing, then continue on down. At the bottom of the rope, George Dunn, John Smolich, and Phil Ershler met me and helped me the rest of the way to Camp III.

I was nearly blind for a week before I gradually began to regain my sight. Fortunately, there was no permanent damage. It just hurt like heck for a few days, then finally let up. It was the weirdest thing that had ever happened to me.

In the meantime, Phil Ershler, George Dunn, and John Smolich had set out as a team, with the goal of establishing Camp VI in the protection of the Great Couloir. They traversed the North Face from Camp V, looking for a tent that had supposedly been left by an Australian team that had gone up the route a few weeks before. They couldn't find the tent and went too far too late in the day. They wanted to descend then but, by radio, Roskelley advised them against it. "You're good mountaineers," he said to Ershler, "you know you can keep each other alive if you bivouac there tonight and come down in the morning. If you try to climb down in the dark, you'll kill yourselves."

After much discussion, they took Roskelley's advice and bivouacked that night. The weather was too extreme to light stoves to melt snow. George began to vomit and became dehydrated. Smolich also got sick. Neither one could eat any food. The next morning, they made their way slowly down to Camp IV. Smolich was spitting blood on the descent from coughing so hard. He recovered but was out of commission for the remainder of the climb.

George's condition worsened. He couldn't hold down liquid or food. We set him up on an I.V., put him on oxygen, and helped him down to Dr. Ed Hixson at base camp for treatment, a move that ended up saving George's life.

At first Ed couldn't find George's blood pressure, he was in such bad shape. George took ten liters of intravenous fluid that night. We hung an insulated I.V. bottle at the peak of the tent and ran the tube down through a pot of heated water on a Coleman stove and then into George's arm. Ed Hixson stayed up all night to keep the stove going so that the fluid wouldn't freeze or enter George's body at too cold a temperature. Two days later, George was up and eating a bowl of red-hot chili. We later learned that he had been suffering from a stress ulcer.

John Smolich did a great job for us on Everest in 1984. A year later, in June 1985, John was gone. He was leading a climb on K2 and got swept away by an avalanche. I sent his family a beautiful photograph of K2 in full moonlight and told them, "This is the view that John now has."

I am continually reminded how hard death is on those who are left behind. It hurts and it's hard to reconcile yourself to the fact that the people you loved won't be around anymore. Fate has moved its huge hand and you had no control over it at all.

On October 20, 1984, after four summit attempts, the hand of fate finally allowed us to gain the summit of Everest. I had chosen John Roskelley, Jim Wickwire, and Phil Ershler as the final summit team. My son Peter was strong and looking good, but I opted for the experience of the other three. It was a hard decision to make because I knew that Peter wanted a shot at the summit. Instead he did an incredible job of supporting the summit team by leading another team through an extremely technical traverse to put in a

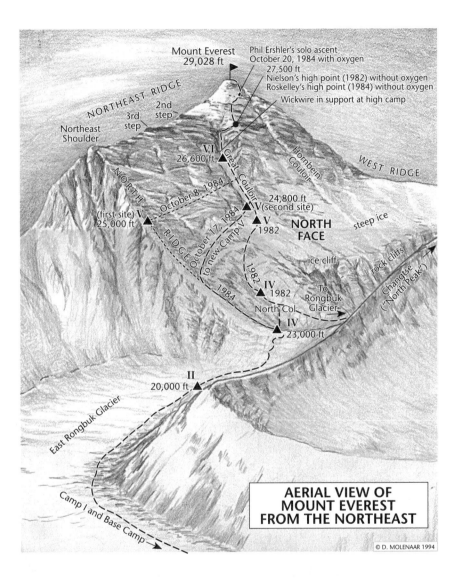

Mount Everest
29,028 ft

Phil Ershler's solo ascent
October 20, 1984 with oxygen
27,500 ft
Nielson's high point (1982) without oxygen
Roskelley's high point (1984) without oxygen
Wickwire in support at high camp

NORTHEAST RIDGE

2nd step

3rd step

Northeast step
Shoulder

NORTH

VI
26,600 ft

Great Couloir

Hornbein Couloir

WEST RIDGE

October 8, 1984

24,800 ft
V (second site)

(first site) V
25,000 ft

RIDGE October 17, 1984

(to new Camp V)

V
1982

NORTH
FACE

steep ice

ice cliff

rock cliffs

IV
1982

To
Rongbuk
Glacier

Changtse
("North Peak")

1982

1984

North Col

IV
23,000 ft

II
20,000 ft

East Rongbuk Glacier

Camp I and Base Camp

**AERIAL VIEW OF
MOUNT EVEREST
FROM THE NORTHEAST**

© D. MOLENAAR 1994

new Camp V. The winds had raked through the old Camp V and blown away our food bags. Peter and his team set up a new Camp V at 24,800 feet, in the couloir.

Ershler, Wick, and Roskelley climbed to the new Camp V, then pushed to 26,600 feet the next day and wedged a small tent beneath a rock and called it Camp VI. From there, they would make their summit attempt.

On their first attempt, all three were turned back when Roskelley began to get dizzy and couldn't maintain his balance. When they reported in on the radio, I was ready to call off the climb, but Roskelley argued against it. He believed that his dizziness was the result of a couple of codeine pills he had taken the night before to treat the pain of some old frostbite injuries. He said he was sure he'd feel well enough in the morning to try again.

There was only one bottle of oxygen among the three climbers. The second bottle had been swept away in a small avalanche. Roskelley's climbing ethic forbade the use of supplemental oxygen, so that left Ershler and Wickwire to decide who would use the single bottle. Wick felt that Ershler was the stronger climber, so Wick volunteered to stay behind in Camp VI while Ershler and Roskelley made a go for the summit the next morning.

They had reached about 27,500 feet when Roskelley decided to turn around. He was becoming hypothermic. Without oxygen, the fire goes out inside your body. Your extremities are the first to freeze. Roskelley told us later that he could feel his body core temperature dropping and that he was shivering uncontrollably. Ershler wanted to go back down with him. As a professional guide, Ershler's natural instincts are to care for his climbing partner. But Roskelley urged him to keep on to the summit. "In three weeks, when you're back home," said Roskelley, "you'll hate yourself for turning around."

It was Phil Ershler's third attempt at the summit of Mount Everest and he made a heroic solo ascent of the last 1,500 feet. On the summit, he buried the mouthpiece from Chris Kerrebrock's horn in the snow, then took time to say goodbye to Marty Hoey. Ershler expressed the feelings of the entire team when he later commented, "It was time to close a couple of circles."

◆ 13 ◆

KANGCHENJUNGA: THE FIVE
TREASURE HOUSES OF THE SNOWS

Our success on Everest in 1984 created lots of publicity. I was interviewed by Bryant Gumbel on NBC's "Today" and by several other talk-show people. The University of Colorado saw one of these shows and in 1985 invited me to lend my climbing expertise to the Rio Abiseo Project, an archaeological dig of a pre-Incan site called the Grand Pajatan. Located in tropical cloud-forest wilderness in Peru, the ruins had been discovered by explorer Gene Savoy in 1963. The dig was being done in cooperation with the Peruvian government in a site on the eastern slopes of the Andes in what is now a national park called Rio Abiseo.

We went in the summer of 1985. I was able to take Ingrid with me, as well as Greg Wilson, one of my guides who spoke Spanish. Carolyn Gunn, our camp manager from the Everest climb, also accompanied us, along with Pamela Roche-Taylor, who worked for one of our sponsors, Allied Fibers. Once again, JanSport was the major sponsor of the trip.

The plan was to locate and map several burial sites on a 1,000-foot, nearly vertical limestone cliff covered with thick vegetation. The tombs were in caves and beneath overhangs covered by foliage. We spent three weeks at the site and discovered about twenty tombs.

We worked with a well-known archaeologist, Tom Lennon of the University of Colorado, and with a Peruvian journalist named Barbara d'Achille, who was covering the dig for a Lima newspaper. While the group explored and excavated ruins among the 400 buildings and temples of stone that had been discovered under the vegetation at the base of the cliff, Greg and I climbed the cliff, looking for tombs and recording their locations with a chart and a Polaroid camera.

One of the tombs we found on the cliff was incredible. It was two stories high. Lining the roof outside were six wooden, nude male statues, all showing an enhanced penis. When we first saw these statues, I said to Barbara, "Looks like the guy was a king looking forward to the future life, with all these statues and phallic symbols around the tomb."

She said, "What makes you think it wasn't a woman looking forward to her future life?"

That made me stop and think, "Why not?"

We couldn't get to all the tombs. A thirty-foot overhang of vegetation on top of the cliff blocked our way. I hacked through the foliage with a machete and tried to come down from above, and then up from below. Greg and I traversed from each side, but we couldn't reach one of the tombs that we knew was there. The rope between Greg and me tangled in the vegetation when we belayed or leapfrogged, so we ended up doing some high-angle, unroped vine and shrub climbing and getting a good scare when a large tropical bird would suddenly burst from the foliage. I did find some vases and other artifacts, which helped Tom determine that they had unearthed a pre-Inca civilization, more than 3,000 years old.

What was especially exciting to Tom was that the area had been unpolluted by subsequent civilizations. Therefore, the artifacts would more accurately reveal the life-style of the original people—including what they had eaten and what diseases they had suffered.

Since 1983, a terrorist group known as the Shining Path had been on an increasingly violent rampage throughout much of Peru. Three years after we left, a couple of the people from the dig were killed. One of them was Barbara. The terrorists had rounded up a bunch of local natives and threatened to kill them. Barbara bravely stepped in front of the group and said, "Don't shoot these people." The terrorists shot her instead.

During our work together, Tom had told me that he'd be happy to spend the rest of his life in this humid, mosquito-infested climate, digging in the dirt and mud for artifacts. That's his calling and he loves it. Archaeologists are tough. I gratefully returned to my calling, guiding on the snow- and ice-covered slopes of Mount Rainier.

After returning from Peru, I began organizing an expedition that had been brewing in my mind since our first attempt on Everest, and one for which Nawang Gombu had been a prime motivator: Kangchenjunga, at 28,146 feet the third-highest mountain in the world.

In 1983, we applied for two permits, one for Kangchenjunga, the other for Namche Barwa. At that time, Namche Barwa was the highest unclimbed mountain in the world—7,782 meters, or 25,531 feet. This mountaineering "plum" is located in Tibet at the eastern end of the Himalaya in an area of heavy snow and high avalanche danger. The mountain features a dangerous headwall almost 2,000 feet tall. Several countries had been vying for the first permit. We had heard at one time that the Japanese, who had been bidding for it for years, had suggested a permit fee of $1 million, just to keep certain countries out of the bidding.

The Chinese had unsuccessfully tried Namche Barwa twice. I wanted to do a joint climb with the Chinese, but our negotiations were endlessly hung up in political goings-on. The Chinese finally hooked up with the Japanese in the fall of 1992, and made a joint climb of the peak. It took them three attempts, but they summitted just before the Japanese emperor's historic first visit to China.

At the same time that we were dealing with the Chinese for the Namche Barwa permit, we also were working with India to grant us a permit to climb Kangchenjunga from the Sikkim side. Kangchenjunga is located in the Himalayan range, in Nepal on the border with Sikkim. The mountain actually has five summits and is known to the Nepalese as the "Five Treasure Houses of the Snows." At the time, it had never been climbed by an American team. Seventeen nations had tried the mountain, sixty-three people had been to the summit, and twenty-two from eight different countries had died trying.

I asked Senator Ted Kennedy to write a letter on my behalf to then Prime Minister Indira Gandhi. She became fascinated with the project and invited us to climb, but was assassinated before she could witness the results of our expedition in 1989.

(A similar thing had happened to Prime Minister Bhutto of Pakistan in the seventies. Bhutto had gone to Harvard with Ted Kennedy, and Ted had written to Bhutto to help get us the permit to climb K2 in 1975. When we came off the mountain, the American ambassador said, "You guys better get out of here. Things are really shaky, so don't count on a visit from Bhutto. It looks like there might be a coup." Soon afterwards Bhutto was jailed. In 1979 he was hanged. Politics is a very dangerous sport—in many ways, more dangerous than mountaineering.)

We wanted to climb the north side of Kangchenjunga, but a Russian team had already secured a permit to climb it in the spring of 1989. We settled instead for a permit to climb the south side during the fall of 1989. Then, to our delight, the Russian team contacted us, asking if we'd like to switch sides. Their goal was to climb all five summits, and that could only be done from the south side. They planned to make their assault in the spring with 40 climbers and 1,000 porters.

We agreed readily, even though it meant accelerating our expedition plans and giving ourselves only six months to organize the trip, instead of the usual year that I like to have. Our consolation was being able to access the north side of the mountain, which was rated as difficult as Everest.

Once again, we rounded up our major sponsors from the Everest climbs, added several others, and also sold T-shirts and sweatshirts. A total of thirty-five companies donated equipment and food. This time the American Alpine Club represented the American climbing community as official sponsor of the expedition.

We also received $80,000 from four Indonesians from Djarkarta who wanted to learn how to climb in the Himalaya. They spent three months with us and got to 22,000 feet. The money they contributed paid for the cleanup of the climb.

EDWARD M. KENNEDY
MASSACHUSETTS

United States Senate
WASHINGTON, D.C. 20510

May 17, 1983

Her Excellency
Madame Indira Gandhi
Prime Minister of India
New Delhi

Dear Madame Prime Minister:

I am writing to you on behalf of a close personal friend,
Mr. Louis W. Whittaker, who recently submitted a proposal to
the Indian Mountaineering Federation for a joint Indian-American ascent of Kanchenjunga, the world's third-highest mountain
and one which has never been climbed by Americans.

I understand that there may be security considerations
which could complicate Mr. Whittaker's proposal to approach
Kanchenjunga from the Sikkim side, but I would greatly appreciate your government's giving this application every possible
consideration. I can personally vouch for Mr. Whittaker as a
man of fine character and great ability who would be fully cooperative with Indian authorities. Therefore, I too would be
enormously pleased if he were given permission to pursue this
joint Indian-American expedition. A copy of the application
submitted to the Indian Mountaineering Federation is enclosed.

I recall with pleasure our useful conversation during your
visit to the United States last year, and cannot help but view
the Whittaker proposal as the kind of joint Indian-American
undertaking which could do much to strengthen bilateral understanding and cooperation. I hope you will agree.

With warm personal regard and appreciation,

Sincerely,

Edward M. Kennedy

Letter from Ted Kennedy

Kangchenjunga
28,168 ft

The
Castle

▲ V
26,000 ft

North IV
Col ▲
24,000 ft

N O R T H   F A C E

▲ III
22,000 ft

20,000 ft ▲ II

**KANGCHENJUNGA
FROM THE NORTH**

I ▲
18,000 ft

To Base
at 16,200 ft

© D. MOLENAAR 1994

The Kangchenjunga climbing team included me, Gombu, and several RMI guides, including George Dunn, Larry Nielson, Robert Link, Craig Van Hoy, Phil Ershler, Ed Viesturs, Greg Wilson, Jim Hamilton, and Eric Simonson. With so many qualified guides available, and many of them with Himalayan experience, the problem was not in choosing whom to take, but how to avoid insulting those we had to pass over.

Skip Yowell of JanSport also joined the team and Dr. Howard Putter became team physician. John Roskelley and Jim Wickwire came on board at the last minute after a climb they had planned to Menlungtse fell through. They took me up on the invitation to join our expedition. John had made an attempt on the north side of Kangchenjunga a few years before, and we would benefit from his knowledge of the route.

Our approach to the mountain was complicated by political problems in Nepal. We first sent Craig Van Hoy over in late February, followed by Eric Simonson in early March, to set up logistical support and staff and to arrange for local provisions. The remainder of the team arrived in Kathmandu on March 18 and flew to Taplejung on March 21, where we met Craig. Eric remained behind to expedite the 3,500 pounds of food and equipment that were stuck in Calcutta.

We had chosen to ship our gear by boat for $1,500, instead of paying the $30,000 it would have cost to send it by air. Then we found out that the ship would be three weeks late. On top of that, India imposed a boycott on Nepal and things got complicated in a big way.

We nearly had to cancel the expedition because of the deteriorating political situation. We ended up buying as much gear as we could find in Kathmandu and heading for base camp. If we stayed in Kathmandu, we had no chance of making the mountain. It was better to take our chances, go to base camp, and pray that the rest of the gear would arrive in time. We had to live off local food on the trip in. As a result, most of the team got diarrhea and were quite sick by the time they reached base camp on April 6.

Gombu and I stopped three days short of base camp, in Gunza, a small village at 11,000 feet with an unreliable Morse-code telegraph key to Kathmandu. We waited there a week, telegraphing Eric for status reports on our equipment, but all we got were sketchy reports, rumors, and speculations from the evening Radio Nepal broadcasts. We didn't know what the hell was going on. We did know that if our equipment came, it would be flown to Gunza. So we waited.

Eric Simonson had traveled all over the world leading his own expeditions. He was, and is, very adept at moving equipment through difficult situations. Because we couldn't rely on the telegraph key in Gunza, Eric sent us progress reports by runner, but each runner arrived several days after Eric had written the message, so we really had no idea if we'd ever get our gear.

After working a bit of behind-the-scenes magic with some crucial palm-greasing of government officials, border guards, and gas-station attendants, Eric was finally able to get half the gear released from India, passed through customs, and flown by a Nepalese army helicopter into Gunza. At one point he had gone from truck number 800 in line at the border to truck number 3 when he had taken one of the border officials into a bathroom and given him $500 in cash.

The practice of bribery actually enables you to get things done. You know that when you hear an official say, "It's impossible," the expected rejoinder is, "How much will it take to make it possible?" We always build into our expedition budgets funds to cover these "impossibilities."

To squeeze in a few more boxes of provisions, Eric had given up his seat on the army helicopter. That meant he also gave up his position on the team. It was a great sacrifice on his part, and one that enabled us to succeed.

Gombu was our other ace in the hole. He acted as interpreter and liaison, he hired porters and cooks, and then he kept them all in line. Without him we'd have suffered even more frustration. When our gear arrived in Gunza, he helped me arrange for porters to carry it into base camp.

Eric had decided to send more rope in place of butter, so we had to do without that essential food. With the equipment we did receive in Gunza—about half of what we had originally shipped from the United States—and the equipment we had purchased in Kathmandu, we figured we had enough to mount our assault.

Ingrid had organized a nine-person trek into Kangchenjunga, and they arrived a few weeks after we had set up base camp. They had a wonderful trek, with great weather and without the hassles and hang-ups that the climbing team had experienced. They hiked over relatively pristine terrain, passed through villages of happy, healthy children, traversed hillsides covered in flowering trees, and walked through massive rhododendron forests.

Ingrid and her trekking group spent only three days at base camp with us before hiking back out. George Dunn's wife, Nancy, had come on the trek. As soon as she arrived, George asked me if he could move his tent about a half mile down into the valley, away from the gathering of tents at base camp. He and Nancy had only been married for about a month, and they wanted to relish their three days of privacy. We later gave George a lot of ribbing about his romantic interlude.

By usual trekking standards, Ingrid's trek was a long journey: a round trip of 240 miles in thirty-three days. When it came time for Ingrid to leave, it was harder to say goodbye to her at base camp than it had been at home.

On this trip, we also acquired a mascot. A few years before, after the 1984 Everest climb, Peter Jenkins had given Skip Yowell an Alaskan malamute dog as a gift. It was strong and husky and reminded Skip of his strong, husky friend Gombu. So Skip named the dog "Gombu," not realizing that, to a Sherpa, having a dog named after you is not a compliment.

On the hike to base camp, a little black puppy followed us all the way in and made itself at home. Craig Van Hoy gave it a bath to disinfect it, and it quickly became used to all the attention—and food—showered on it by a bunch of homesick climbers. Gombu came up to me the first day in base camp and said, "Lou, this dog's name is Skip."

Skip was a faithful, loving companion to us throughout the climb. Afterwards, he followed us back out of base camp and took up residence in one of the high villages. By the time we left, Skip understood English, but I doubt that anyone has since told him to sit or roll over in Nepalese.

Our experiences on Everest in 1982 and 1984 had shown us how to climb without Sherpas, relying only on our own resources. I had planned to also climb Kangchenjunga without Sherpas, but several of Gombu's Sherpa friends came in to base camp after we had arrived and offered to assist on the climb. Of course we welcomed their help.

To set up our high camps on Kangchenjunga, we used porters to help stock Camp I, and six of the Sherpas to help with the difficult carry to Camp II. Above Camp II, only three of the six Sherpas were able to handle the technical climbing and only two of them carried a load to Camp V.

In mid-April, during the establishment of Camp II, I discovered that the ten oxygen cylinders that had been flown to Gunza by the Nepalese army did not fit our regulators. Without oxygen our hopes of gaining the summit became very slim.

I had done the Russians a favor by switching sides of the mountain. Now I needed a favor from them. I dispatched a porter to the south side of the mountain. He had to travel a foot trail around the base of the mountain, about ninety miles one way. With Wick's help, I composed a letter to Ed Myslovsky, the Russian team leader, asking if he would sell us six oxygen bottles and two regulators. I included $3,000 with the note.

Knowing that it could be three weeks or even longer before we received a reply, we got back to work establishing Camp III. John Roskelley played a crucial role in establishing the route to Camp III at 21,500 feet and Camp IV at 24,000 above the North Col. This was the crux of the climb, involving more than 3,000 feet of very difficult climbing, much of it nearly vertical. It was a more difficult route, but it was safer than climbing in icefall and avalanche areas.

We preferred the near-vertical wall to the ledges that created hanging glaciers that, in turn, created icefalls. Hanging glaciers and icefalls are called objective hazards, and you can get killed real easily climbing in those areas. We knew that Kangchenjunga normally received a lot of snowfall, even during the pre-monsoon season. Our climb had begun pre-monsoon, in late spring, when there was less buildup of snow and ice. But each day we were delayed pushed us closer to the monsoon season and the arrival of heavy storms.

On a steep wall, snowfall only accumulates about an inch deep before it sloughs away and cleans off the wall. On a wall like this, it's your own ability—or lack of it—that will kill you, rather than objective hazards. We preferred to trust our own ability and tackle the wall.

Our climbing team fixed nearly 4,000 feet of rope on this section. A fixed rope allows you to get back down quickly if the weather changes or you run out of time. You don't rappel because the rope is anchored to the wall. You attach your ascender, move down to the next anchor, switch your ascender to the other side of the anchor and move on down to the next anchor, and so on. You can descend several thousand feet very quickly this way. And when you're carrying a load back up, the fixed rope gives you the extra anchor and security you need. You don't have to rely as heavily on climbing technique.

Fixing that rope was also key to the success of the climb. It takes time to place that much rope, and we spent two weeks getting it all in. The climbers agreed that it was some of the most difficult climbing that they had ever done on a high mountain. It was technical ice climbing at its most challenging, requiring several hours of continual front-pointing.

After Camp IV had been established on May 10, Jim Wickwire contracted pneumonia and had to descend. I agreed with Jim's decision to leave the mountain, and John Roskelley decided to leave with him. Their departure left it up to our team of RMI guides to finish the job.

With everything that had gone wrong for us—the delay of equipment and food, and people getting sick—if we hadn't had a compatible team we probably wouldn't even have made it to base camp. We had all climbed and worked together on Mount Rainier for many years. Many of us had been on other expeditions together and had been through some stressful situations and higher danger. As guides, we were used to relying on each other. Instead of drawing apart on Kangchenjunga, we became even more close-knit. One of the climbers likened it to a commando group going in under high risk. The climbers were so well trained and worked so well together that they were able to quickly overcome any obstacles they encountered. With a group like that I didn't really need to lead.

Other Perspectives: John Roskelley

I've been with quite a few other leaders on different types of climbs and large expeditions. I think there have been expeditions that have failed because of the leadership. Despite the expertise of the

climbers you might have on an expedition, leadership is crucial to success. I've been on two expeditions with Lou, and he's impressed me with his ability to relate to people. He gets along well with the climbers, he takes into consideration the whole group, the strength of the group, their weaknesses, their technical abilities, and he puts all of this into some equation of his that seems to work every time.

Lou is in the unique position of being an expedition leader with the majority of the climbers under his employ, which is an advantage in some ways. I was very impressed with the guides he chose to go on Everest and Kangchenjunga. They were very strong, very determined, and good team players.

On Everest in 1984, it was pretty commendable that Lou didn't choose his son over Phil Ershler for the last push. Phil had had his chance, really. He had been on Everest twice before and I think that's why Lou let him go again. Lou could have said, "All right, Peter, it's your turn." Peter was really strong, and definitely summit material. It was a tough decision and Lou deserves a lot of credit for having made it.

On that 1984 Everest expedition, Lou had no problem with my climbing without oxygen in a group of people who were determined to climb to the top of Everest with oxygen. To me, getting to the summit is not as important as how you get there. That's my own ethical baggage. Lou was able to accept me as an individual and accept my differences, and also keep all the other people on the climb focused in one direction. Some leaders have a tendency to lose that focus and allow their team to also lose focus. With the kind of people Lou chooses to climb with—his guides and others who are generally self-sufficient, self-driven, and determined—it can be hard to hold a group like that in a straight line toward a common goal. I haven't seen anybody in the American climbing scene do a better job than Lou.

When I think about Lou, I see a guy with a great big smile on his face, a laugh as big as he is, and a person very sure of himself.

Opposite: *Phil Ershler front-pointing on ice wall at 23,000 feet; Kangchenjunga, 1989 (Photo: George Dunn)*

Meeting him, you come away knowing that this guy knows where he wants to be in life.

Lou loves people. I saw that in Tibet and Nepal. He gets around the "common folk" of these villages and he's lovable. And they love him back. He's not afraid to touch or hug them, where a lot of people will not touch them. They've got a lot of yak smell to them, they wear old, stained, and licey-looking clothes. Lou would never embarrass another person.

On Kangchenjunga, I had a hard time with the Sherpas carrying loads on the mountain. I know the climbers were doing a certain amount of work, too, but there were days when the Sherpas were carrying loads to the higher camps. It was difficult for me to take because it's not the Sherpas' goal to get to the summit, it's our goal. To use oxygen or have Sherpas carry loads for me is not part of my climbing ethic. But that wasn't Whittaker's baggage, it was mine. I had done almost all the leading on that face. I'd been to 26,000 feet on a climb on that mountain a few years before and I knew the route really well. Once I set my mind on an expedition, I pretty much follow through on it. This time, on Kangchenjunga, I felt torn because I wanted to get that peak, but I couldn't sit there and be a bummer to the whole expedition. Either you get out or you live with it. I have to walk my talk, so I chose to get out.

On 8,000-meter mountains, the decision to use or not to use oxygen usually determines the success of a climb. From a leader's viewpoint, I had to take into consideration John Roskelley's earlier request on the 1984 Everest expedition to climb without oxygen, and how the other team members would react to his request. John is really a hell of a strong climber, one of the best in the world, and, unlike some misguided critics have written, a great team player. I had told John that I'd like him on Kangchenjunga with us, without oxygen—or even without clothes—whichever way he wanted it. He had been key to our Everest 1984 success, and I hoped that he could give us some time on Kangchenjunga.

Generally, if you don't use oxygen at higher altitudes, you risk frostbite and the sacrifice of some toes and fingers. At higher altitudes, oxygen also helps boost your energy and keeps you from getting rummy. On Kangchenjunga, we were blessed with good weather in between some big storms. Our late start had placed us closer to the monsoon season, so we knew we'd be getting some storms. But during the streaks of good weather, you could sometimes go above 24,000 feet without gloves or a face mask. It was nice to be able to stand at Camp IV at 24,000 feet with a cup of coffee in your bare hands and not get blown all over the place.

By the time Roskelley and Wick left, we began to feel an urgency to get to the summit before the monsoon season set in. The ascent of the final summit pyramid involved more difficult technical climbing. Several storms lashed the team as they fixed rope up a prominent rock step on the north ridge called "The Castle." Time was running out. We needed oxygen if we were to press on to the summit.

Luck was on our side. During the first week of May, less than three weeks after I had dispatched him to the south side of the mountain, our porter returned with two other porters and a letter from Myslovsky. It read, "We think that the air is not to sell. It doesn't depend on whether it is the air from Moscow or Seattle, so we are happy to send you some air from Russia." Myslovsky had sent the extra porters to help carry six bottles of oxygen and two regulators. In his letter, Myslovsky asked that we bring the empties back to Kathmandu at the end of the climb. He also enclosed our $3,000 and added, "If something will be lost, don't worry—you'll be able to pay the penalty in whiskey.... We hope to celebrate together our ascends!" Both our teams were due to arrive back in Kathmandu around the end of May.

The Russian oxygen bottles were made of titanium and were incredibly lightweight, about seven pounds each, compared to ours, which weighed about eighteen pounds each. Myslovsky had shown one of the porters how to use the regulators and he, in turn, showed us. We were back in business.

To pick the first team, I looked at who had been climbing well together. A sort of natural selection had occurred just from working together on the mountain, and the climbers had already divided into smaller teams of two and three. We had two, and possibly three, waves of teams ready to attempt the summit.

The first team of Larry Nielson, Greg Wilson, and Robert Link

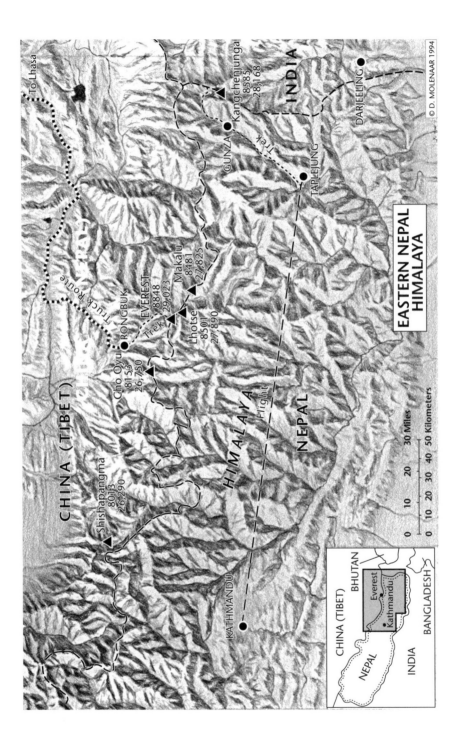

EASTERN NEPAL HIMALAYA

© D. MOLENAAR 1994

got stuck at Camp IV for five days during a bad storm. At that altitude, they grew weaker each day and eventually had to bail out and let the second team come up for a try.

The second team, Phil Ershler, Craig Van Hoy, and Ed Viesturs, got a break in the weather and easily made it to 26,000 feet to establish Camp V on a beautiful, calm evening. They radioed down to base camp and said that it looked good for the summit the next day. It was. On May 18, they reached the top of Kangchenjunga. Phil used oxygen, but Ed and Craig made it without.

I was especially happy for Craig, because the week before he had told me that he wasn't ready to attempt the summit. He thought it was too dangerous. I worked on him for several days. I finally asked him, "When we leave the climb, will you feel that you gave it everything you had?" He decided to go for it, and did a great job.

The second team's success inspired the first team to give it another try. The weather blew back in and it looked like they would be jinxed again. On May 21, the day of their summit attempt, all we could see from down below were clouds and snow blowing around the peak. It didn't look good. We got a radio call at seven that night from Larry Nielson. He said, "Lou, we had the worst weather, the worst wind, the snow was really deep and crusted up higher. We just gave it our best shot. Do you copy that?"

"Yes, I copy."

Then Larry added, "But, Whittaker, we made it!"

Incredible! Six Americans to the top of the third-highest mountain in the world. And all six had honored the belief of the native peoples, that the gods dwell on the summit of Kangchenjunga and to tread on the highest point would offend them. All the climbers had stayed several feet below the actual uppermost point of the summit. They reported that the Russian climbers who had made it to the top appeared to have done the same.

The religious beliefs of different native populations are very interesting. After we first reached base camp, one of the Sherpas had started limping with a bad hip. He caught a chicken that had been carried in and rubbed it against his hip in the belief that would make the pain go away. The next day he was no longer limping. I don't know if the chicken was limping instead, because it was missing.

Whatever garbage we couldn't burn was to be carried off the mountain. We had cleaned up every climb since K2 in 1975 and, on Kangchenjunga, we hired eighty porters from Gunza, both men and women, to help with the carry. The day before we were to begin carrying out gear and garbage, the porters came up to our camp to spend the night. It snowed during the night and, at one time, I thought I heard a baby crying. The next morning, Gombu said that he had heard it too. We discovered that one of the women porters had had no one in the village to care for her four-month-old baby, so she had brought it with her to 17,000 feet, wrapped in a basket that she had strapped on top of her pack basket.

The porters secure their pack baskets with a single strap, called a tump line, around their foreheads. All of the loads weighed 50 to 55 pounds—we weighed each one and paid the porter according to the size of the load. Imagine all that weight pulling at your head! A couple of our climbers tried it, but couldn't balance the load. The native mother, who weighed less than 100 pounds herself, carried a 55-pound load off the mountain, with her baby strapped up top.

The Nepalese had advised us not to burn any of our garbage until the end of the climb, to appease the gods. They told us that if we made a fire sooner, we would create a big storm. So we had dug a big pit and let the garbage collect. A couple of times I had asked Gombu if we couldn't just go ahead and burn it—the ravens had discovered the garbage and were driving us nuts. Gombu had said, "No, we must honor the local beliefs."

On the last day, after the last team had descended to base camp, we collected all of our burnable garbage in the pit and set it afire. That night the monsoon rains hit. It rained like crazy for eight days and three trails got washed out. So much for the cynicism of the Occidental mind.

The hike off the mountain was not as pleasant for us as it had been for the trekkers. They had left before the monsoon season and had experienced warm, balmy weather. We left at the beginning of the monsoon and experienced the hike through hell.

On our way out, we were introduced to an ingenious animal: the leech. Leeches lie dormant for several months during the dry season, then wake up with the arrival of the monsoons. A built-in

Native woman porter carrying fifty-five-pound load plus four-month-old baby; Kangchenjunga, 1989 (Photo: Lou Whittaker)

heat sensor alerts them to the arrival of any warm-blooded animal in their vicinity.

We hiked out through the beautiful, wet rhododendron forests of Kangchenjunga with leeches dropping on us in droves from the branches and leaves above us. You couldn't feel them bite, because they secrete a deadening agent similar to Novocaine. They also secrete an anticoagulant to keep your blood from clotting and to ensure them a steady flow.

The first time we saw a leech on Larry Nielson's hand, we all cried out in alarm as Larry ripped it off and threw it into the forest. Within a few days, we had become used to having them all over us and we'd say, "Look, there are seven of them on my hand. Take my picture."

We used the surgical scissors from our first-aid kits to snip the leeches in half. You couldn't kill them just by stomping on them. Once they were engorged with blood, they'd just roll out from under your boot. You'd wake up at night in your tent and feel them hanging from your earlobes. Your face would feel slippery and you'd know it was blood. In the morning, the inside of the tent would look like someone had machine-gunned the inhabitants.

It was one of the harder parts of the expedition to endure, but we were rewarded in Kathmandu when we met up with the Russian climbing team. We celebrated with them for three days before we finally left for home.

Both Ingrid and I had a metaphysical experience on Kangchenjunga that we didn't mention to each other until we were back in the United States. After arriving at base camp with her trekking group, Ingrid came down with a terrible altitude headache. She had it the whole three days she was there. She took some medication but nothing seemed to help.

Ingrid spent a lot of time in our tent, trying to rest and keep warm. A two-dimensional Nepalese woman appeared in the tent. The woman manifested as a dark shadow, but recognizably dressed with a scarf over her head like the women we had seen in the village of Gunza on the hike in. The woman helped Ingrid turn over, she placed her hand on Ingrid's forehead in a soothing way, and she stayed with her in the tent for the entire three days that Ingrid was in base camp. Ingrid felt very comforted by her.

Ingrid thought she had been hallucinating until I got home from the climb and we started recalling our experiences. When she told me what had happened to her, I said, "After you left, I'd climb into the tent at night and have the sensation that somebody was there. Every time I came to the tent, I'd look to see if someone were there." It hadn't been an intimidating feeling at all. It had been comforting, as it had been for Ingrid.

Maybe it had been a gift from the gods of the "Five Treasure Houses of the Snows."

◆ 14 ◆

CONTINUUM

There are very few high or inaccessible unclimbed peaks left on earth. It's easy to get jaded and feel that, therefore, there are no great challenges left for those of us who choose to "go up high." On the other hand, if you seek satisfaction from the standpoint of individual human achievement rather than from the focus of the worldwide media, there are more than enough adventures left to challenge the human body and soul.

Ever since Sir Edmund Hillary became the first person to ascend to the highest point on earth in 1953, Mount Everest has been climbed every which way but naked. Even so, to the mountaineering world Everest remains the "Super Bowl of Climbing." The first time you lay eyes on that great beauty and touch her flanks, you know that, for you, it *is* a first, and nothing can diminish that feeling.

Unfortunately, most Americans don't place much commercial value on the achievements of U.S. mountaineers, the way they do on the heroics of their baseball, basketball, and football heroes. The high-risk endeavors of climbers get major media attention when someone gets killed while climbing. Otherwise, except for coverage in the specialty press, climbers are left pretty much on their own. This is good news for those who climb solely for the love of the adventure and prefer uncrowded routes. But if you're a climber trying to make a living as a sponsored athlete, the going is tough.

Mounting a large expedition gets more expensive each year, as different countries attempt to reduce the environmental impact on their most prized peaks. In the fall of 1993, the permit for Mount Everest was set at $50,000 for a team of up to five members, plus $10,000 for each additional member up to a maximum of seven. There is also a $4,000 trash disposal deposit, which is refunded to the team if it cleans up after itself, including shipping home all oxygen bottles and batteries. And of course there is the expense of the expedition itself.

An experienced expedition leader has a better chance of securing sponsorship for a climb. Each expedition stands on the shoulders of the preceding one. A successful expedition helps build confidence among the sponsors you will be relying on to support your next endeavor.

Among individual mountaineers as well as teams from various countries, there is always competition, but I believe that, on the whole, most mountaineers feel they are part of a world community. We share a lot of the same experiences and the same concerns. We are inspired by each other's feats.

After our 1982 Everest expedition, the Australian climber Tim McCartney-Snape asked me for photos and details of our route. He was also planning an expedition on the north side. I gladly shared the information. As it turned out, in 1984 his team was on the mountain at the same time as mine. They climbed from the bottom of the Great Couloir, as we had in 1982.

A couple of times the Australians joined us at advanced base camp for tea, and we swapped stories. They had a rough climb. They suffered major frostbite injuries and part of the team was nearly swept away by a major avalanche. They summitted before we did, and we celebrated their success, knowing that each expedition benefits from the one that goes before it.

In 1980, when Reinhold Messner became the first person to summit Mount Everest alone and without the use of supplemental oxygen, his supreme human effort changed forever the intimidation factor associated with the world's highest mountains and launched a new era of exploration. Now we're seeing an era of "super-alpinism," individuals and small groups in high-speed ascents of difficult routes on big mountains, as well as in unusual descents—such as by hang glider, parachute, and snowboard.

This evolution is natural, as people seek new and different ways to express themselves in their pursuits, but it's also dangerous. Many super-alpinists die young. I've always felt that no mountain is worth a life. To me, the mountains have more to offer than just high-risk challenge.

It may sound trite, but when I go up high, the problems of my everyday life diminish. I see how small I am in relation to the planet, the universe. The experience has broadened my perspective and made me more accepting of people's inherent differences.

It can be a real culture shock to mountaineers, coming back to the United States after a long climb in a foreign country. Almost everyone in the United States looks overweight. In addition to getting back our strength and health, we also have to adjust to the luxuries of heated buildings, electricity, tap water, an indoor toilet that flushes. And rich food. It's not unusual to get intestinal distress just from returning to a regular diet.

I've observed many different cultures and religions of the world, and I've come to realize that there are many levels of existence. There's much I don't understand and never will. But I believe that I've gained a better respect for the beliefs and life-styles of other human beings.

A few years ago, a reporter asked me to recall the last time I had prayed to God for help in a dangerous situation. I told him, "When I was six years old." I forget the situation. But I do remember clearly that I learned early on to be self-sufficient and that I liked the confidence it gave me.

A life in the mountains has not only made me self-reliant, it also has reinforced my spirituality. There's a big difference between religion and spirituality. I don't subscribe to an organized religion and I don't go to church on Sundays. I worship nature and recognize a Supreme Being. The laws of nature are constant. Snow melts at the same temperature and an avalanche occurs at the same angle of slope in the Himalaya as it does on Mount Rainier. Nature's laws are the same wherever you go. I think many of the ills of the world are caused by the imbalance between our natural lives and the everyday lives we create.

Death is the hardest natural occurrence for most people to accept. Not long after Marty Hoey died on Everest in 1982, I was asked to give a lecture to a hospice group. I talked about how death is half of nature, how life and death are balancing forces, and how the death of a young person is especially hard to accept because it happens out of the context of our daily lives. When we look at the natural world, it seems that things happen out of context all the time. In reality, what we're witnessing are natural occurrences. Many tribes and so-called primitive religions derive their beliefs from what they see happening in the natural world. We also can find some answers in nature, if we just take the time to observe and learn.

Climbing has taught me to accept death as a natural part of life and has lessened my apprehension of it. It has not lessened my grief at losing someone I love. Death is hardest on those who are left behind, but it also sharpens your appreciation for life. As Shakespeare wrote, "Ne'er the rose without the thorn."

I like the pace of my daily life. It's steady and fun. Ingrid and I spend a lot of time together on our construction projects and also have time left over to enjoy other interests such as skiing and traveling. After the Mount St. Helens eruption in 1980, when the house in which Ingrid and I were living in Ashford, Washington, got covered in a foot of ash, we decided to go underground. We wanted the protection but also liked the idea of blending in more with our natural surroundings. We designed and built an underground home on a nearby twenty-acre parcel, about three miles from the entrance to Mount Rainier National Park. The main part of the house is built into a bank at the top of the property, with three feet of earth on the roof. The house is built of basalt rock and logs taken from the hill where we placed the house.

I always tell people that my business is climbing mountains and my hobby is construction. Ingrid and I did most of the labor on the house, and hired some of the guides and a couple of contractors to help during certain phases. Construction is a bit like mountain climbing. There's a lot of satisfaction in watching your vision, or goal, become reality.

Ingrid can pour concrete, build rock walls, and pound nails with the best of 'em. She has a good sense of design and knows what she wants. We've traveled in Europe a lot and are always looking

Lou and Ingrid working at their favorite pastime, 1992 (Photo: M. Olaf Lundstad)

at old architecture for ideas. We built the house with rock walls and floors and arches, just like a lot of the old European buildings that have stood the test of time. We even have a rock shower. We drew the line at a rock toilet. We get enough opportunity to use those in the mountains.

We sloped the roof of the house at twenty-two degrees, the same angle as the sun during winter solstice, to let the sun into the back of the house during the cold months. The sun hits the basalt rock floors and generates heat. The walls are a foot thick for insulation. In the summer the walls keep the heat out. In winter they work in reverse. It takes only one cord of wood each winter to heat the house.

Because we live next door to a national park, we get elk and deer in the yard almost every day. Raccoons are regular visitors. A stream runs through the property and into a large trout pond, where blue herons, ducks, and other birds congregate. Because the water comes off a hill, we don't need a pump. We don't have the upkeep of a lawn—the property is covered with trees, indigenous rocks, grass, and sword ferns. We've tried to fit our home into the environment rather than strip the land to make room for the house.

Having a home we love means a lot to me and Ingrid. We both travel a lot, and it's nice to come home to a place that you love. We've skied in Sun Valley, Idaho, regularly for more than twenty years. We finally bought a condominium there a couple of years ago. We ski together all day long, we do each run without stopping, and we go fast. We used to like skiing moguls; now we enjoy cruising down open slopes. It's easier on the knees. Skiing is a great recreational sport, and great for couples. You can put in a good day of exercise and then enjoy a social evening. Mountain climbing is more of a solo sport, not too social and quite a bit more work. You're usually not coming down to a warm lodge and a couple of hot buttered rums at the end of the day. In mountaineering clothes, you can hardly tell a man from a woman. They look and smell the

Peter, Ingrid, Lou, and Erika in New Zealand on a trek led by Peter, 1992 (Photo: Aija Ozolin)

Win, Peter, and Lou celebrating a climb at the Gateway Inn; Ashford, 1992 (Photo: Laura Evans)

same. Skiing is much different, but it still allows you to get the feel of the mountains.

Most of our friends in Ashford are non-climbers. We've formed a sort of "breakfast club" with a few of them. We try to meet at least once a month at a different restaurant in Ashford. It's a good, supportive group. You can be yourself, be in whatever mood you're in. We kid each other, cheer each other up, help each other out. Ingrid calls me and Frank Paul, one of the men in the group, soulmates. She claims we share the same dirty mind. Frank and I respect each other and value our friendship. We like to hang out and joke, talk about women. Ingrid just rolls her eyes and laughs. She says we remind her of the story about the man who comes home from the doctor and tells his wife that he's been advised to cut his sex life in half. His wife asks, "Which part are you going to give up, talking about it or thinking about it?"

When I'm not hanging out in Ashford, climbing, or lecturing, I often get involved in conservation work. I'm careful how and with whom I align myself. Several years ago, I mistakenly came out in support of former Secretary of the Interior James Watt. Boy, did I fall for his snow job! Now I steer clear of politicians and try to focus on local or grassroots groups. I recently became a member of the board of directors for the newly established Olympic and Rainier Fund. Its purpose is the betterment of both national parks, through funding and education.

I like to work with groups of young people. They're very receptive to the call for conservation. We adults have been fouling our nests with no regard for the consequences to the next generation. The only way we're going to preserve the wilderness areas on this planet is to get the kids outdoors and let them see what wilderness is, what it feels like. Then after they grow up, you've got more advocates for preservation. If they've never experienced nature, they don't develop the passion to want to preserve it.

Most people in the United States have no concept of wilderness or nature preservation because they never get out. In Europe, walking and hiking are a natural way of life. Most Americans have an umbilical cord that's about thirty feet long, attached to their cars. If they can't get to it from their cars, Americans are not really interested in it.

I've done a few walkathons representing New Balance. I've noticed that two-thirds of the people who turn out are women. And each year we see more and more women on Mount Rainier. This is encouraging, because women are prime motivators of their husbands, children, and friends. It's interesting to watch how quickly some people turn on to the outside world through a simple activity like walking or hiking in the mountains.

Being up in the mountains and having to learn to be self-sufficient makes you realize that you are responsible for your environment. If you break a law of nature, you're going to pay for it. There are no loopholes; the laws of nature are the same for everyone.

Environmental conservation is becoming a global concern. You hear about it in third-world as well as in developed countries. Ten

Inside the house Lou and Ingrid built, 1985 (Photo: Dee Molenaar)

years ago, the environment was not a political issue in the United States. Today it is, and it will continue to be right up there on the agenda, next to the federal deficit and health insurance reform. We all need to understand that everything we do in our daily lives has some sort of effect on the natural world around us.

Several years ago, when I was planning the 1982 and 1984 Everest climbs, I hired Dan McConnell to make sure that our sponsors got what they expected from their involvement—endorsements, press coverage, and such. Out of my association with Dan came the idea for The Mountain Summit, a yearly gathering of conservation-minded outdoor people, with the goal of "helping to ensure a future for personal adventure in the world."

The Mountain Summit has attracted every big name in mountaineering and other areas of outdoor adventure, from British mountaineer Chris Bonington to Iditarod champion Susan Butcher, from Yuichiro Miura, the first man to ski down Everest, to actor Robert Redford, who hosted the 1990 summit at his Sundance resort in Utah. It is mainly a consciousness-raising effort, but it works, and has attracted participants from all over the world. Each time a summit convenes, the media is invited to get a chance to meet people who make their living in the outdoors and who are intimately acquainted with wilderness.

I see my involvement in these events as ways that I can give back some of the time and energy that was generously invested in me by my mentors when I was a kid, learning to climb and appreciate the outdoors.

One thing I never thought would happen to me is that I'd be put in a museum while I was still living. But sure enough, at the Mount Rainier Visitor Center, there is not only a statue of me, but also of my twin, Jim. Jim is dressed in the clothing and equipment that he used on Everest in 1963, and I'm wearing the gear that I used on Kangchenjunga in 1989. The Park Service called me in to

Lou and Ingrid's home in Ashford (Photo: Lou Whittaker)

consult on the proper way to dress the mannequins, to make sure that the ice axes were held properly, that the boots and crampons were correct. I discovered that the mannequin they used for me was female.

This bothered me until a friend reminded me that, supposedly, we all have both a masculine and a feminine side. I always have appreciated the fact that there is a feminine side of life, so, after thinking about it, I decided to accept the choice of mannequin as a compliment.

Another thing I've never envisioned happening to me is having to stop climbing. In many ways, it's a lot easier to climb to the summit of Mount Rainier now, in my sixties, than it was when I was younger. I've learned a few tricks. I know what to expect, both from the mountain and from my body. I've learned to protect my knees. That's what usually goes first on older mountaineers. You can walk uphill all day long, but coming down puts tremendous pressure on your knee joints. A lot of my guides have learned this early on and have stopped plunging down the slopes, to conserve their knees.

In the fall of 1995, I'm planning to lead an expedition to Masakhang, an unclimbed peak in Bhutan, a restricted country that borders Sikkim. My good friend Nawang Gombu will be co-leader. He helped me secure the permit through his friend, the prime minister of Bhutan.

Masakhang is a 7,400-meter peak. It's not among the treasured 8,000-meter peaks like Everest, K2, and Kangchenjunga, but at this time it is unclimbed and, therefore, a plum. It's also in a pristine area that's not commercially traveled, and that's one of the major attractions to me, Gombu, and Ingrid. We'll go post-monsoon and plan a two-month climb. We'll round up our sponsors and a small team of climbers. As she did on Kangchenjunga, Ingrid will lead a trek into base camp. Ingrid and I enjoy sharing time in the mountains of other countries.

To some people, this expedition may seem an unnecessary venture. Why risk your life, they might ask, when you've already achieved so much? All I can say is that sometimes the risks we choose are so intensely personal that we don't even know why we're doing what we're doing—we only know that we have to do it. Many people would view Jim Wickwire's return to K2 in 1978 and Larry Nielson's return to Everest in 1983, when they each almost died, as foolhardy ventures. But we can't judge the validity of someone else's risk by our own boundaries. Only Wick and Larry understand what personal challenges they have conquered, and what challenges still lie ahead.

The results of the risks we choose to take during the course of our lives are usually measured in terms of success or failure. I think what matters most is what we have learned and how much we have grown as the result of taking these risks.

I'm strong enough to summit a 23,680-foot peak like Masakhang, and I'll give it my best shot. It will be a great adventure—just one of many that I feel are yet to come.

> *They have cradled you in custom, they have*
> *primed you with their preaching.*
> *They have soaked you in convention through*
> *and through;*
> *They have put you in a showcase; you're*
> *a credit to their teaching—*
> *But can't you hear the Wild?—it's calling you.*
> *Let us probe the silent places, let us seek*
> *what luck betide us;*
> *Let us journey to a lonely land I know.*
> *There's a whisper on the night wind, there's*
> *a star agleam to guide us,*
> *And the Wild is calling, calling ... let us go.*
>
> *From "The Call of the Wild"*
> *by Robert Service*

GLOSSARY

Acclimatize: To gradually become accustomed to higher altitudes.

Anchor: A point or object where fixed ropes or belays are secured to rock, snow, or ice by various means; i.e., by piton, sling, or ice screw.

Ascender: A lightweight mechanical device used to move up and down fixed ropes by sliding up the rope, but gripping to prevent slipping back.

Belay: A method of protecting a climber whereby one climber controls slack in the rope to arrest a fall by passing the rope around his waist or through a belay device to create friction.

Bergschrund: German word for a large crevasse at the head of a glacier, usually found at the bottom of a steep slope.

Bivouac: French word for a temporary camp, usually with some sort of makeshift shelter; used in an emergency situation.

Bollard: A short, thick mound of snow or ice formed by digging a horseshoe-shaped groove in snow or ice; used as an anchor.

Buttress: A prominent section of mountain or cliff, usually flanked by a gully on each side.

Cairn: A pile of stones built to mark a trail or other feature in navigation; a monument.

Carabiner: Oval or D-shaped snap link made of steel or aluminum with a spring-hinge gate; used to clip a climbing rope into pitons, anchors, and harness; also used to carry gear and haul loads.

Cerebral edema: See *edema.*

Cirque: A steep-walled valley or natural amphitheater at the head of a valley.

Col: A pass or major gully in a ridge.

Cornice: An overhang of snow along the crest of a ridge formed by wind.

Couloir: A gully.

Crampon: Metal spikes that can be attached to the sole of a climbing boot to give traction on snow and ice.

Crevasse: A split of varying dimensions in the ice of a glacier.

Dulfersitz: A friction wrap used to rappel; the rope runs from the anchor to between the climber's legs, around a hip to the front, over the opposite shoulder, and into that hand.

Edema: Altitude-induced accumulation of fluid in the brain (cerebral edema) or lungs (pulmonary edema); can be fatal.

Fall line: The vertical line of a slope.

Figure eight: A belay device through which the climbing rope passes; also a type of knot.

Fixed rope: Rope anchored on a slope to enable climbers to more safely carry gear up a mountain or to climb up and down over a period of time.

Friction wrap: A method of running a rope around your body to create friction and help control your descent in a rappel.

Front-pointing: Climbing on steep snow or ice by kicking in the front points of crampons and using an ice axe or ice hammer in each hand to create handholds in the slope or wall.

Frostbite: Frozen tissue, most commonly on toes and fingertips; gangrene can result.

Glacier: A river of ice on a mountain.

Harness: Nylon webbing worn by a climber and to which a climbing rope is attached; various types of harnesses include waist, chest, and a combination of the two; a waist harness often includes leg loops for more security.

Ice axe: Tool with an adze or blade and pick mounted on a wood or metal shaft; used for balance and to chop or scrape steps in hard snow or ice.

Ice hammer: Similar to an ice axe, but with a hammer head.

Ice screw: A piton with a screw shaft for use as an anchor in ice.

Jumar: Also called jumar ascender. See *ascender.*

Kicking steps: Creating steps in firm snow by kicking the boot into the snow; a function performed by the lead climber.

Lead climber: The one who ascends first, setting the route for other climbers to follow.

Monsoon: In the Himalaya, the monsoon season begins in late May and usually extends to the end of August, and is accompanied by higher precipitation.

Moraine: A ridge, mound, or irregular mass of boulders, gravel, and sand deposited by a glacier.

Pitch: A section of a route between belays.

Piton: A metal blade with an eye at one end for attaching a carabiner or sling; can be hammered into a crack or screwed into ice to act as a belay or anchor point.

Pressure breathing: A method of maximizing air intake and exhalation to aid climbing at high altitude.

Prusik: A knot tied into slings onto a rope; usually used to ascend a rope.

Pulmonary edema: See *edema*.

Rappel: A method of descending a vertical face by using a rope secured above and placed around the body and paid out gradually in the descent.

Rest step: A method of walking uphill to conserve muscle strength.

'Schrund: See *bergschrund*.

Self-arrest: A method of stopping yourself from falling by digging into the slope with ice axe and feet.

Serac: A vertical promontory of ice that has broken away from a glacier.

Sling: A short length of nylon webbing or rope tied or stitched in a loop; used for belays and anchor points.

Soloing: Climbing unroped.

Spindrift: Powder snow blown by the wind.

Suspender sitz: A friction wrap used to rappel; the rope is doubled and split behind the climber's back, with each piece going in front to opposite shoulders and one hand.

Suspension traverse: A rope anchored above each side of a crevasse with a pulley attached; climbers attach their harness to the pulley and slide across to the other side.

Swami belt: A rope or nylon webbing tied around the waist, to which a climbing rope can be attached.

Tie in: To attach yourself to a climbing rope by means of a knot that is clipped or tied directly to your harness or swami belt.

Top rope: A climbing rope anchored to the top of any steep wall or serac and used by climbers to ascend safely, usually with a belay from below.

Traverse: To cross a slope horizontally or to contour a slope.

RESOURCES

Books

Bass, Dick, and Frank Wells, with Rick Ridgeway. *Seven Summits.* New York: Warner Books, 1988.

Jenkins, Peter. *Across China.* New York: William Morrow and Company, 1986.

Molenaar, Dee. *The Challenge of Rainier.* Seattle: The Mountaineers, 1979.

Ridgeway, Rick. *The Last Step, An American Ascent of K2.* Seattle: The Mountaineers, 1980.

Roskelley, John. *Nanda Devi, the Tragic Expedition.* Mechanicsburg, Pa.: Stackpole Books, 1987.

Rowell, Galen. *In the Throne Room of the Mountain Gods.* San Francisco: Sierra Club Books, 1977.

Videos

"Everest North Wall." Directed and produced by Laslo Pal. Seattle: Pal Productions, 1983.

"The Winds of Everest." Directed and produced by Laslo Pal. Seattle: Pal Productions, 1985.

Instruction and Guiding

Rainier Mountaineering, Inc.
c/o WBH P.O. Box E
Ashford, WA 98304
Phone (206) 569-2227

Summits Adventure Travel
Attn: Peter Whittaker
51902 Wanda Road
Eatonville, WA 98328
Phone (206) 569-2992
Fax (206) 569-2993

Lodging

Whittaker's Bunkhouse Motel & Espresso
30205 State Route 705 E
Ashford, WA 98304
Phone (206) 569-2439

Index

Andrea Gabbard and Lou Whittaker

Andrea Gabbard spends her time writing about or participating in her favorite outdoor sports, including mountaineering, backpacking, paddling, and skiing. She has been senior contributing editor of *Outdoor Retailer* magazine for over ten years, and works out of her home in the foothills of the Sierra Nevada near Yosemite National Park. *Lou Whittaker: Memoirs of a Mountain Guide* is her second book.

THE MOUNTAINEERS, founded in 1906, is a nonprofit outdoor activity and conservation club, whose mission is "to explore, study, preserve, and enjoy the natural beauty of the outdoors...." Based in Seattle, Washington, the club is now the third-largest such organization in the United States, with 14,000 members and four branches throughout Washington State.

The Mountaineers sponsors both classes and year-round outdoor activities in the Pacific Northwest, which include hiking, mountain climbing, ski-touring, snowshoeing, bicycling, camping, kayaking and canoeing, nature study, sailing, and adventure travel. The club's conservation division supports environmental causes through educational activities, sponsoring legislation, and presenting informational programs. All club activities are led by skilled, experienced volunteers, who are dedicated to promoting safe and responsible enjoyment and preservation of the outdoors.

The Mountaineers Books, an active, nonprofit publishing program of the club, produces guidebooks, instructional texts, historical works, natural history guides, and works on environmental conservation. All books produced by The Mountaineers are aimed at fulfilling the club's mission.

If you would like to participate in these organized outdoor activities or the club's programs, consider a membership in The Mountaineers. For information and an application, write or call The Mountaineers, Club Headquarters, 300 Third Avenue West, Seattle, Washington 98119; (206) 284-6310.

Send or call for our catalog of more than 300 outdoor books:
The Mountaineers Books
1011 SW Klickitat Way, Suite 107
Seattle, WA 98134
(800) 553-4453